Praise for *A Manual for Being Human*

'Clear, accessible wise advice for modern minds.'

Matt Haig

'Dr Soph is the therapist and best friend that the world deserves ... this book is a crucial and life changing one that should be placed in everyone's mental health toolkit. *A Manual for Being Human* is an amazing read and a gift to the world. I can't wait to give it to every single person I know!'

Scarlett Curtis, *Sunday Times* bestselling author
of *Feminists Don't Wear Pink (and other lies)*

'A truly wonderful, warm and wise one-stop shop for any inquisitive human. Packed full of prompts, practical tips and pep talks that will guide you through any situation.'

Emma Gannon, *Sunday Times* Business bestselling
author of *The Multi-Hyphen Method*

'An incredible manual to navigate these testing times, Dr Soph is compassionate, knowledgeable and kind – this book is for everyone who wants to live the life they deserve.'

Elizabeth Uviebiné, author of *Slay in Your Lane* and *The Reset*

'*A Manual for Being Human* is the motherlode, enlightening on why you might feel and behave how you do.'

The Times

'Finally! A book which takes psychological wellbeing across the lifespan out of the therapy room and into the mainstream. Dr Soph's warm, reassuring and frank style will have you understanding yourself, your actions and your relationships without a hefty therapy price tag.'

Dr Karen Gurney, author of *Mind the Gap*

'Absolutely brilliant. A gold mine of coping skills to get us through life. I will be keeping copies in my therapy room and my own home. Do not skip this one.'

Dr Julie Smith, clinical psychologist

'Dr Soph breaks down therapy in a way we can consume and learn from. A powerful voice for people to learn about their mental health ... I wish I'd had this book years ago!'

Poppy Jamie, author of *Happy Not Perfect*

'Through her book, Dr Soph manages to not only help us understand ourselves better but shares the therapeutic tools we can put in place to make life a little easier too. Insightful and robust and yet also, warm and personal, this book will stay with me for years.'

Lucy Sheridan, author of *The Comparison Cure*

'Psychology at its most accessible and usable! Sophie takes us on a journey through our lives to make sense of how we think, feel and behave then helps us build a strong path to go forward and live our future lives well.'

Dr Emma Hepburn, author of *A Toolkit for Modern Life: 53 Ways to Look After Your Mind*

ABOUT THE AUTHOR

Dr Soph has a bachelor's degree in psychology, a masters in neuroscience and a doctorate in clinical psychology, and is one of the few clinical psychologists in the world right now taking psychology out of the therapy room. After seeing the staggering decline of the nation's mental health, she left behind her traditional role as a clinical psychologist in the NHS in order to provide more people with the access they need to have good mental health. Since 2018, she has helped thousands manage their emotional wellbeing by sharing her psychological knowledge on Instagram, on her blog and through her online private practice. Dr Soph is an expert for the mindfulness app Happy Not Perfect and has been featured in many global outlets.

A MANUAL FOR BEING HUMAN

What makes us who we are,
why it matters and practical
advice for a happier life

DR SOPHIE MORT

GALLERY BOOKS UK

G

First published in Great Britain by Gallery Books UK,
an imprint of Simon & Schuster UK Ltd, 2021
This edition published in Great Britain by Gallery Books UK,
Simon & Schuster UK Ltd, 2022

1 3 5 7 9 10 8 6 4 2

Simon & Schuster UK Ltd
1st Floor
222 Gray's Inn Road
London WC1X 8HB

www.simonandschuster.co.uk
www.simonandschuster.com.au
www.simonandschuster.co.in

Simon & Schuster Australia, Sydney
Simon & Schuster India, New Delhi

A CIP catalogue record for this book
is available from the British Library

Paperback ISBN: 978-1-4711-9749-9
eBook ISBN: 978-1-4711-9748-2

Typeset in Bembo by M Rules
Printed in the UK by CPI Group (UK) Ltd, Croydon, CR0 4YY

MIX
Paper from
responsible sources
FSC
www.fsc.org   FSC® C171272

What caused people distress was not so much their own mistakes, inadequacies and illnesses as the powers and influences that bore down upon them from the world beyond their skin.

—DAVID SMAIL

This book is for the human-curious, psychology-curious and therapy-curious – it is for humans unable to access therapy and also those who are paying for long-term support.

I wrote this for people who are looking for an answer to how they are feeling. For those who are interested in understanding themselves more fully and for those who are hurting and have no place to turn to make sense of their experience. I am writing it for the thousands of people who speak to me each day on Instagram, the brave souls that reach across the electronic divide sharing how lost they feel, at sea without a framework to underpin and explain their experience.

Contents

Part Two:
What's Keeping You Here

Part Three:
How You Can Move Forward:
Your New Toolbox with Go-To Techniques

Introduction:
Why People Are Struggling

Hi, I'm Dr Soph.

You can call me Soph or Sophie.

I'm a clinical psychologist.

A few years ago, I was working in a London hospital, in a brain injury outreach team for adults. One day I was driving away from an appointment with a new patient and I realised something. I realised that over the previous eight years, across all the services I had worked in, I had witnessed the same thing in all of my new patients: people in extreme distress who had sat on a waiting list for a long time (sometimes for over a year) and had never been given the fundamental psychological ideas that are considered common and obvious among psychologists.

I realised I was spending the first few sessions with every person I saw destigmatising their experiences and giving them the same basic information.

If this information had been accessible much earlier on, it would have eased some of their anxiety and pain while they were on the waiting list.

I thought about what I'd heard on the news that morning about rising numbers of people seeking help, the overwhelmed mental health services trying to manage, and concerns that the mental health of the population of the UK, and the world as a whole, was in decline.

I also thought about the questions I was hearing among my friends, my family and the people who contact me each day on Instagram: *Why do I feel so bad? How did I get here? How do I move forward? Who should I listen to? How can I afford to help myself when therapy and other forms of support are so expensive?* I too have asked these questions. That's actually why I trained as a psychologist.

And then I suddenly understood.

There is a damn good reason why people are struggling. We are not raised to understand ourselves.

We are not taught to understand our emotions or who we are at a young age. Instead, we are raised to fear them and experience shame whenever any kind of distress arises. Rather than being taught simple and effective coping strategies, we are usually taught to put on a brave face; told to 'be good', 'snap out of it', or that 'it's no big deal'.

Instead of being encouraged to embrace all of who we are, including imperfections and weaknesses, we are expected to create a personal brand to show to the outside world at all times. We hide how we truly feel, even from ourselves.

This means we are totally ill equipped to manage the stresses of life and what it means to live inside our emotion-filled bodies.

Without knowing how to understand ourselves, the odds are stacked against us. When distress inevitably comes knocking at our door we have no useful ways to respond. We pretend everything is fine. We keep busy, burying ourselves in work. We use sex, alcohol, drugs or Netflix as fun but temporary distractions. Distractions that don't solve the problems or help us move forward. Distractions that just delay the inevitable for a little while, until the next wave of distress hits.

We then blame ourselves for the way we feel, which makes us feel worse, and the cycle continues.

I think we have been set up to struggle.

Well, not anymore! On that day of realisation, I pulled my car into a layby, grabbed a pen from my bag and wrote a list of all the things I'd cover off in most initial sessions with clients. This book is the result of those notes and the answer to the questions I hear every day.

I'm going to share with you the information usually kept behind therapy room doors, in the ivory towers of academic buildings and in dusty old textbooks.

If you have ever asked the same questions my clients, friends, family and I have asked, this book will help you answer them and will give you the information you need to understand the very core of who you are and how you came to be, well ... you.

What you will find in this book

This book is a manual for the human experience. It is not a dry and dull psychology compendium (don't worry, I read those for you). It's a book filled with psychological ideas from a mix of traditions, including my own theories and tips that you can put to use immediately. It starts with our earliest experiences and moves through to adult life.

For example, do you want to understand how your

childhood affects who you are today? How it affects your relationship with yourself and others? Do you wonder why there are experiences from that time that you feel you should be over but don't quite seem to be able to let go of? If so, you'll find the explanation here. Do you wonder how social media, marketing and the advertorial content you consume each day affects your emotional wellbeing? Do you want to know what your emotions actually are, where they come from and how to manage them when they threaten to overwhelm you? I will give you useful advice for how to have a healthier relationship with these facets of life. Do you want to believe in yourself and your ability to be content with who you are? If the answer is yes, then it's all in here.

This book will show you how your environment shaped you. How society may actually be the thing that needs to change and not you. It will give you a foundation to understand your whole life experience and emotions, and the skills to get you onto the path of healing, whatever that word means to you.

When people come to therapy, they always ask me different versions of the same three questions: how did I get here? What's keeping me here? And how do I move forward? This book is therefore structured to help you answer those questions in exactly that order.

Part One: How You Got Here
This first section of the book will help you understand how you developed to be who you are. It will also help you identify problems arising from your past experiences and current life events that we know cause distress. This part starts the moment you come into the world.

Part Two: What's Keeping You Here

This next section will help you identify what you are doing right now – the very normal patterns, bad habits and negative cycles that may be keeping you stuck and holding you back in your life.

Part Three: How You Can Move Forward: Your New Toolbox with Go-To Techniques

The final section in the book offers scientifically backed techniques that you can put to use immediately. You will find some quick tips littered throughout the book, but the majority of them are in Part Three.

This book is not a quick fix

It isn't for times of crisis and it's not to be used in place of speaking to your local mental health service. It also isn't a diagnostic tool or even a book about specific diagnoses. This book will convey the foundation of the human experience. It will offer you an insight into yourself through the mind of a therapist and will give you the tools you need to understand yourself and to heal from whatever it is that has been causing you pain and keeping you stuck.

This book isn't just about healing yourself; it is about getting to know yourself intimately so that you can get the most out of your life. It is also about creating community and joining voices with others so that we can stand up against the structures and life events that undermine our ability to be human.

How to use this book

Within these pages, you will find theories that resonate with you, and others that don't so much.

To help you personalise your experience I have filled each chapter with questions for you to answer as you go along. They are the kinds of questions I would be asking if you were in a therapy session with me. They are the kinds of questions I ask myself when I'm trying to understand why I feel or have behaved in a certain way. They will give you a chance to really investigate your lived experience.

Equip yourself with a pen, highlighter or other tool that will help you mark out the sections of the book that mean something to you. If you mark up this book with your own notes you'll be able to return to the bits that speak to you. The longer you stick with an idea the more likely it is to sink in. So, don't be afraid to make a real mess as you go along. Grab a notebook too. The answers to the questions in this book may not come to you in a flash. They may emerge slowly, and a notebook is a great way to capture your thoughts.

I have interspersed the chapters with recommendations of related books that I love, just in case you find yourself hungry for more information on a topic.

Also, look after yourself as you read through. Take your time. It may bring up emotions that you don't expect, as it is a deep dive into your past and present. If certain topics or questions bring up upsetting thoughts or feelings, I recommend putting the book down for a moment, or longer, and trying a breathing exercise (see Chapter 12) or another self-soothing strategy from Part Three. Come back to reading whenever you feel ready, as it will always be there for you.

This book comes with a trigger warning

In these pages we will touch upon serious issues, such as bullying, prejudice, death. At the top of each chapter I will let you know what, if any, sensitive themes are going to be discussed and then you can choose how to proceed.

Please remember, if you are struggling with something, if it ever becomes intense, speak to someone. Consult your GP or your local mental health team, and know that there are 24-hour crisis lines available, and you are not alone.

Trigger warning over, are you ready to begin?

Let's begin.

Dr Soph xx

Part One

How You Got Here

Emotions, relationships and negative self-beliefs – the three main topics that bring people to therapy. One might think that, because of this, I should start this book telling you what emotions are, how best to approach relationships and how to get positive about yourself.

However, the way each of us struggles in each of these areas is deeply personal. For example, how we feel our emotions is down to our genetic make-up, how stable our early life experiences were, how we were taught about emotions and soothed when young, and what stresses and strains we live through.

If you want to truly understand who you are, and why you may struggle, we need to start right at the beginning.

Before we learn how to manage these deeply human experiences, we will go on a journey through life, discussing the two biggest influences that shape who we are and what each of us struggle with: the environment we grew up in and the life events we have experienced.

9

The first part of this book will take you on a tour of these two influences. The first four chapters cover the aspects of our environment known to be responsible for shaping our biology, brain development, emotions, beliefs and behaviours. These are our early home environment, our school years, the media and marketing around us, and structural inequality. The fifth chapter focuses specifically on the life events that distress and derail us.

If you want a comprehensive understanding of how you grew into who you are today, and which moments of life may have left you feeling sad, anxious or like you aren't good enough, I recommend working through each chapter one at a time.

It is important however to know that . . .

We do not come into the world a blank slate.

Siblings are not the same even if they grow up in the same place. As the cognitive psychologist Stephen Pinker says, if a little sarcastically, it's the reason that your pet and your child will not both learn language irrespective of how much time you devote to teaching them and nurturing them in the same environment.

The wheels of who we are are set in motion before we're born. DNA reportedly accounts for 20–60 per cent of temperament – how sociable, emotional, energetic, distractible and tenacious we are. However, full-term babies are born when their brains are a third of their adult size, and brain development isn't complete until our mid-twenties. Similar to the way architects adapt blueprints to fit the terrain they build upon, you and your brain developed and adapted to your specific surroundings.

It wasn't just your family that shaped you; it was all of your early experiences. School, friendships, the media you consumed, the society and culture you grew up in, and the life events you experienced, all played a part.

You might have evolved to be shy. This could be for a million reasons. Perhaps you were predetermined to be that way. Or perhaps you were taught that shyness was 'becoming' (was the right behaviour for who you are). Or perhaps no one taught you how to socialise, making it feel scary. Equally, you could be shy only on occasion, like when you meet someone dreamy that makes your heart beat faster and your mind go blank.

You might have a short fuse for many reasons too. It could be down to your DNA. Or because you grew up in a high-stress environment that taught you to be on high alert at all times (for an angry caregiver or a sudden change at home). Or because you weren't taught how to manage your emotions, meaning they bubble over on occasion.

Equally, it might have nothing to do with your past. Maybe you have a lot on your plate and have reached the limits of what you can cope with. Suddenly the smallest thing is enough to set you off.

I can't tell you which parts of you were predetermined. I can, however, share the main factors I know shape people, starting from the moment they take their first breath.

With this in mind, I invite you to read this book, and to hold the information lightly. Do not assume it explains everything. Or that everything you do has a deep psychological meaning.

There will be things you do that are indeed linked to your upbringing, and things you do that you simply enjoy, or that come to you on the spur of the moment.

1. Caregivers, Siblings and our Family Environment

* Warning: look after yourself while reading this. If you start to feel overwhelmed, take a break, breathe, and come back when you feel more centred. There is no shame in any of this.

We are not survival of the fittest. We are survival of the nurtured.
—LOUIS COZOLINO

When you emerged into the world, you cried out. Not bloody surprising! You came out of your warm, cosy, food-packed womb and into the blindingly bright, noisy and cold world. Suddenly you were vulnerable and in an alien environment, reliant on others for your safety. You cried firstly to get the mucus out of your lungs, and secondly to make your caregivers notice you.

You needed a human to keep you alive. But you needed them for more than food and shelter. You needed them for connection and to soothe your overly active fear system that was constantly triggered by this unknown world. You also needed them to help teach you about the world, and to help your nervous system (the brain structures that respond to stress) develop.

The attachment – the bond – you formed with your earliest caregivers helped shape your brain development and your nervous system, gave you your first understanding of emotions, and provided the blueprints of relationships that you use to make sense of others right now.

Even though you can't remember that time, as first memories tend to date back to three and a half years old, whatever happened then is likely still affecting you now – affecting how strongly you feel your emotions, whether you understand them, how you understand and interact with other humans, and who you choose to date and befriend (but we won't get to this part till Chapter 10).

Safe, soothed, seen and secure

A baby's primary goal is to stay close to their caregiver. Throughout this book I use the term 'caregiver', instead of parent or parents, as not everyone is raised by their birth parents. Caregiver includes anyone who is the responsible adult and guardian of the child.

Good news: while babies may not be able to do much, they are not passive receivers of care from the people around them. They are primed to initiate it. Think of those facial expressions and endearing little moves babies do – they are, in a good way, manipulating you into being there for them.

They learn to adapt as quickly as they possibly can to their environment, crying out and responding to the reaction of their caregiver. Adapting to ensure that whatever happens they will not be left alone. The rest is up to the caregiver.

Daniel Siegal, Clinical Professor of Psychiatry at UCLA School of Medicine, says babies and children need to be safe, soothed, seen and secure.

When it comes to development humans need attention the way plants need sunlight

Safe

Babies and children need to grow up in a safe-place and have caregivers that are not dangerous.

Grow up in safety and your first experiences teach you that the world can be a safe-place. People too. It also teaches your developing brain that it doesn't have to be on high alert for threat.

Grow up in amongst danger, violence or neglect, and your brain will adapt to help you survive. It may keep you in a state of anxiety and hypervigilance (hyperawareness for any potential future threat that may arise). It may keep you pumped with adrenaline so you are ready to run from danger, to fight against it, or it may numb you out so that if you can't escape threat you can endure it.

Soothed

Even in a safe environment, all novel experiences can be scary to a baby. Their first experiences of light, hunger, pain, cold or loud noises are threatening because they are unknown. When anything feels dangerous, they cry and kick out. If an adult comes to soothe them, they (eventually) relax. This is co-regulation, the wonderful ability to use another person's calm nervous system to soothe our own, and the reason hugging the people we care about, even as an adult, can make a real difference to our emotional state.

The next time the same experience arises, they feel less scared; they have learned they are not in danger and, importantly, should potential danger arise again, other people will be there for them.

Seen

Babies and children need an adult to see their distress, and not only soothe them but make sense of it for them.

You can imagine this process as a caregiver acting as a mother bird. You know how birds catch worms, chew them up and then regurgitate them into baby birds' mouths in a pre-digested and manageable fashion? That's what our caregivers are meant to do with our emotions and experiences across our childhood. They make sense of our internal worlds for us by explaining what is happening in and around us.

Through this we learn what causes us distress, what certain sensations mean and what we can do to soothe or meet our needs in the future. For example:

'Aw, you're crying because you must be cold. Don't worry, Mummy's here. I have a blanket and a hug to warm you up.'

The baby learns: this feeling is 'cold'. Blankets and other people can warm you. It may feel scary, but I'm not in danger. If I cry someone will help me. Next time this happens I don't need to be as afraid.

'You scraped your knee, it hurts right now but it'll heal.

Let's put a plaster on it together and do something nice to help you feel better.'

The child learns: this feeling is 'hurt'. It happened because I have a cut. It's temporary and it will heal. I'm not in danger. Next time it happens I don't need to be as afraid; I can understand it and know what to do.

'You're frustrated because I told you that you couldn't have the sweets you wanted. It's okay to be frustrated. Do you want to run around the garden to let the emotion out? Or come for a cuddle?'

The child learns: this feeling is 'frustration'. It happens when I don't get what I want. It's okay to feel this. I have options to manage this.

We also needed our caregivers to make sense of how they behaved towards us, for example: 'I was cross. I'm sorry. I had a busy day and didn't mean to snap. It's not your fault.'

The child learns: when adults snap it is because they are angry. This can happen when they're busy. Adults can apologise when things go wrong and they have ways to manage their emotions, which I can try. And importantly, it was not my fault.

The more children experience this, the more they understand themselves and, over time, learn to self-soothe. They also become more adept at understanding others, recognising the tell-tale signs of certain emotions on people's faces.

Sometimes I meet clients who struggle with their emotions, as they were simply never taught how to understand them, and therefore don't have the words for their experiences.

It's never too late to learn, however.

Making sense of how you feel

Quick tip 1: if you struggle with understanding how you feel, start keeping a journal. When you feel any kind of emotional change (stress, anger, numbness) write down the sensations you feel in your body: 'My chest is tight.' 'I feel teary.' 'I feel nothing.' Write down the emotion labels that might explain these feelings, and also note what is happening in your life – 'I had an argument.' 'Someone spoke over me.' Over time you will start to see patterns. You will start to make sense of when and why you feel certain ways, including what helps you to feel better. Chapter 14 will give you clear details on journalling. Chapter 6 will help you understand your emotions more deeply.

Quick tip 2: if you struggle with understanding other people, what they may be thinking or feeling, mirror their movements. Copy their gestures, their posture, pull the facial expressions they pull. This will trigger your mirror neurons and may give you a taste of how they feel. Mirror neurons are brain cells that mirror other people's experiences, making it feel like their experience is happening to you too. Have you ever winced when you saw someone stub their toe, flinching as though it happened to you? If so, your mirror neurons did that to you. Subtly copying someone's gestures will also signal to the person you are with that you are attuned to their experiences.

Secure

Babies and children need consistency.

We needed to know that we could rely upon our connection with our caregivers – that they would be there when we needed them and would be in tune with our needs.

Our caregivers didn't need to do any of this perfectly.

Making mistakes and getting cross are deeply human experiences, and although, as children, we might not fully realise it, our caregivers are humans too.

Whenever an adult makes sense of a child's emotional experience for them, explaining what emotion they may be feeling and why, they give that child a gift: the language they will need to understand themselves and their internal experiences, that will help them for the rest of their lives.

What mattered in those moments was that our caregivers took time to make sense of what happened, to then soothe us and heal the rupture.

In fact, seeing our caregivers get it wrong from time to time, and seeing them manage this and talk us through it, showed us that messing up is inevitable, survivable, human, and that we can learn from our mistakes.

If you felt safe, soothed, seen and secure as a baby, as you got slightly older you acquired your very own and first coping skill: an internalised image of your caregiver. Whenever you felt distressed you conjured up their image and, assuming this person was consistent and nurturing, suddenly you felt soothed.

Slowly, over time, you were able to move away from your

caregiver. They became your 'secure base', a safe-place from which you could explore the world and learn about more than just what happens when you were in their arms.

You can see this exploratory behaviour in all young children. They look to their caregiver and then slowly move away (maybe to another part of the room, or towards another child). When they reach a certain point, they will suddenly return to them. Kids do this, getting further away each time, knowing their caregiver will be there to soothe them when they get back.

The primary people in your life taught you whether you were safe in the world, whether other humans were safe, how keenly you needed to look out for threat, how anxious you needed to be, how to understand your own experiences, whether you made sense, and whether you could explore by yourself. They gave you the skills to manage all of this.

Attachment Styles

If you had the experience described above, bloody marvellous! A caregiver(s) continuously attuned to your needs causes people to develop what therapists call a **secure attachment style**.

As an adult, this means you are likely to feel safe and relaxed around others. It means you will feel safe to share your emotional experiences and understand how to self-soothe. This means you feel secure in relationships and worthy of the love and support of others. You are likely to find dating and friendships manageable.

About 50 per cent of people have this attachment style.

You can think of it as a kind of calm and centred version of relationship programming. Unfortunately, we didn't all have caregivers attuned to our every need.

There are many reasons why adults may not be in tune with a baby or child's needs. They may be actively cruel and intentionally harmful. Or they may be trying their best, love their kids to the ends of the earth, but still can't quite be there in the way that makes us feel secure. Maybe, for example, they are managing their own mental or physical health; maybe they're repeating the way they themselves were raised, or maybe they have to work 24/7 to put food on the table, which keeps them away for extended periods.

Whatever the reasons, some of us learned early on that adults couldn't be there for us consistently, that they weren't always reliable. More than that, we may have learned that connection with others can feel dangerous and that the world is emotionally fraught because of this.

People who learn this have an **insecure attachment style** and can feel anxious or shut down when in the presence of new people or anyone who might reject or dismiss them.

Is this you? If so, don't worry – it's me too. I am outing myself now so that if you fall into this category, you'll know you're not alone. You are a person who had to adapt to manage the distress caused by growing up in such an environment. You are a person who found ways to survive this and stay close to the people you needed in order to stay alive. Amazing work!

The two most common styles of insecure attachment are: **avoidant** (23 per cent of the population) and **anxious** (20 per cent). There is another insecure attachment style: **disorganised** (2 per cent of population), which often arises if neither the anxious nor the avoidant style worked to keep you close to, and also safe from, your caregiver, and you couldn't pinpoint a consistent way to keep yourself emotionally safe. If this is you, you may notice that as an adult the drive to be close is matched by an overwhelming feeling of panic when people *do* get close. As this is much less common, it is not discussed here. If you want more information on the disorganised attachment style, I recommend reading *Why Love Matters: How Affection Shapes a Baby's Brain* by Sue Gerhardt.

Avoidant attachment: feeling like a cat

An avoidant attachment style usually arises if one or more of your caregivers are predictably unavailable to meet your needs.

You may have an avoidant attachment style if you learned as a young child that no one came if you cried out. Or if, as you got older, you felt consistently rejected or dismissed any time you showed emotion or a need for closeness and comfort. Maybe you were told you were 'just tired', or that you needed to 'get over it' when you said you were struggling.

If this happened to you, you would have experienced high levels of childhood anxiety because the secure connection you needed – to dampen down the threat activity in your brain – wasn't there.

But you were smart; you adapted in order to survive and stay close to the human you needed in your life. You were given the message that your emotions would not be attended to, so you learned to minimise or – 'even better' (I say this ironically as, while this helped us fundamentally as kids, this is something that can really mess with us as adults) – get rid of any display of emotion, feeling or need for emotional support and closeness. To do this, any time an emotion, or a need for closeness, arose, your brain tried to squash it.

You will also have found other ways to deactivate your attachment system. For example, you may have been careful to spend time in the vicinity of your caregiver without initiating any contact for fear of them rejecting you. You may have focused on logic over emotion, distancing yourself from your feelings at the same time as becoming self-reliant, fixing your issues by yourself without the support of others.

Unfortunately, these strategies only numbed the conscious expression of the anxiety you felt. You still had all that distress going on inside of you.

Adults with an avoidant attachment style usually feel extremely self-reliant or 'pseudo-independent'. I say 'pseudo' because the self-reliance isn't really because of a desire to be alone – it's because of a fear that others won't be able to meet their needs, and this feels so overwhelming that they shut all that down and keep people at arm's length.

If this is you, you may seek out friendships and connections but feel overwhelmed when someone needs you or gets too close. You may feel a little like a cat – a creature that interacts on its own terms, leaning in when you want to, but needing to retreat and take time out on your own the moment you feel overwhelmed. You may feel your best around people who are calm and give you space to live how you want and need to.

You may notice that you sometimes feel a little superior to others, seeing another's 'neediness' and emotionality as something unnecessary and something you are relieved you don't have. This isn't because you're arrogant or overly confident. Quite the opposite. This is your mind's attempt at keeping you

Learning my attachment style was one of the 'ah ha' moments of my psychological journey. Suddenly my extreme self-reliance and other relationship behaviours made sense.

safe and your self-esteem up. It protects you from your (maybe unconscious) fear that you may not be someone another person is able to, or would want to, be there for.

Can you see how the adaptations a child makes in order to stay safe might affect how they are as adults?

Anxious attachment style: feeling like a puppy

An anxious attachment style develops if one or more of your caregivers was unpredictable in meeting your needs, sometimes getting it just right and other times totally missing the mark.

You may have developed an anxious attachment style if your caregiver listened attentively to you, and effectively met your needs one moment, but then the next moment, for example, unexpectedly emotionally or physically disappeared, leaving you wondering what their behaviour meant (do they care? Or not?). Or they became over-protective, making you feel like the world and whatever you were worried about was extremely dangerous. Or they required you to behave in ways that suited their needs, e.g. 'I threw this birthday party for you, so please act well and make me look good' or 'I'm struggling right now, soothe me, I know you want to see your friends but I need you more'.

Like the avoidant person, the person with an anxious attachment style learns that other people can't be trusted to consistently meet their needs. If this was you then, unlike the person with an avoidant attachment style, who focused on logic and shutting down, you adapted in a different way.

You couldn't use logic to know when your caregivers would be consistently present, so you learned that the best way to continue the connection you needed with your caregivers was to stay as close to them as possible, continuously initiating interaction, as you knew at some point this would work; they would respond in the way you needed them to. They became the centre of your focus, which may have led to you being described as a clingy child. This is not a negative. It was your very smart way of staying connected.

You may also have found that sometimes, when your care-givers did meet your needs – offering the listening ear, or the kind words and actions you needed – you were already so overwhelmed that their actions didn't soothe you. You desper-ately craved them, but the brief interactions weren't enough, which meant it was hard to feel genuinely calm and safe, as you were sure they would disappear again or change what they needed from you at any moment.

As an adult, you may have high hopes for other people. You may put them on a pedes-tal, seeing the best in them, and sometimes the worst in you, as

Those of us described as needy, aloof or shut down often have, at heart, the exact same desire and fear: the desire for deep human connection and the fear that no human could, or would, want to be truly there for us. We just differ in the way we try to keep ourselves safe in the world.

your early experiences may have affected your self-esteem. You may sometimes feel let down by others, as you have them in your mind often and think about doing kind things for them, yet notice this behaviour isn't always reciprocated. If this is you, it can be helpful to remember that people with different attachment styles may show they care in other ways. If someone doesn't always hold you in mind, it isn't a sign that they don't care.

You will feel at your best when surrounded by people who genuinely show you consistent care and support: people who are available for you. You may notice that when you are around people like this, you feel centred and calm, rather than anxious or preoccupied with them. The standoffish people in your life may bring back those earliest feelings and ways of connecting.

In Chapter 10, I will tell you how these styles show up in our adult lives, how they can affect our relationships, particularly while dating, and how you can make your attachment style more secure.

Working out your attachment style

Quick tip: If you don't already know your attachment style, go online and take an 'attachment style quiz'.

Siblings

It isn't only our caregivers who affect the first few years of our lives. If you had siblings, these relationships also shaped who you are.

Siblings can be a gift for our development. They offer you company, a place to learn sharing, compromise, secret keeping, and lots of opportunity to practise conflict and resolution.

Seriously, did you know that siblings aged two to four years old get into a fight on average every nine and a half minutes? I believe it. My brother used to shout, 'Pinch back-of-the-legs time!' and then chase me around the house. Thank you, David!

The birth order of siblings has also been shown to have an effect on emotional development. The first-born child has the direct attention of their caregivers when they come into the world. Then another comes along, replacing them, which can be a serious fall from grace, as they now have to share their caregivers and get given more responsibility. First children often receive praise for being responsible and for supporting their sibling(s), meaning they often grow up to be the serious and more mature one of the family, enjoying leadership roles in work, feeling comfortable when in charge.

The next child then gets the direct attention until ... another comes along.

Many middle children report receiving less attention than they would have liked. They are not the first child, who is listened to or given responsibility due to their age, and are not the youngest, who usually requires the most attention. The middle child often adapts to this by developing relationships outside the family. They are often good at socialising, and also often become the peacekeeper of the family, a loyal negotiator who is good at compromise and able to communicate with the older and the younger people in the family. If this was you, does it resonate?

By the third child, the caregivers have usually relaxed a little. Either because they are exhausted or because they now believe children are more robust than they had previously dared imagine.

The youngest child therefore tends to get away with more as the rules slacken. This sometimes causes resentment amongst the other siblings – 'It's not fair! It was way stricter when I was your age!' To manage this, the youngest often uses charm and humour to disarm their older siblings and stay part of the gang. The youngest is therefore usually seen as the cheeky risk-taker, the lucky one, and this can carry on into adult life.

Irrespective of where you were in the pecking order, it's important to remember that siblings constantly vie for the attention of their parents. They lock onto what they're good at, and they strut it around in front of their parents like peacocks. This is why siblings often take on roles, e.g. he is the smart one, she is the sporty one, they are the funny one.

If your caregivers gave more praise for certain activities – such as being academic over being creative or vice versa; being a rule-follower over a spontaneous child who did things their own way or vice versa – then you may have fought to be best at that activity. Or if you felt that your caregivers showed any kind of favouritism over one or all of your siblings, you may have felt a little 'less than' or on the outside of the group. Sad times.

I have worked with many people who have felt on the outside of every group they're in as adults, and that they will always be left out, not favoured by the most popular person in the group. For many of them, their first experience of this happening was with their siblings, where they felt their parent loved the others more. They started to see themselves as outsiders when they were children, then, during times of stress as adults, they felt that way again.

Not so fun fact: my clients are right. Research shows that caregivers do often feel closer to one of their children, and that feeling you are not the favourite, or that someone else is, can affect our self-esteem all the way into our fifties.

However, even when children grow up they do not always guess accurately which sibling is preferred in the family. Indeed, research has found that adult children were only correct in predicting who their mother favoured less than half of the time (44.6 per cent to be exact) and guessed correctly who their mother was most proud of only 39 per cent of the time!

And this is the case with so much of our childhood experience – it isn't just what happened to us that affects us, it's how we made sense of it, but sometimes the way we interpreted our experiences wasn't quite correct.

> **Questions for you:** did you grow up with siblings? What did they bring to your life? Which aspects of your behaviour could you say stem from them being in your life? Where were you in the order of the siblings? How did you adapt to that? What role did you take on in the family? Was it one of the ways I mention above or another way? Are you an only child? How was that for you? How does talking about it make you feel?

I will do anything to keep you close

I hope I have got this message across: babies and children are smart. They are constantly adapting to keep the relationship with their caregivers alive. The behaviours we adapt in those early years often become the foundation of who we are and how we act as adults. And there are further adaptations some of us made in order to do this. For example, children who fear abandonment, punishment, or that they are not accepted, may start to people-please. They may ignore their own wants and wishes, put other people's needs first, and say yes to everything requested of them, in hope that if they get it all right, they will be accepted, loved and safe.

Other children may manage this experience by becoming a perfectionist (you can be both a perfectionist and a people pleaser), hoping that if they do everything correctly, they will be seen as enough. Adopting either of these behaviours can give a child a sense of control in an uncertain world.

Children who are not listened to, or who have found that neither people-pleasing or perfection helps in any way, may learn that the only way they get the attention they need is by getting angry and/or shouting louder, escalating their behaviours until they have broken enough rules that someone comes to stop them. This is something caregivers rarely understand. If this was you, you may have been labelled as 'bad', named as angry or difficult when actually you just knew (unconsciously) that it could be better to have an angry interaction than no interaction at all. When children adapt like this, these behaviours usually follow them into adult life.

I had an adult client who was extremely sociable, considered the 'life and soul' of her circle of friends and any party she attended. She swore like a trooper and was known and loved for her crass and unorthodox ways. When calm, she felt deeply connected, loved, and able to be her wild, unfiltered self at all times. During times of stress, however, she noticed feeling 'paranoid' (her words), sure that her friends would suddenly turn their back on her. She started second-guessing what they might be thinking. 'I know they say they are having a good time, and that the food I cooked was delicious, but what if they are just saying that and don't mean it?', 'Is that smile they just gave me genuine or is it fake?', Do they really want to be here or are they just humouring me?'. These fears also came with a strong need to people-please and act perfectly.

Swearing gone, 'Please', 'thank you', 'sorry' suddenly became her most uttered words.

What my client was going through made sense. She had grown up with caregivers whose moods were highly change-able – some moments she was the golden child who could do no wrong; other times, she was ignored, or shouted at, used as the scapegoat for any mishaps in the house, pulled up for any imperfect behaviours on her part. To manage this, she developed a superpower in terms of predicting when their moods may suddenly swing, adapting her behaviour to try to please them in order to get them back into a good mood.

We spend most of our lives repeating the patterns we adopted when young. The ones we adopted to keep ourselves safe and to stay close to the adult(s) that raised us.

Now, when stressed, she slipped back into this early way of managing stress and started overpredicting threats. For an easier life she needed to update her coping strategies to ones that fit her current life, with mindfulness and self-compassion at the core.

Before you start assuming

that all of your behaviours that arise during times of stress relate to childhood, I need you to hold in mind that children don't only adapt for these reasons. Some kids are natural people pleasers, some natural perfectionists, and some natural rebels. Some were praised any time they showed these qualities and, like we all do when someone tells us we did something right, they simply engaged in those behaviours more. Also, some were told that certain behaviours were expected of them. For example, a friend of mine who is first-generation British Asian was told from a young age that only perfection would be enough for them to be seen as equal to the white children in the UK.

If you identify with any of the labels discussed here, don't assume there's something dark or mysterious underlying these behaviours. It may just be that you are this way or that you were told this was important. What matters is how strongly you feel the need to engage in these behaviours as an adult, and to what extent, if any, they affect your life.

If your perfectionism is useful, and not so strong that it leads you to burnout, then no problem. If your people-pleasing simply means you have stronger relationships, also wonderful. If shouting louder helps you in a job where everyone fights to be heard, brilliant!

However, if these behaviours are getting in the way of your relationships, or leading you to exhaustion, you may need to consider letting go of them. I realise this can feel scary, especially if you believe you need these long-held behaviours to prevent abandonment and ensure love. So, don't suddenly try dropping your long-held behaviours. Simply note where and why they may have started, recognise that they helped you adapt to the world you grew up in, and then gradually introduce a new skill from Part Three of this book. Chapter 8 (coping skills that make things worse) will talk you through perfectionism and people-pleasing in more detail, so you can truly feel safe to let the old ways go.

With this in mind, can you think of any behaviours you might have adopted during the first few years of your life? Do any of the above labels resonate with you, or did you become:

- **The mediator** in your family, sitting between arguing caregivers, trying to defuse their arguments.
- **The protector** – the person who shielded your siblings or other family members from family arguments or harm.
- **The funny one** – clowning around, as making people laugh ensured connection or diffused tension.
- **The enabler** – the person who had to support a caregiver who used substances.
- **The golden child** – this one sounds great, as it means you are the 'hero' of the family, with a deep sense of responsibility, but, if you mess up, it's a disaster.

Or were you expected, as a child, to act as the parent? Sometimes children have to take on adult roles earlier than they are able. For example, when they become the caregiver of a family member. They may have to cook, clean, take care of their siblings, get themselves and their siblings to medical appointments and school, or be the one to support their caregiver through times of emotional distress.

If this was you, you may notice that you find play hard as an adult, as you missed this important childhood phase. You may notice you expect yourself to always know how to complete a task, even when you don't exactly know what is expected, as when you were a child you had to put on a brave face and make it work.

Okay, phew, we are nearly done with talking about the first few years of life. How are you doing? Have I poured an ocean into your cup or are you still with me? I have only one more thing to share with you, and then I recommend you put the book down and take a few minutes to move your body.

Goodies and baddies

In the first few years of life children cannot hold the idea of good and bad in mind at the same time. 'Good mummy', 'bad sister', 'good dog', 'bad floor' (that scraped my knee): everything had to be one or the other. Think of the fairy tales you heard or watched as a kid. Remember the goodies and the baddies?

Children believe their caregiver is a 'goodie'. If a caregiver misses their needs, children often interpret it as being their fault, that they are the 'baddie'. They don't have the nuanced reasoning to understand that sometimes caregivers miss their needs because they're stressed or have to make ends meet, or because they have an avoidant or anxious attachment style.

Even children who are harshly treated, even physically, by their caregivers usually continue to love them, but they can stop loving themselves, sometimes believing they must deserve everything they get – if this is you, I promise that you did not deserve this. You deserved better. You are good and worthy of love.

If you are a parent reading this, thinking, *Oh God, what if my child thinks they are bad? What can I do?* Don't worry. The solution is simple. Try to teach your children that they are loved, that they are not responsible for the difficult times (such as divorce) and continuously show them that things are rarely ever simplistically 'good' or 'bad'. For instance:

'Sweets can be good for your mood, and sharing them can be fun to do with friends, but sweets can also be bad for your teeth. They are both.'

'The dog sometimes wees inside, doesn't he? Weeing inside is bad, isn't it? But he does so many lovely things and lets us cuddle him, we think he's good, don't we?'

Teach them that while an action they engage in may be bad, it doesn't mean *they* are bad.

Questions for you: who were the main people in your home life as a child? Did you stay with one set of caregivers or more? Was the first year of your life calm-ish, do you think? (I realise this is very difficult to know unless you grew up in a war zone, or know that during this time there was violence or neglect at home.) How about the following years? What did you learn about emotions when you were growing up? Were they acceptable? Were they soothed? How were they soothed? Did you feel like part of something? Wanted? Or did you feel on the outside and like you might have to change to fit in? In what ways did you adapt? What attachment style might you have developed? Did you people-please or use any other strategy to gain the love and support you hoped for in your family? What meaning did you take away from those years about who you are? What were the best things about you? What things were praised? Who was your greatest source of support or inspiration? Who or what made you feel seen and safe?

The new rules

I believe that one of the reasons many of us struggle in life is because we haven't been given the right information to help us understand ourselves and to know that we are okay. Therefore, at the end of each chapter, I will present you with a set of new ideas to take on board. Here's your first set:

- **You are a unique mix of your DNA and life experience.** Who you are today, how sensitive you are to stress, how easily you understand your emotions, what you expect from other people and how you act around other people is in part determined by your DNA, and in part determined by the environment you grew up in.
- **Our human drives are survival and connection. Love and acceptance.** Even those of us who seem not to want love and acceptance publicly. Even those of us who seem disconnected, prioritising work over connection, control and status and perfection over relationships, often reached this point as we were taught this was how to gain approval or the pinnacle of social acceptance.
- **We needed love but we also needed boundaries.** Children need care, they need space to make mistakes and they need someone to show them where the limits of *acceptable behaviour* lie. Children feel safe when they know there are rules and limits and that someone is in charge.

- **As a kid you likely worked extremely hard to gain the attention you needed and deserved.** There will have been behaviours that you took on as a kid that kept you safe and some of these will be still be observable today. You can be extremely proud of yourself for the ways you adapted back then, even if they are ways you don't necessarily value now.

- **You were deserving and worthy as a child and you did not need to prove this.** You are deserving and worthy today too.

- **It is possible that two seemingly opposite things can be true at the same time.** For example, it is possible that your caregivers were trying their best but still missed your needs. It is possible that you feel hurt by the experiences you went through as a child and that you also still love and respect your caregivers. It is possible for you to feel angry and devastated, in fact, and still care about them.

- **We all have stories that we tell about ourselves.** I call them stories, as they are beliefs rather than facts, and the stories were shaped early in childhood. For example: 'I'm not enough, otherwise they would love me more.' 'I will be enough if I can be perfect.' 'If I show someone I care, they won't be there for me.' These stories are carried with us through our lives. We'll dig more deeply into your beliefs soon but, for now, if any of these examples resonate with you, start looking for the exceptions now. For example: who shows you love and care right now? Was there a time you didn't act perfectly and it was okay?

- **If you can't remember much of your childhood, don't assume something is wrong.** Our earliest memories are extremely fragile and are easily lost due to their age. Even if we keep our earliest memories, we may lose the ability to date them correctly. The way we make sense of what you went through (and go through today) is more important than what actually happened to you.

- **You are an adult now.** One of the most important things we can all remember is that, whatever happened in our childhood, we get to choose what happens in our future. Even though what happened then may still affect us, we now no longer need our caregiver's approval at all times in order to stay safe in the world. We don't need them to teach us how to self-soothe. We can do it ourselves – how satisfying is that!

- **Children know something adults sometimes miss.** That is the joy of curiosity and awe. Can you go outside right now and look at your surroundings as if for the first time? Look for the patches of light and shadow. Look for patterns in the scenery – the leaves or the trees. Focus on the big picture then zoom into the smallest thing you can see. Really get involved. Look for anything you haven't noticed before. Can you hear birds? Stand at the bottom of a skyscraper or a tree and look up. I like to do an 'awe walk' each day, looking for things I haven't seen before, getting involved in nature, seeing the world as if through a child's eyes. Maybe you will like it too.

A Note to You

Hello!

Chapter 1 is done. How do you feel?

I would like you to do something for me. Take a moment to think about someone from your childhood who made you feel *good* about yourself. Someone that was there for you. It could be a person. It could be a pet. Your god. It could be a character in a book or in a film. It could be an imaginary friend or a place you escaped to that brought you peace during times of chaos or fear.

Bring that person to mind. Think about how they made your life a little better. What did they teach you? Did they show you that some people could be kind, reliable, fun, supportive? Did they teach you places that can be calm and safe? Did they teach you to cook, fish, read, cry or do any of the things you still do today? How did you feel in their presence?

Psychologists are obsessed with problems. But ... we are not just shaped by bad experiences. The person/being you brought to mind just now influenced who you are today. In fact, every small positive interaction you have affects who you are and how you feel.

We are shaped by everyone we come across, especially those who make us feel seen, heard and accepted. So, if this book or any other psychology-related text you read ever starts to feel a little heavy, remember this.

Dr Soph xx

2. The School Years

All children are artists. The problem is how to remain an artist once he grows up.

—PABLO PICASSO

Education is an incredible thing. It has been shown to disrupt the cycle of poverty, enable people to gain paid work and improve life expectancy. It gives young people structure, routine and an opportunity to meet others, so they learn how to advocate for themselves and gain experiences and skills outside of what we would naturally come across in our day-to-day lives.

The learning environment is usually the first place we are shaped by influences and kids outside of our immediate family – in my case, a new set of people who hadn't heard of, and didn't want to play, 'pinch back-of-the-legs time'. Phew!

As a self-confessed nerd, I think schools and teachers are

nothing short of miraculous. However, as this is a book to help you figure out and overcome the challenges of life, I will focus on some of the problems we may have faced during that time that can still affect us now.

When we start school, playtime and engagement with others suddenly has structure. It isn't solely about curiosity and joy. It isn't about imagining a million and one impossible possibilities before lunch or making mud pies (my preschool activities). School is about performance, accuracy and speed.

You get given tests and grades and are maybe told where you rank compared to others in the class, the year, the country. You are told to fight your way to the top.

Rather than being taught how to manage your emotions and relationships – our most common stumbling blocks as adults – we are usually taught that there is a hierarchy in school subjects. For example, languages and maths are often seen as boring but 'real' and 'important' topics, while dance and drama are seen as fun, creative pastimes, but not 'serious' subjects.

The focus on speed, performance and vocational learning is because free education was shaped for the Industrial Revolution of the late eighteenth century, and set up to teach young people, as fast as possible, the skills they would need to get into industry and make the country money. Taking your time, learning through error, creativity and joy did not help industry so, to put it simply, they weren't valued.

I tell you this not to undermine schools. I say it because so many people I meet feel they're not productive enough, that they haven't made enough out of their lives academically. While this message can come from our families – and, as I will show you later on, the media too – school is often the first proper introduction kids have to the capitalist idea that they will spend the rest of their life being measured by their productivity. Deeper than that, it may be the first time they learn to conflate their worth (and the worth of others) with their productivity.

Your grades do not tell you who you are

How do you feel about your academic ability? Your answer may link to how you were talked about in school.

Our grades and reports are supposedly a reflection of who we are, and what we're able to do. However, there are a number of factors that influence how we fare in school. For example, we do our best when:

- Our school feels safe, is accepting and nurturing of our personal culture, and meets our physical needs (e.g. feeds us).
- Our classes are interesting, structured and meet us where we are at, providing us enough of a challenge to keep us motivated but not so much of a challenge that we become overwhelmed.
- Our teachers are motivated, use multiple teaching methods to keep us engaged, and make us feel like they care about and believe in us.
- We can see ourselves, and people who are like us, reflected in and thriving in the books we are given and the teaching staff who support us.
- Our caregivers are supportive, involved and take an interest in our schoolwork and lives.
- Our home lives are calm and safe.
- Our peers make us feel accepted.

There are so many factors that affect how we fare in school but, more often than not, we are tested as if these things *don't* exist or matter.

If you were seen to do well in school and were interested in the 'right' subjects, you may have had letters sent home praising your achievements. There may have been gushing praise, and suggestions of a bright and shining career ahead of you. Your self-esteem and self-belief may have been boosted as a result. I hope you had this.

However, I have worked with lots of young people who were described at school as 'disinterested', 'disobedient' and/or 'not very bright' because they didn't get high grades or good reports, and because they were fidgeting or distracted in class.

These labels followed them everywhere but ignored important facts that explained what the teachers saw because, as you are about to see, sometimes the behaviour we see on the surface does not explain what's happening beneath.

Some kids couldn't concentrate in class as their skills lay elsewhere; for example, they could act beautifully but maths simply didn't make sense to them. They'd be anxious and fidgety if they were called upon to answer a question in front of their classmates.

Others needed to fidget their body in order to focus their mind – an experience sometimes but not always associated with attention deficit hyperactivity disorder (ADHD) – and as this wasn't allowed or understood by teachers it was interpreted as bad behaviour.

Others had home or school lives that were extremely distressing – perhaps due to loss of family members, poverty and food insecurity, abuse at home, bullying in school and many other reasons. All of which meant they were understandably distracted in the classroom.

These kids all needed different kinds of support but started to believe the stories they were told: 'I'm not bright', 'I'm stupid', 'I can't achieve', 'Something is wrong with me'.

When people in positions of power tell stories about us (our parents, teachers, bosses, the people we respect and fear), we tend to believe them. We start seeing information that confirms the story is true and ignore anything that contradicts it. Particularly when we're young, as this is the time we are learning about ourselves and when we trust the opinions of adults.

Stress isn't a bad thing, in small doses

I am not saying that tests, competition and feedback are bad. They can be very useful driving forces that help us learn.

You may have noticed that when you feel under pressure, there is a small window of opportunity, a moment when your performance actually improves. This is a biological fact. There's a sweet spot where adrenaline and cortisol enhance our abilities, especially our ability to focus and perform.

In the previous chapter I told you that the way we respond to stress depends on whether our caregivers were in tune with our emotional needs. It also depends on being exposed to manageable amounts of stress, which we learn to tolerate and overcome. This teaches us resilience.

Once we surpass that perfect level of stress, our abilities diminish rapidly. It's as if we hit a red zone. A mist descends and our ability to think clearly and act efficiently goes totally out of the window. Once we are in this state, the smallest thing can make us give up or react with anger or tears. I'm sure you can think of a time when this has happened in your adult life – a time when your stress levels suddenly got too high and something small happened which made you snap.

If you felt like you were under high pressure in school because your family would only accept straight As, you may have had the empowering belief that your family believed in you ... coupled with a potentially paralysing fear of what would happen if you failed.

If you were being heavily monitored, as you had been in detention many times before and the next time would be 'your last', you may have been desperate to prove that this time you would and could do better, but noticed that your best attempts at being 'good' were scuppered by how anxious you felt when you tried to apply yourself.

If you were told to be 'more like the other kids' (for example, young people with autism may be put under pressure to 'behave' as if they do not have autism), you may have noticed the stress levels of trying to be different from who you were naturally.

If you now feel you aren't academic, or 'good' at things, it may not have anything to do with your ability. It may be that you were interested in or skilled in the areas that didn't fit what the school system valued, or that you were (mis)judged as being 'not very bright' when actually you had wonderful talents that happened to be in areas not prioritised by the school.

While we were learning about the World Wars, the Kings and Queens of England, how to solve quadratic equations, how we fared against our classmates, and what our academic strengths were (or equally weren't), we were also learning about something else: who we were.

Questions for you: what was school like for you? Can you remember some of your school reports? Some of the things the adults or teachers told you about how you measured up against your school peers and your siblings? What was the general feeling you got about your abilities at that time? Were you ever singled out by teachers for your ability or seeming lack of ability? Did you feel under pressure to perform? Was it helpful? Who supported you? How do the answers to these questions link to how you see yourself now?

Quick tip 1: you are not defined by your school grades or any grade or how quickly you can perform any task. You can be proud of your natural talents even if they were not valued in school. Are there any activities you were put off doing in school because they weren't valued? Maybe art? Drama? When you think about these subjects, do they give you a thrill? If so, could you try them again?

Quick tip 2: making mistakes is the fastest way to grow. If you get something wrong, focus on what can be learned from this to help you in your next attempt. As very young kids, play was the place we learned about the world, making mistakes without consequence. Could you bring a little play back into your life? Choose a hobby or something you're already doing that you would be happy to see solely as for fun. Allow yourself to drop the idea you need to do well at it, see what happens when you allow yourself to make mistakes. Also, fun fact: mistakes lead to the best opportunities for learning, and sometimes the mistakes we make change the world. For example, Post-it notes, penicillin, X-rays and the microwave were all discovered following a mistake made by their now famous creators. You can't make decisions without ever making a mistake.

Who am I?

Adolescence brings physical changes such as growth spurts, weight gain, hair growth, breasts, periods, balls dropping, acne, voices breaking and wet dreams. It also causes emotional changes such as mood swings.

Adolescence starts when you hit puberty, typically between the ages of nine and seventeen, and ends in

One of my friends works as fast as Jack Flash getting things finished and done in a jiffy. The other works as slow as a snail, taking her time, meandering towards the finish line. I love them both equally. Why? Because these things don't matter when it comes to who is a person worthy of love, time and respect.

your mid-twenties, when your brain structures, such as your pre-frontal cortex (the part we use to focus our attention, make complex decisions, put ourselves in other people's shoes and inhibit our impulses) have finished developing. It used to be widely accepted that teenage impulsiveness was due to the underdevelopment of this part of the brain. However, research shows this isn't the full picture.

The adolescent brain

Have you noticed that adolescents suddenly seem bored by the people and activities they used to find fun? Moping around the house, talking little to their family, coming alive the moment a new friend calls the house, or when they are invited to do something new or that seems downright terrifying to an adult?

This isn't because they are immature or 'HATE YOU', as so many teenagers have shouted to their caregivers. It is because baseline levels of dopamine (the brain chemical that makes you feel good and want to repeat an action) drops during adolescence but spikes any time you engage in a novel activity, meaning adolescents may only feel truly alive and excited in the face of something new.

Also, have you noticed that some adolescents may walk straight into danger: take alcohol into school, shoplift, break curfew, throw themselves down a hill on a skateboard – no helmet, no brakes, eyes wide open – and not flinch?

Adolescents *can* understand risk. They can also at times (like all humans) overestimate the danger of certain actions – 'My friends hate me, my life is over', 'Oh my God, I nearly died'.

The adolescent brain will, however, downplay the risk of a new scenario if there are any possible positive gains – 'Yeah, I could get caught drinking, shoplifting, staying out, and I could get hurt, but imagine how fun it'll be doing it!'

Overall, this means that adolescents are driven to novelty, and can feel wildly alive in the face of the new and the dangerous, especially if their friends approve of said danger (more about the power of friends shortly), and may take risks (e.g.

drug-taking, fighting and driving too fast), sometimes with serious consequences.

However, we learn more about the world and what it's really like by testing the boundaries and rules given by teachers and parents, to see if they really are true and what'll happen if we break them: *How much trouble will I really be in if I get home late? How much danger will I really be in if I drive too fast? Or if I go to a party and get off-my-face drunk?*

My need to break rules, added to my desire to fit in, is the reason is why I, like most teen clichés, started smoking at thirteen (sorry, Mum), and when I got caught and didn't want to get punished, lied about it, saying, 'They're not mine, they're my friends'.' (Sorry, Beth!) And it's also why I engaged in a brief spate of shoplifting, which ended with a visit to the police station. Whoops!

This search for novelty and the downplaying of risk motivates adolescents towards independence. It means they turn towards their friends, determined to find out who they are outside of their family. It means they're able to take risks that help them initiate new friendships, try out for new sports or activities, sign up for courses, perform in front of huge audiences. It's the reason adolescents are able to do death-defying stunts on skateboards and snowboards, and many other kinds of activities that adults, who are only too aware of their own mortality, would never dare do.

The positive effects of risk-taking can be seen in the teenage activists who are standing up for what they believe in and are making real change in the world, such as Malala Yousafzai, the youngest person to win the Nobel Peace Prize, and Greta Thunberg, climate change warrior.

Finding out who we are and what we are capable of is easier when we aren't afraid of taking the risks required to do so.

Identity

Few adolescents are aware of these brain changes, feeling instead a slave to the biological changes happening underneath the surface (moody one moment, happy another, bored, enamoured, vulnerable, wild the next – a constant shifting cycle for many).

What they may be aware of, however, is the question, Who am I (outside of my family)? Where do I belong? What is my identity?

Identity includes every aspect that we use to define ourselves, including our beliefs, our ethics, our style, our taste, our racial identity, gender identity and sexual identity.

It continues to develop and evolve throughout our lives and as our roles change (e.g. if you become a parent, lover, sister, brother, friend, employee, business owner, volunteer, hipster, goth, part-time bum etc.). However, we become truly aware of it, and really shape it and own it, in our teens.

Some of us know core aspects of our identity from our earliest memories – 'I'm gay', 'I'm trans' (although not all people who identify this way know immediately), 'I'm religious', 'I care about justice'. As long as these areas of our lives are supported, they will flourish.

Some are told their identity from an early age by their family – 'You're a hard worker who will take over the family business', 'You're a sports star, you'll practice every night.' If the adolescent agreed with these designated life roles, then fine. If not, conflict possibly arose in the family, and rebellion may have ensued as the adolescent fought to find out their true self.

Some of us had to experiment with different beliefs, ethics, styles and tastes to find out who we were. I had a grunge phase, a hippy phase, a stoner phase, an uptight phase, a (possibly overly) wild phase, an angry phase, an anxious phase. I belonged to different groups for each of these times of my life. They didn't happen one after the other; they overlapped and merged, and ebbed and flowed. In fact, they weren't really *phases* – they were significant life periods that were important to help layer different aspects of who I am now.

You perhaps know a teenager experimenting with their identity right now. Ask them one week what their favourite band is and what's in fashion, mention their answer to them a week later and they'll look at you shocked: 'What! That band/ those clothes are so last year.'

While experimenting, we are looking for an identity that works for us, and for validation. We want people to show us in no uncertain terms that our true selves are accepted, deemed to be good and worthy. If we gain this, we can develop a strong sense of self. We can feel proud and sure. We flourish.

Why we care what other people think

Our earliest ancestors survived by existing in communities. A tribe meant access to food, people to procreate with and safety in numbers. Being out of the tribe meant almost certain death, as loners had to fend for themselves in a dangerous world, finding food and fighting off tigers solo. Therefore, even in the twenty-first century, any time we perceive we may be 'out of the group' our brain perceives: 'LIFE-THREATENING DANGER'.

Have you ever noticed that, even though you're an adult who can feed and fend for yourself, you can still feel anxious or hurt when someone dislikes your life choices, or when no one likes your latest Instagram picture, or where you see pictures of the people you know and love having fun without you (the fear of missing out, aka FOMO)?

Or have you noticed that when you feel lonely and like there's no one to share your secrets or your time with, that it hurts? If so, you are normal. We may be modern humans, but we have an ancient need to connect. For teenagers, whose emotional states are already heightened, this experience is even more pronounced.

This is why adolescents may focus on the items that connect them to their peers as if their life depends on it: 'I MUST have that top/iPhone/go to that party', as part of their brain believes that their life does indeed depend on it, and why Instagram and other places where people can like and comment on your pictures can be an extremely anxiety-provoking place for a teenager, whose life stage means they are particularly sensitive to social feedback.

Factors Affecting Our Identity

Our biggest fear isn't being rejected, it's being invisible.

—ROY PETITFILS

Many factors affect our identity, but here are some of the most influential.

Our culture

The culture and the time we grow up in shapes what information we are taught about multiple aspects of our identity. Many of us growing up in the UK were taught:

Humans are hardwired to connect. If you care what other people think about you, feel pain in response to a perceived rejection, you are normal.

- **There are two genders:** male/female, which are dictated by the genitals you are born with. Even though the Office of the High Commissioner for Human Rights states that the number of babies who are born 'intersex' (1.7 per cent of world population) is as almost common as people having red hair (2 per cent of world population), and the fact that not everyone identifies with the male/female binary and some people will transition genders in their lifetimes. This is not a new phenomenon. For example, in the Indian subcontinent, 'Hijra' (or 'Khawaja Sira' as referred to in Pakistan) are officially recognised as a third gender and have historically been revered as demigods. And many other cultures have a long history of a third gender and/or non-binary people being held in high regard, for example 'Two Spirit' people, in Indigenous North American groups; 'Māhū' in Native Hawaiian and Tahitian cultures; 'Fakaleiti' in Tongan Culture and 'Bakla' in the pre-colonisation Philippines.

- **There are roles for each gender, which we must assume:** girls are feminine, pretty, kind and accommodating. They are concerned with relationships. They are the embodiment of sexuality but are also vulnerable and emotional. They should cover up and not go out for fear of what will happen to them. Boys are strong, independent and make great leaders. They are confident in their abilities and are competitive. They don't need help, as they don't struggle. Big boys don't cry. They are 'trouble' and can't be trusted to manage their sexual urges – 'boys will be boys, after all' – which is an incredibly dangerous message for people of all genders. Also, did you notice the boys' gender traits (leadership, confidence, competition) are the ones most highly valued by society at present (vs. kindness, vulnerability and an understanding of relationships)?

- **Sex is one thing and is risky:** Sex means penetrative penis-in-vagina sex, which is engaged in by men and women who are in love. Sex leads to teenage pregnancy and STIs, which gives a clear message that sex should just be avoided in the first place, as it is dangerous and/or could lead to the biggest mistake of your life! In truth, sexuality is much bigger than these things. Sexuality can be fluid, with people of all genders enjoying it. It includes intimacy, curiosity, play, consent, respect, and can be between people who are in love or people who have just met. The safest way to enjoy and explore your sexuality is through learning what you like and what you don't (self-pleasure rules, but, like I said, this is rarely supported in our society), how to express this (sharing your 'what's hot' and how to say no or absolutely not) and how to listen when someone says no. Unfortunately, self-exploration was stamped out for a few of us at a young age. Many children unknowingly discover self-pleasure at an early age. My friend, for example, once 'rode her bed post' pretending it was a pony. When she realised how good it felt, she kept on doing it. Upon realising their avid little rider was getting a little more pleasure out of the game than they'd initially realised, her parents panicked and shouted at her, 'Shameful, sinful girl!' The way kids are treated in response to this will shape how they think of self-pleasure going forward. Support a child to understand this behaviour and you give them a chance to have a healthy relationship with self-exploration. Shame a child (which is what often happens) and create a connection between self-exploration and 'I am bad'.

And, unfortunately for women, attempts at sexual exploration are often labelled as 'slutty' behaviour.

In case you didn't get the memo ... people masturbate and you can too. Shame free!

These teachings have real-world consequences. They tell us there is one way to be, meaning many of us may have grown up with a limited idea of what and who we *could* be. Also, these narrow views mean we are more likely to police ourselves and/or others who are different from what we're shown is expected/approved. Bullying and prejudice start this way.

They also mean we are left ill-equipped in an area of our life (sexuality and physical intimacy) that at best can be mind-blowing, earth-shatteringly good or, at worst, utterly dangerous (when there is no understanding or respect for consent).

What did you grow up hearing about gender and sexuality? Was it like this or was it something different? In terms of sexuality, did you feel empowered? Confused? Scared? Were your gender and sexual orientations seen in a positive light? What words were thrown around the playground about gender and sexuality? Did you hear slurs like 'lezza' and 'slut' in the playground or at home? And how was your sexual debut? Did people support you through this time?

Hopefully your first sexual encounter was a positive one (respectful, exciting, liberating, with only a smattering of awkwardness) and discussed only with people you trusted. For some of us, sadly, the experience was a source of gossip for others, or we were slut-shamed (men are rarely shamed for their sexual activity), or we had to come out hoping desperately that the people we shared our sexual identity with would support and love us. Whatever happened at this stage further affected how proud we could feel about this aspect of our identity.

The effects of this early miseducation can affect us right through life. Psychologist Sarah McClelland, who writes about 'intimate justice', found that young women rated their sexual satisfaction depending on how satisfied their partner was. Young men, however, rated their satisfaction depending on whether *they* orgasmed or not. Interestingly, women's satisfaction based on partners was present irrespective of partner, meaning when women were intimate with women the orgasm gap disappeared! And when people were asked to describe what sexual experiences at the low end of satisfaction would be like, the young women described these experiences using labels including 'depressed', 'emotionally sad', 'pain', and 'degradation'. Whereas the young men described such experiences in terms of 'loneliness', 'having an unattractive sexual partner' and 'insufficient sexual stimulation'.

I recently worked with a straight couple. They had been together for eight years and came to therapy to talk about sex. Any time the woman told the man what she wanted, an argument ensued and sex stopped. When we talked this through, the man said: 'As a man, I should know how to please my woman. I should be confident, I shouldn't need to be told, otherwise this means I'm bad at sex and have failed in the unmanliest way. When she suggests that I touch her in a certain way, I think she's telling me exactly this: I am bad in bed. I am not a man.'

In this case, the mixture of schooling (learning that we need to do things perfectly otherwise we've failed), gender norms (learning that men should be confident leaders who never need help) and the limited knowledge we are taught around sex had merged to create problems in their relationship. But, once understood, these were possible to overcome.

Good news: research shows that gender is slowly becoming more fluid (yay!), and that more girls are taking on 'traditionally masculine qualities' such as showing confidence and leadership skills (qualities that should never have been gendered in the first place).

Bad news: research also shows that caregivers and peers are more likely to punish and shun 'gender violations' in boys than in girls. The power imbalance set up between genders is kept in place by the punishment of people who act outside of their predefined roles. If we are to reach a place of equality, we need to show people of all genders that they can succeed and be taken seriously. AND we need to show people of all genders (particularly boys) that showing emotion, being kind, caring and open to being taught by others is not a threat to their manhood but is in fact deeply important.

Ruth Bader Ginsburg said, 'A gender line . . . helps to keep women not on a pedestal, but in a cage.' I believe this is utterly true. But I would argue it keeps almost everyone in a cage – not just women.

Can you see the link between what we are taught and how we feel as adults? Have you ever thought of yourself as a slut after having a one-night stand or two? Have you ever felt ashamed after having a wank? Or like you aren't having enough sex and that this somehow means you are less as a person? What foibles do you have about sex? Does it link to how you learned about it?

A quick exercise

Your sexuality and how you find pleasure alone or with others is not only normal, it's fantastic. Desire, pleasure, power – you can explore them all and you deserve to feel pleasure, not pain or shame. If shame or embarrassment arises around sexuality or your body, this feeling likely did not start with *you*, so why not shake off all that baggage and begin exploring your sexuality with pride.

And …

There is no such thing as being 'bad in bed'. Clinical psychologist Dr Karen Gurney told me that: 'Phrases like "he's bad in bed" or "I have a low sex drive" are statements that prevent people from under-standing that sex is only ever a dance between people, not a state that one person can own. It's not possible to be "bad in bed", as sex is a communication, not a learned skill (though many of us can be bad commu-nicators!)' This means we need to start learning how to communicate what we like, want and need, and get comfortable with asking what others desire too.

Decide one thing you can do today to start learning what you like or don't like. Maybe retire to bed early today for a little self-exploration. Maybe buy yourself a sex toy (you can tell yourself it was doctor's orders!). If this feels too big a step, could you buy a book to help you learn more about sex and sexuality? Once you find something that feels good, practise saying you like it out loud. I know it sounds weird, but we have to start being able to speak our desires. Alone is often the best place to start when we feel a bit shy. Do the same with the aspects of sex you don't like.

Sticks and stones will break my bones ~~but~~ and words ~~will never~~ can absolutely hurt me.

Bullying

In the UK, one in five young people report being bullied in school. Of those, nearly two-thirds were bullied due to their appearance. Young people with long-term illnesses, additional educational needs and disabilities, and those living in single-parent homes, are some of the most likely to be targeted. And almost half of LGBTQ+ pupils report being bullied.

Do you notice these incidents link to *difference*? Or, more accurately, diversity that we may not have been taught to understand or embrace?

While most of you reading this right now are no longer in school, these statistics suggest that a large portion of you may have experienced bullying. Bullying can have wide-ranging and wide-reaching effects, and doesn't just happen in school, therefore it's important that you know how to identify it, how to stop it, and how to prevent past bullying from affecting how you feel today.

Bullying can be physical, and it can be verbal. Many of us remember hearing terms of abuse in the school playground, e.g. 'slut', 'fatso', 'nerd', 'loser', 'idiot'. Today, the slurs are often much worse.

Bullying can also be done online – someone leaving harassing comments on a person's social media page or sharing and laughing about photographs or videos they've posted *is* bullying and can be devastating for a young person, especially when they know they'll be facing their classmates – who will have seen the comments – the next day.

Bullying can be silent – for instance, someone excluding you from their group or a certain activity, or ignoring you when you are in their presence, cutting you out. This can happen at any age.

If these things happen once or twice, or if you have friends who support you through the experience, buffering you from the comments (ideally stopping them), you may be hurt for a while, and then move on. If it happens repeatedly, and no one steps in to help you, anxiety, sadness, loneliness, possibly sleepless nights can arise.

Bullying has caused and continues to be a cause of suicide. It can have seriously damaging effects on everyone who experiences it. It isn't confined to the playground or childhood, either. Many people experience bullying in their adult relationships, at the office and/or in other areas of their lives.

People who are bullied can find it hard to trust others, assuming they will bully them too. They may also start to believe the words and actions of the bullies. This makes sense, especially if people stood aside and watched what happened without trying to stop it. When this happens, it can seem as if everyone else agrees with what is occurring, meaning we must deserve it, or that we are not worthy of being protected or treated any better than this. If this is something you have been thinking, or have thought in the past, I promise you that you deserve(d) better. Bystanders usually don't step in because they feel afraid to, or because they think they can't do anything to help (factually untrue), not because they agree with what you're going through. You do not deserve to be bullied.

Have you ever been bullied? In school? In work? How has it affected you?

Managing the effects of bullying

Know that the words and actions of bullies are not your fault. Bullying behaviour often arises when the perpetrator has either been bullied by others, making them believe it's normal, or when they want to make someone else feel smaller because something is happening in their lives that compels them to behave this way. Knowing this can help us see their words and actions as a reflection of their lives rather than due to a fault of our own.

Speak to someone you trust. Ask for their support to manage the bullying. If you are still at school, can this person help tell the school what is happening? If you're an adult in the workplace, can you share what's happening with a trusted colleague who will support you if

---

you make an official complaint? Even if they cannot do something about the situation immediately, sharing how you feel will help you know you are not alone.

Do not respond to bullies (unless you have a specific plan of action). If possible, walk away from them and identify safe people who you can turn to when it arises again. If the bullying is happening online, Chapter 3 will tell you how to manage this.

If you have been bullied at any point:

Look out for the times where you talk to yourself or treat yourself in the ways the bullies did. At any age, the words and behaviours of others affect us. The words uttered or spat at us burrow their way into our psyche, and can become words we use against ourselves. If you now have an inner critic that speaks to you as the bullies did, Chapter 9 will talk you through why this is normal, as well as giving you ways to separate from and overcome these words. I still hear 'flat-chested, anorexic-looking bitch' on occasion when I look in the mirror, the choice words of my personal bullies when I was thirteen. Thankfully I now place little value on those slurs.

If thinking about bullying has left you feeling a little anxious right now, bring to mind the being you thought of at the beginning of the chapter – the person or pet that made you feel safe. Let them soothe you. Take a moment to imagine them with all of your senses. They believed and believe in you. Remember, you internalised their words too.

Fun fact: You are even internalising my words right now, creating a miniature Dr Soph in your mind, whose words can speak to you and support you when you feel uncertain or afraid in the future.

Finally, if you know someone being bullied, please intervene.

Our caregivers

Adolescents are obsessed with their friends, but they still need their caregivers' support.

They need them to be role models, to offer their wisdom, experience and a knowing ear, as they have already been through all of this. They need encouragement to help them thrive, and not be judgemental if they want to explore their identity.

I have many clients who, during adolescence, heard their caregivers slut-shame, fat-shame and use homophobic language about other teens in the neighbourhood, sending a clear message about what would and would not be tolerated within the family. I also have many clients who had this language used against them too, or who were punished for wearing clothes not traditionally meant for their gender, or who were routinely weighed through their teenage years, their calories counted and diets put in place. As this happened during the period when they were still figuring out who they were, the message that something was 'wrong' or 'unacceptable' about their appearance, or that they were 'fat', left a lasting impression. They still feel those slurs when they think about their body or clothes now.

Teenagers also need caregivers to instil and keep boundaries. They need to know that someone is still ultimately in charge and can swoop in if there's danger, as well as being clear what the limits are and how those rules will be enforced.

If you are parenting a teen now, my friend and fellow clinical psychologist Dr Ann-Louise Lockhart summarised this experience so well, and maybe you will find this helpful:

> When you sit on a roller coaster and you pull down the head restraint, what do they tell you to do? They tell you to push on it to make it secure. They tell you to do this because they want to keep you safe. You want to make sure that you are safe. This is such a beautiful analogy and example about parenting a teenager. As we push in and lean in, they push back. Why? They want to make sure you are a secure and stable base they can trust.

This can be a very difficult time for caregivers, as most of us were tricky as hell as teenagers, slouching around the house, unimpressed by anything outside of our friends, getting angry at the slightest things. And our caregivers had to manage this while also grieving the loss of their little one, who used to look up at them as if they were the centre of the universe.

The bottom line is, as we struggled through our teens,

trying to become the people we are today, most of us wanted our adults to be close to us, to see us and support us, even though we didn't necessarily show it. (That reminds me, I should probably take a moment to say, Sorry, Mum. I was a nightmare, wasn't I? Love you to bits!)

Developing a Personal Brand

Authentic validation inoculates us from the ravages of shame.
—ALAN DOWNES, *The Velvet Rage*

If we struggle to find our identity during our teens, or if we cannot find a place to fit in, 'Who am I?' can become, 'What's wrong with me?'

As adolescents, if we felt shame for any aspects of who we were, it may understandably have affected our mood and how we felt about our place in the world. It may have also affected our behaviour.

Remember I said that humans always find a way to cope? The teen that feels shame or alienation for an aspect of their identity, and isn't shown how to manage and process their feelings, finds other ways to manage.

They may withdraw – if you don't have another clear way to cope, pulling away from something upsetting may feel like the only safe option.

They may find ways to numb out – teens rarely know how to manage big emotions; they haven't been taught the skills, so numbing through alcohol and drugs may be where they turn.

They may, like a chamaeleon, change their appearance to blend in, becoming more like the people deemed 'acceptable' by their peers or society, adjusting how they speak, act and express themselves in order to fit in.

For example, the adolescent alienated for their ethnicity or race may assimilate to be more like the archetypal white child in school, rejecting parts of their culture that may have previously felt important. The teen whose identity or sexuality is seen by others as making them less of a 'man' may try to become more like the 'manly man', potentially rejecting their sexuality or the deep knowledge of how they wish to act, dress, date and live.

Many of us during adolescence tried to construct a new identity or 'personal brand' that we show the world – one that doesn't hold any of the bits we've been told not to show.

We may work on becoming 'perfect'. Working to get 'perfect' grades, the 'perfect' body, the 'perfect' clothes, etc. I put this in quotes, as there is no such thing. We may become the 'comic' of the class, the 'quirky' one, the 'flamboyant' one, the 'aloof but interesting' one – anything to detract from the things we fear other people will find out about us.

A young man, a client of mine, felt that no matter how much he achieved, or how much praise he gained, he couldn't shake the feeling that he wasn't 'enough'. To the outside world he looked to be 'killing it'. He had 'the car' and a six-figure salary; he was tall, muscular, always well turned out (like someone in a Hugo Boss advert), always working overtime, giving more than was asked for in his job, and he knew all the on-trend topics to talk about. He was often told how hot, smart, successful, funny and overachieving he was. Other people envied him, and yet, on the inside, he felt insecure. The issue was that he felt the perfect exterior was a façade he adopted after being shamed for being gay by his peers and his father when he was growing up. He had believed, *If I can be perfect, people will love me; they won't think about my shameful parts.* And people had indeed praised him since that time.

No matter how much others heap praise on us, sometimes it never hits the spot. Why? Because part of us is always thinking, *If they knew the real me, they wouldn't be saying that.*

Not everyone feels this way, obviously. Some people feel great being on their own, and some people have no interest in 'fitting in' at all.

> **Questions for you:** did you feel that you fitted in with your peers at school or outside of school? Did you have a friend or friends? Did you feel accepted? Did you belong to a group? What group did you belong to? Were there parts of yourself you felt you had to hide in order to be accepted? How hard did you try to hide these parts? Did you have multiple friendship groups, adjusting yourself slightly to fit into each? Did you sit on the edge of many groups and therefore not really feel like you fitted into any? How did this shape how you saw yourself? Do you think you created a version of yourself that made you more acceptable to others?

The new rules

- Who you think you are today and how you feel about your identity may indeed link to who you were told you could be as a teenager and the amount of validation, support and boundaries you received at that time.

- Feeling anxious about not fitting in, feeling FOMO and caring what others think is normal. Remember: mostly everyone wants to fit in. Most people are worrying about the same things. Worrying about how they look, come across, will perform, will be judged. Most people are focused inward and not on you. This can be a liberating realisation.

- You do not have to conform to gender or other expectations. The world is slowly moving towards a more fluid way of understanding gender (and sexuality too). If you are 'meant' to be 'masculine' but want to engage in something traditionally seen as 'girly', such as being emotional, know that you are more than allowed to do that. Likewise, if you do not want to conform to a gender binary, you don't have to! I recommend reading Alok Vaid–Menon's book *Beyond the Gender Binary*, if you're looking for more reading on this.

- If there are parts of yourself that you had to pretend did not exist, or have had to push away, you don't have to do that now. When those parts arise, you can say hello and welcome them in. I know this may sound hard. If it feels daunting, try to find a community of like-minded or like-identified people. Instagram and other online communities exist for almost everything, so if you can't find people who make you feel good and safe in the real world, online might be for you.

- **Our identity feels most stable when we nurture multiple aspects of it.** If you rely on one area and something gets in the way of it, who are you then? For example, base your identity on your job and lose your job, or base your identity on your relationship, your looks, your beliefs, and something challenges these, you may find yourself struggling with your sense of self.

- **If you're a caregiver, please support your young people to know all of this.** Be the listening ear, and the place our future generations can turn to. Be the person who says 'Let's go for a haircut' (or another thing they would like to do). Ask, 'What would you like me to call you?' to the young person who tells you they think they are trans. Be the person who says, 'You can always come to me when you feel sad and teary' to the boy who tells you he is struggling. Be the person who says, 'Thank you for telling me. I am so happy you did. If this is a secret, you can trust me to keep it. Who else knows, so I make sure I don't out you?' to the young person who tells you they are gay, or bi, or queer, or pansexual. Be the person who says, 'You can be a badass leader and I will support you in whatever role you choose' to every young person that crosses your path. Most importantly, be the person who says 'I believe you' to any person or people who tell you they have been harmed. Let them know they matter, and that you will support them to find justice and/or whatever steps they wish to take to find safety and peace after danger and fear. Show them they can be everything they already are. And that the insecurities many of us had drilled into us do not have to be theirs as well.

A Note to You

Hi!

I think it's time to reiterate that not everything can be explained by childhood.

Sometimes you'll strive for perfection simply because you want to do a good job. Sometimes you'll want to please people because you've met someone you really like. You believe that putting a bit of extra effort in will give your relationship a better shot (and you would be right). Sometimes you'll find yourself mediating between arguing friends, family or others simply because you genuinely want to help.

Sometimes we do become the perfectionist, the clown or 'the aloof', or something else, as a way of surviving. Sometimes . . . we just are those things.

Sometimes we just do stuff because we do! There may be no hidden metaphor and no secret link to the past.

You are not a robot. You do have free will. Spontaneity is real.

OK, let's get to another layer of life that shapes us and can often make us feel distressed: the media, marketing and social media.

Dr Soph xx

3. Advertising, Media, Social Media

You can still believe you are lacking, even if your childhood was great and you grew up surrounded by supportive people who were in tune with your emotional needs.

Why is that?

Advertising, the media (newspapers, magazines, films and TV) and social media, notably Instagram – all these things can be inspiring. For instance, I love clothes, and I get my ideas and stay 'on trend' through the advertisements, media and social media I consume. However, they can leave us feeling rather inadequate.

Films and TV share imaginative and exciting stories that we can escape into at the end of a tough day. But they often promote and reinforce prejudiced ideas. For example, many ads, films and TV programmes lack diversity and often replicate sexist, heteronormative, fatphobic, ableist, racist and other prejudiced tropes that are already rife in society (such as the Protein World adverts targeting women with the slogan "Are you beach body ready?", and the racist portrayals of 'Blackface' and 'Yellowface' in *Little Britain*), and they often include negative storylines about mental health. All of this can lower self-esteem and lead to anxiety, depression, restrictive eating and the other forms of emotional distress that I regularly see in my clinic.

The previous two chapters built upon each other, moving from birth through your school years, exploring how the messages you received from your immediate family, caregivers and teachers as to what was 'acceptable' behaviour when you were growing up may have shaped your thinking about yourself and others. This chapter is slightly different. Advertising, media, and social media can have detrimental effects at any age. During our childhood and teenage years we are most sensitive to the information given about who is worthy and lovable. The magazines, adverts, movies, TV and social media we are exposed to growing up will have affected what we expect for ourselves. And these incredibly powerful media influences continue throughout our lives.

Advertising

In 2019, Chloé Michel (an economics PhD student at Zurich University) and colleagues demonstrated that when a country spends more money on advertising, there is a subsequent 'significant' dip in life satisfaction across the nation. They predicted that if a country doubled its advertising spend, it could expect a 3 per cent drop in life satisfaction across its population.

The relationship between advertising and life *dissatisfaction* is because we are in a constant state of wanting more. Save up to buy a new phone, car or outfit, and you'll feel pleased for a short while ... until a newer version comes out. Feel fine about how you look, then open a magazine and realise you haven't quite got the abs or the pore-free skin of the models in the adverts. So you reach for your wallet – for the new gym membership, new clothes, new-fangled diet or the facial treatment that promises to get rid of all evidence of ageing.

Many of the people I see in my clinic say they feel a failure. When I ask them why, they often say they don't match up to the images they see in magazines or movies. They feel too ugly, too fat, and like they haven't acquired enough status symbols that would signal they have a good life.

I will use the beauty industry and advertising to demonstrate how these feelings of inadequacy can start.

Selling perfection

Think about the ads you saw growing up, when you were a teenager. Did you read magazines or see ads on TV when you were a teen, or did you have social media? Do you remember what the images you saw were like at that time? Do you remember any brands you particularly liked? How did the people in those images look?

How were they gendered (were they clearly shown to be male vs. female)? How did they act? Were they thin? Toned? Muscled? Were they beautiful? If so, what made them beautiful? Were they ageless? Only one race? One skin tone? Were they presented as 'perfect'? Were they an extremely narrow representation of human life and experience? Is the shorthand for what you saw: tall, white, thin, toned as hell, buff-as-hell men ('manly' men), and feminine and pretty women ('girly' girls and 'womanly' women)? Did they have the beauty and the body that you think of as the ideal that you need to compare to?

This is what I saw in *Mizz* and *More!* magazines, my favourite teen reads, and in my mum's copies of *Vogue*. Everyone seemed glamorous and as rich as Scrooge McDuck swimming around in his piles of money. And they were constantly having

sex or getting themselves ready for sex (in a very heteronormative way). Perfume ads were the worst, showing supermodel
bodies dipped in gold or lounging in elite hotel rooms.

As well as turning to their peers, teenagers look to the
media and film to find out what is expected of them and what
is 'normal'. What you see growing up matters.

The description I just gave you, the beauty ideal in the UK
at that time, became the template in my mind for 'attractive,
worthy human' (yes, I linked 'worthy' with 'attractive' as this
was what I saw everywhere). I therefore believed that if I could
look like the people in the ads, refine myself in the gym, wear
the right clothes, buy the perfume they were selling, I could
have that life too. Advertising works.

I didn't notice that the models in the photos and media
didn't match up to the level of 'perfection' portrayed. I didn't
think about the fact that they were made up or adjusted with
lighting and further technology in post-production (I'd never
heard of this). I didn't think about the fact that these ads were
specifically designed to sell me something. And I didn't think
about the fact that if *they* don't even look like that in real life,
no one can.

I, like so many people, became preoccupied with how I
looked, and I also noticed that no matter what I bought, it
didn't quite scratch the itch.

The amount to which each of us is affected by advertising
varies. Some people feel mildly but manageably inadequate,
while others feel totally devastated. For example, they
might not see themselves represented in this marketing,
and start to wonder, 'Am I an anomaly? Is something wrong
with me?'

How much we are affected by advertising and beauty standards depends on a number of factors, including:

- **Gender**: Women are under significantly more pressure to conform to a thin body type, and subsequently report twice as much weight-based body discrimination as men. However, male body issues are on the rise too, with research showing that increased exposure to images of muscular male bodies directly links to decreased mood and higher levels of physical dissatisfaction in countries where muscles are the gold standard of male beauty.
- **How we believe we measure up to the images we are shown.**

Social comparison theory

Leon Festinger, the father of social comparison theory (1954), says comparison is one of the ways we learn about ourselves and make sense of where we are in the world. We look around, see what others are doing, then ask, 'How do I measure up?'

If we feel we are doing better than others (this is called downward comparison), we will feel a boost and our self-esteem will go up. If we feel we aren't doing as well (upward comparison), but feel that with a little practice or effort we could achieve that level, we may feel inspired.

If we see a large discrepancy, we may feel inadequate, defeated and lose motivation.

From an evolutionary perspective, this will have helped our ancestors learn their place in their tribe, inspiring them to learn the skills needed to grow and be better at surviving in their environment, and may have helped them know when a fight wasn't worth picking, as the opponent was bigger and clearly stronger.

In the days before global media and the internet, we solely compared ourselves to our family, our local community, colleagues and the Joneses up the street. Nowadays, we can compare ourselves to people we know, celebrities and influencers, 24/7. How you respond will therefore depend on how closely you feel you measure up to the images shown.

When we see the images of airbrushed, 'perfect' people, living 'perfect' lives, in magazines, movies and heavily curated Instagram feeds, we have an impossible benchmark. The people that feel they *are* close to the images they see may strive for the impossible benchmark, not disheartened but excited by the possibility they can achieve this goal.

However, for those who feel far from the idea portrayed, the benchmark may switch quickly from being a carrot of opportunity to a stick with which they beat themselves when they find themselves falling short. And these images are everywhere. Bombarding us every second of every day. For many people this leads to feelings of inadequacy, de-motivation and even devastation, which can show up as low self-esteem, anxiety and depression, and can be one of many reasons people develop eating disorders.

For those of you who do not feel affected by beauty ads, and who have no body image issues, you may notice social comparison affects you in other areas instead. Maybe you grew up seeing images of people who had cars, planes and jewels, and you now compare yourself to the super-rich. Or maybe you have recently seen someone gain a promotion and felt inspired, as you believe you could reach that level of success; or maybe you're de-motivated as it feels out of your league.

Or maybe you've noticed that even when you achieve the thing you hope for – e.g. the promotion, the new car, the latest iPhone – you feel good about it for a short while, but then, moments later, when you see someone else has an even bigger promotion, an even more impressive car, the next model of iPhone, you suddenly feel like your achievement meant nothing.

Advertising exploits the human drive to compare ourselves with others. It thrives by keeping us in a state of wanting more. If we felt we were 'enough', we'd buy much less.

Quick tips to protect yourself from the negative effects of advertising

The next time you start to criticise yourself for your looks, or something you own that isn't the newest model, take a moment. Don't automatically reach for a new quick fix or the 'buy' button. Ask yourself: 'Who's profiting from my insecurities?'

When you notice negative social comparison arise at any time, know that it's a normal human experience. Then reframe your thought. For example, if it occurs in relation to an ad, and you think, *I'm ugly because I don't look like that*, remind yourself that people in advertising are nearly always filtered, photoshopped and edited. Remind yourself that no one's worth is based on how they look, even though we've

78

been told many times this is the case. If it arises in relation to seeing someone attain a goal you have yet to achieve – *They are incredible, I'm a failure* – consider if there's a way to see their achievement as something to aspire to, rather than as a sign of your failure. If self-criticism is something that plagues you, Chapter 9 (The Inner Critic) will help you manage this, and Chapter 13 (Mindfulness) will help you notice and let go of upsetting thoughts, including comparison.

Use social comparison to your advantage. If you need motivation, look to people who are doing slightly better than you, who you feel you could aspire to. If you need a boost, look at the people you feel are equal to you and are impressed by (it's always easier to be proud of someone else's success than our own), people who are behind you on your journey – perhaps a rung lower on your career ladder – so you can be reminded of how far you've come. Or maybe compare yourself to yesterday's self.

The good news

Even though models are now generally younger and thinner than they were twenty-five years ago, the media and advertising does become slightly more diverse year on year.

You may have noticed that a slightly different message has started to appear in advertising in recent years. For example, more 'in touch' beauty brands, such as Dove, espouse a more 'authentic' and diverse set of values, and the singer Rihanna's make-up and lingerie brand, Fenty, has one of the most diverse beauty campaigns I have ever seen. Both brands have also pledged they will never airbrush and edit their images. It is definitely a positive change, and one we need to see more of. Yet we still have a long way to go, as 70 per cent of women say they do not feel represented in the ads they see.

The bad news

Advertising is becoming increasingly difficult to spot. Previously, you could turn off the TV or put down a magazine and know that you wouldn't see an advert until you returned to them. Now, ads are targeted to you specifically and pretty much follow you around on social media.

Our brain uses short cuts to make sense of the world. One of these is social proof, the idea that if other people like something it must be good, and if lots of people follow someone they must be right. These short cuts can have us idolising people with huge followings, taking their words and ideas as gospel, wanting to buy anything they are selling, whether what they are selling works for us or not. They can stop us questioning what is right and true.

You Google something you need to buy once – a kettle, a toaster, a holiday, or look for advice on a personal matter such as acne, weight issues, low libido or erectile dysfunction – and suddenly the solution is offered to you again and again, as if by magic, the instant you open your social media.

Sometimes the advertising on social media is so subtle we miss it. Influencers are often paid to promote products. Most worryingly, advertising carried out via influencers (even if not paid for) doesn't have to comply with the trading standards that traditional ads have to, which is especially worrying for health- and beauty-related products, as I have seen so many laxative teas and laxative lollipops, which are not only unnecessary but can be downright dangerous.

Being able to identify advertising, and also any potential editing, has been shown to decrease the negative impact on self-esteem. Start familiarising yourself with the telltale tricks of these industries. Consider that someone talking excitedly about a brand may be secretly trying to sell you something. And start paying attention to the difference between the people you see in your real life and those you see in ads. People have pores, wrinkles, lumps, blemishes and asymmetrical bodies. If someone looks too smooth and has no pores, lines or marks, it's likely they've been edited.

Pay attention to adverts and editing

Spend the next 24 hours on the lookout for edited, airbrushed ads. And look for images on social media that might sneakily be selling you something. What do you notice? Who is represented? What is the idea that you're being sold? What item(s) are they selling you? Are the people edited? Then turn your attention towards yourself. Notice how you feel when you look at these ads. Scan your whole body. Is there any part of you that has a sinking feeling?

Or is there a part of you that feels inspired? Or motivated to buy the item? Be curious about the effects of advertising on your thoughts and your body. If you become overwhelmed, remind yourself of this chapter and choose a soothing skill from the back of the book.

You are good enough

I had a client who knew the ins and outs of advertising and the beauty industry. She could spot an edited image a mile off, was part of a body-positivity campaign and her social media was full of activists who spoke of loving the skin they were in. During one therapy session she confided in me: 'I truly believe all people and all bodies are deserving of love and are worthy, yet when I look in the mirror and see I've put on weight my heart sinks and I feel shame. I feel bad because of my appearance AND because it makes me feel like a fraud, someone who pretends they believe all bodies are equal but who doesn't really mean it.'

My client wasn't a fraud. She struggled because until the fat-shaming, age-shaming and other shaming messages we see in other forms of media disappear, it's going to be very hard for any of us to shake the feeling that we need to be 'perfect'.

So many magazines and newspapers still run articles shaming celebrities for being 'caught' without their make-up or without their hair 'done', for having wrinkles or a double chin, or for having cellulite, and many others straight-up fat-shame celebrities.

These articles are not only bullying, they also serve as a stark warning of what we are to contend with if we want to dare to be human and act outside of the beauty ideal of our time. They are the modern-day equivalent of a head placed on a spike – a warning that, should we dare veer away from the prescribed (impossible) standards, we will be 'punished'.

Research shows that fat-shaming celebrities in the mass media leads to a spike in anti-fat attitudes. And that people aren't always aware they implicitly believe 'fat is bad'. For example, if I asked you, 'do you believe fat is bad?', you might say, 'NO! I vehemently disagree. People of all sizes are worthy and good.' However, you might show that you unconsciously do agree with this statement by making knee jerk assumptions that thin people are more likely to be good, or by instantly preferring someone who's thinner to someone who is bigger.

This is an important point. It means that even when we vehemently disagree with shaming stories in the media, and feel understandable outrage, we still internalise the underlying message we are being given: 'fat is bad', 'fat is shameful'.

When we learn new information that is accompanied by a strong emotion such as shame, it's almost as if it is stored in our memory and tagged with a red-hot label, a PICK ME marker, making it the first piece of information that gets chosen when your brain is trying to make sense of the world or what it sees. So, even if you don't feel you have internalised fatphobia, it's likely that the belief is still lurking somewhere in your subconscious. You will know this is the case if, like my client, you ever put on weight and you feel shame that seems to come from nowhere, or if you see someone else put on weight and feel suddenly and unexpectedly judgmental of them.

This is one reason why you can follow a trillion and one body-positive, body-neutral, acne-positive, age-positive, sex-positive and a million other kinds of activists, believe in everything they say, feel empowered and ready to see yourself as worthy exactly as you are, and then look in the mirror, or at yourself and your behaviour, and panic that you are not good enough.

If this latter point resonates with you, keep following the activists. Use mindfulness to notice and let go of the thoughts as they arise, remembering the thoughts were never yours but came from the media. Offer yourself self-compassion and know that, over time, these conditioned beliefs will slowly fade.

So many of us judge people based on their choice of clothes, style and accessories rather than based on their heart; decide if someone is good or bad based on how they look rather than how they make us feel; aspire to be like those whose life looks good in pictures, rather than those who make a true difference in the world. I don't think we intend to think this way. I think we have been socialised to do so. Whatever the cause, it is up to us to undo this way of thinking.

Film and TV

If you can see it, you can be it. And I believe in that.
—ELIZABETH MARVEL

Film and TV has a significant problem with a lack of diversity and accurate storytelling, which affects how we think about ourselves and what we believe we can aspire to. Research shows that white boys' esteem is improved when they watch TV and film – they link this to the fact that white men are usually cast as the heroes, who have power, money, incredible jobs, a glamorous lifestyle. And that girls' and Black boys' self-esteem is decreased, as their roles are usually sex object, sidekick or villain.

It isn't just girls and Black boys who are cast in restricted roles. So many people are shown in a single and stereotyped way in TV and film. Too often, the gay character in the sitcom is super 'camp', the person with a fuller figure in ads is unhappy about their weight or is bullied, there's one Black person in a soap opera and they're cast as an 'angry young Black woman'. Or there's one disabled person and they are shown as the surreal character or portrayed as a hero or 'an inspiration' for living their life. And usually each of these roles are supporting roles in TV and film, never the lead.

Sometimes, whole communities are misrepresented too. The popular British TV programme *EastEnders* has been widely criticised for this. It is set in the East End of London, an area known for its ethnically diverse community, yet the majority of the characters are white.

In 2014, an email from an unnamed producer to Sony chairman Michael Lynton was leaked. The email stated that diversity didn't pay and it was a financial risk to include Black people in leading roles.

The idea 'diversity doesn't pay' has been one excuse for the extremely slow process of diversification in TV and film. It's a fallacy, as was shown by the box-office smash hits *Black Panther* and *Crazy Rich Asians*, but that's not the point. Deciding who deserves to be seen and represented should not be about profit.

It should be about humanity. It is very hard for people to feel good about themselves when they can't see themselves living full lives, experiencing love and joy, doing everyday activities, working hard and being respected. It is very hard to know that there are multiple paths open for you in life, when you never get to see people like you living those multiple paths.

Understandably, this lack of representation is making people miserable, which can show up as anxiety, low self-esteem, depression and other forms of negative thinking.

I worked with a Black, queer woman in her sixties. She came to therapy because she was deeply unhappy with her body weight and felt ashamed of how she looked. Her self-esteem was low in general. I asked her to tell her story starting with when she first noticed these feelings. She went right back into her childhood. She spoke of growing up bombarded with images of thin white girls. In storybooks, it was the white children who had the adventures. In films, the Black women she saw were sexualised, angry or 'matronly'; she never saw characters that were Black and thriving. The fuller-figure women were often the butt of the joke, and in the news they were always shown in the back of the shot, headless and under a headline such as 'Obesity on the Rise'. She never saw a queer woman, except in porn, and that wasn't the role model she was looking for. She said that all of this had caused her to question her own validity and made her wonder if she would ever be allowed to take a centre role in her own life. It made her wonder if the world could ever value her at all. It was a clear example of each of the issues outlined so far in this chapter.

Her job (she was a lawyer) had helped her feel more

worthwhile, as it was socially valued, and she knew she was great at it. However, now she was sixty and experiencing the effects of ageism (women rarely feature in valued and empowered roles in film and advertising after the age of forty, when they are usually cast as the 'caring older woman' who wears comfy sweatshirts and looks after everyone) and was starting to feel invisible; the old feelings of inadequacy were re-emerging.

Telling her story was part of the therapeutic process, as was normalising her experience by showing her how it mapped onto the way advertising and film had taught her to see herself. The other antidote involved finding a community of women she could be inspired by and who made her feel represented. She connected with other Black women, queer women and women in their sixties. She shared her story and heard theirs. With them, she started a social media account, sharing images of themselves as living their full lives, together. She became a mentor for young queer Black women who didn't know that being a lawyer was a path available to them. She hadn't seen herself represented while growing up, so she widened representation for future generations.

Not all therapy is about learning to manage emotions; sometimes it is about learning you are normal, connecting to people with shared experiences, and increasing your self-esteem by doing things you are proud of. (Making change in the world certainly made this woman feel proud.)

Questions for you: when you were growing up, did you see yourself represented in movies and TV? What roles did people with your identity have? Were they empowered? Living a life of joy? Or were they shown in a singular way? How did that make you feel?

Mental health on screen

There is also limited representation in film and TV when it comes to mental health.

What we *all* needed to hear in our lives growing up was: anxiety, fear, distress, sadness, anger – *all* emotions are normal, and none are a sign of weakness. All emotions can be understood. There are ways to allow them in, to soothe yourself and let the negative ones pass. A mental health diagnosis can be understood, supported and usually recovered from. In cases where the diagnosis is considered life-long, there are lots of people (e.g. therapists, support groups, psychiatrists) and organisations to help you manage.

Unfortunately, few of us are taught this, and when we look at films, the news and drama series, that message of recovery is largely absent.

Questions for you: think about the films you grew up with and the stories you read. Did you see or read about people who were struggling? If so, were those people shown displaying panic, sadness, anger or fear, or overwhelmed in a way that was described as normal? Did they have people around them supporting them to make sense of their experience and move forward? Or were they portrayed in a different light?

The reality is few of us grew up with media that showed people struggling or experiencing real, understandable emotion. We were shown people who were happy and succeeding, but when we were shown people experiencing 'negative' emotions, they were usually placed under the category of 'mad' or 'bad' or otherwise failing.

Famous movies referencing mental health and illness are *Psycho* (1960), *Friday the 13th* and *A Nightmare on Elm Street* (1984), Heath Ledger's Joker in the *Dark Knight* trilogy, and Joaquin Phoenix's *Joker* too, all of which show people with mental illness as violent, unpredictable and dangerous. *One Flew Over the Cuckoo's Nest* (1975) shows psychiatric hospitals as a form of inescapable prison.

However, it isn't just films that perpetuate negative stereotypes and beliefs surrounding mental illness. Over the last few decades, news and newspapers have continuously reported stories that directly link mental illness and violence. They focus on the rare forensic cases where people with mental health diagnoses commit violent crimes, rarely ever covering the very common experiences of recovery and rehabilitation. The reality for people with schizophrenia diagnoses, the diagnoses most often associated with these kinds of news articles, is that they are approximately 14 times more likely to be victimised by others than they are to be the perpetrator.

Mental health on screen shows us that:

- The emotion we are meant to show (or get if we deserve it) is happiness.
- Emotional distress means mental illness or that you are 'mad'.

- Mental illness means you are going to be dangerous.
- You will never recover.
- 'Good' people don't struggle with their mental health.

These negative portrayals are stigmatising and they create fear around distress. These myths mean that we constantly strive for happiness and joy, worrying about what it means if any other emotions arise, suppressing any we view as 'undesirable'.

This means when people struggle they don't think of it as normal or understandable; they often panic and ask, 'Am I going mad? Is this the end of my life as I know it?' It also means they feel terrified to share their experiences in case others judge them for it.

I see this fear a lot as a therapist, and I have also experienced it myself.

When I had my first panic attack, at the age of eighteen, the media was the only frame of reference I had to turn to. I really believed it was the end, as I thought I would become dangerous, like the characters I saw in *Friday the 13th* and *One Flew Over the Cuckoo's Nest,* who were trapped in a distress that would never go away. Luckily I found a therapist who showed me that panic could be understood, was a normal feature of being human, and gave me the skills to move forward.

Seeing men express emotions and receive support is even more rare in the media. There are so few options for them to see themselves thriving as someone who struggles or feels. This, coupled with the way we socialise men and boys to be strong and not cry, means men learn that they must not feel or ask for help.

Training men not to feel is killing them. In the UK, men

are three times more likely to die by suicide than women; in Northern Ireland the number rises to four times more likely, and this is the same in the USA. To the men reading this: *you are allowed to feel, cry AND ask for help.*

Crying releases stress hormones and increases endorphins. Crying is an act of self-care.

Quick exercise

Ask yourself what your immediate thoughts are about mental health and emotional distress. Do you think it's okay to experience emotional distress? Anxiety? Panic? Is it okay for other people to struggle? For you to struggle? To ask for help? How would you feel telling someone that you're struggling? Do you ever think emotional distress is a sign of weakness? A sign of being mad or bad? Where did you first learn about mental health? Who do you know that has struggled with their mental health and is still managing to live a life that suits them?

Look up five celebrities who openly talk about their mental health, who show it's possible to struggle and still live well. Do they challenge the ideas about mental health often shown in the media? Do they change your beliefs around mental health?

Repeat after me: 'Experiencing distress does not mean I am mad, bad or abnormal. It's okay to ask for help. There are people who will understand how I feel, coping skills that will help ease my pain and, even if it starts to feel dark, the future is bright, it will just take time.'

This whole book is designed to show you that it's normal to struggle, to need to ask for help, so should you suddenly experience a panic attack in the future, you won't have the same experience that I did.

Social media

Social media offers a low barrier space – it's free, 24/7 and global. People use it for many different things:

- To share pictures of their lives and loved ones with friends and family.
- To advertise their work, share and gain information (including about mental health!) and to organise politically.
- To connect with like-minded people they may not be able to meet in real life.

During COVID-19 and the lockdown, many people found solace in the ability to take to their phones and computers and connect with other people they could no longer visit. Many people used it to connect with new people and gain new skills and ideas for how to manage the time stuck inside the house.

However, social media is being shown to have detrimental effects on our mental health. Not only because of concealed influencer advertising, but because of the endless opportunities for comparison: *Why don't I look like that/have that? Why didn't motherhood look as beautiful and easy for me? Is there something wrong with me?*

The Royal Society for Public Health reports that, out of YouTube, Twitter, Facebook, Snapchat and Instagram, Instagram has the worst effect on our mental health. And frequency of use of Instagram had been directly linked with increased FOMO, bullying, poor body image, low self-esteem, loneliness and high levels of depression and anxiety.

None of us are immune to the harmful effects of social media; it can have a negative impact on all of us in some way, but as with each aspect of this book so far, those already struggling with things like anxiety and low self-esteem may be most at risk.

Your personal brand on social media

Remember learning about the personal brand in the previous chapter? The idea that some of us create a new identity to show the world, that we believe other people will see as worthwhile, lovable and acceptable, makes us feel good in the short term, as it impresses others. But then it leaves us feeling sad, as we worry what would happen if people knew the real us? Well, social media gives us a chance to really build upon and hone that ideal exterior.

Those highlight reels we put up ... they aren't us. They're

snapshots, usually of fragments of our lives that we think friends and society will be most impressed by. On social media, not only can we post images and videos that show us living our best life, we can filter our images, make our eyes bigger, our mouths fuller, alter our bodies and get rid of our pores.

This is adding to our misery offline. Especially if we feel there's a large gap between the images we post and what we see when we look in the mirror or at our life. In my clinic people often tell me how others looking at their Instagram feeds would never know how miserable and lacking they truly feel, and often say they would be horrified if people knew the truth behind the pictures. I've also had clients say they're scared to meet new love interests they've only met online, as they're terrified the person will see how they really look and think less of them when they realise they don't match up to their well-posed selfies.

Many people now feel their real selves need altering and mustn't be seen as they are. In fact, cosmetic surgeons have seen a change in what people are asking for. Their clients used to bring pictures of celebs; now they bring their Snapchat-filtered selves, asking for things such as 'no pores', which is impossible. This phenomenon even has a label – 'Snapchat dysphoria'.

Even the #nomakeup posts are often not quite real. They are well lit, well posed, and still give off a form of perfected image. Likewise, a recent piece of research shows that approximately 12 per cent of #nofilter images are indeed filtered. Very few people are likely to post a truly shit photo of themselves online. We know this is true for ourselves, so why

Someone may look perfectly preened but be struggling deeply on the inside. A perfect exterior does not mean a perfect life. We are so fixated on the exterior that we often miss what is going on underneath.

do we forget that what we are seeing is heavily curated when we look at other people's posts?

What I've realised since being on the 'Gram is we say we want authenticity but, when we see it, we actually don't want it at all.

Quick tips to free yourself from the tyranny of social media

Ask yourself: what kind of image are you trying to portray on social media? Is there a big or small difference between who you present online and how you are in real life? Who are you making these changes for? What would you be risking if you showed people the real you?

Choose to do one thing that will decrease the gap between your personal brand and your real life. Make a pact with your friends to post at least one picture or story a week that is real. Something that shows the mess and mundanity of real life. Something that doesn't have a filter.

Remember other people are sharing their personal brands too. They are unlikely to show that they feel miserable, aren't always living life to the full and, like all people, on occasion run out of toilet roll and tooth-paste and have to trudge to the shops and queue up like the rest of us. But I guarantee they do all these things.

Unfollow the people who consistently make you feel bad about yourself.

Social media is addictive

'It's a social-validation feedback loop,' says Shaun Parker, one of the founders of Facebook, who has subsequently spoken out about his decision to make something that 'exploits our psychological vulnerabilities'.

Every time we post a picture or a video and someone likes it, we get a kick of dopamine (a neurochemical that, when released, makes us want to repeat a behaviour). We get a little reward for our actions, making us more likely to repeat behaviours, such as checking our phones, opening our apps and posting more pictures.

The developers behind these apps are all about exploiting this neurochemical, knowing that if you can give people something that triggers it, you will get people hooked. They also know that the best way to get people hooked is to give them dopamine hits irregularly and unpredictably.

You know slot machines? Bright flashing lights? Most of the time you lose, but, on occasion, just as you're about to give up, you win? People get hooked on them because of the addictive properties of the intermittent win – this is why we get hooked on our phones and on our social media, hungry for the likes that we cannot be sure will come.

When we take time away from our phones, we can go into a dopamine deficit, making us feel miserable and in need of the next hit. This is one of the reasons so many of us spend so much time on our phones, swapping real-life conversations with people for a quick interaction on social media. This is why, as a world, we have never been more connected. However, we are at an ever-increasing risk of becoming lonely, as we disconnect from the people in our lives.

Quick tips

Repeat after me: 'My worth is not measured by the number of likes I receive or followers I gain, or by any other external metric.'

Remove the notifications from your phone. They are designed to make you spend more time on your phone, not to notify you in a helpful way. If someone needs you, they will call, or message multiple times. Switch them off now; it will help.

Keep your phone out of sight, not just face down or turned off when you're not using it. We have less capacity when our phones are in sight. Research shows that the mere presence of our device (switched off or on) affects our ability to think, hold information in mind, and carry out our usual tasks. It's like being addicted to gambling – choosing to sit in a casino all day and assuming we'll be able to carry out our usual social/work/life tasks and won't be affected by our environment.

Schedule regular social media breaks. Delete the social media app from your phone to limit temptation.

And finally, there are lots of nasty comments

Social media is rife with nasty comments. When some people put their pictures online, hopeful for a supportive comment, a like (or a thousand), instead they receive hate speech. Trolls and cyberbullies are everywhere. It's a global trend that is gaining pace, and insults range from subtle snarky comments to all-out death threats. Having already talked about bullying and how it affects us, I will keep this brief: *the internet and social media is riddled with bullying.*

One reason bullying is so rife is that people can become disinhibited when online because of their ability to remain anonymous when they comment, the time gap between one person commenting and the other responding, and the fact that they are not able to see the physical person they are communicating with – making them seem far less human or real – and here's the scary part:

John Sula, the person who coined the term 'the online disinhibition effect', says that some people feel as though they are an imaginary character, existing in a kind of make-believe world when they are online. A world that doesn't have the same rules or obligations as real life.

Meaning that when people are online they feel like they're playing a game. And then, when they go offline, they don't feel responsible for their actions, as they didn't happen in reality.

Groups like Glitch UK are working hard to make online spaces safer to use. If you are experiencing cyberbullying:

- Don't respond to cyberbullies.
- Share your experiences with people you trust.
- Keep evidence of the comments.
- Block the bully and report them, either through the social media app you're using or to the website or service provider they are contacting you through. If any threats are made, report this to the police. Share the evidence you have collated with them.
- Unplug. Make sure you have a full life offline too.

The new rules

- **Know that marketing and subtle messages about how you should look, how you should act, what you should own and who you could be are everywhere** – and quite often they link to someone making money off you.
- **You do not need to change your body, your face or your scent, or have the newest, shiniest item, to be enough. You already are enough**. If you still want to change something, that's fine too! But please promise me that you won't wait until that thing has changed to celebrate yourself. For example, wear the

clothes you want to wear right now; don't wait until something is different to do this. And, please, start telling the people you know how glorious they are as they are. Maybe send them the occasional text out of the blue, or stick a Post-it note on their bathroom mirror – 'You are just so wonderful' – for them to find and smile at. Never underestimate the effect of a small gesture.

- **Wanting the next upgrade to something is fine but, at the same time, know this: when you get it, there will be another newer, better item,** and the thing you just bought may suddenly pale in comparison. This is not because the thing you have isn't good. It's because marketing plays tricks on us, and leaves us constantly wanting more.

- **Recognise that comparing ourselves to others is normal but can undermine our emotional wellbeing.** Advertising, the media and social media will distract us by trying to make us focus on what we own, how we look and how successful we seem. Use mindfulness to help you observe and not be carried away by your comparison thoughts, and work out what you truly value in life (Chapter 16 will help you with this), so you can choose where to focus your energy each day, and act in accordance with what matters to you rather than what your social-comparison brain tells you to do!

- **Fill your social media feed with activists and role models** but expect that you won't feel better immediately.

- **Campaign against stereotypes and misrepresentation in the media, and cyber bullying.** In Chapter 17 there are some tips on campaigning that may help you think about how to get involved.

- **Know that whoever you are, you deserve a life full of joy, ease and love.** You are a three-dimensional human being and you deserve to live a three-dimensional life, even if the media misses this. Start thinking about how you would like to see yourself if you were in this media. Look for people who are already doing this. You deserve to take up space and be seen.

- **Experiencing distress does not make you mad or bad.** It makes you a normal person who lives in a distressing world. Please look after yourself, seek professional support when you need it, and help the people around you to seek support should they need it too.

A Note to You

Are you starting to see how many areas of your life could affect how you feel today?

The more you become aware of the areas of your life that get you down, or make you feel not enough, the more control you can take back over your life; you can understand why you feel the way you do and what the causes are. Then, instead of criticising yourself for feeling low, which most people do, you can decide how to act. Will you choose a coping strategy to improve your mood (such as a breathing exercise from the back of the book) or resolve to do something differently (such as minimising your social media use or filling your bookshelf with sex-positive literature)?

Now we are going to talk a little more about the stuff that shapes us and potentially hurts us and, again, this isn't a breezy chapter. Sorry. Always take breaks when you need to. I will be here whenever you're ready to pick this book up again.

This chapter focuses on prejudice and the systems that keep prejudice alive.

As a white, cis-gender woman, I learned nearly every single thing in this section from someone else: from Black women who write about their experiences of racism and of sexism (misogynoir – a term put forward by queer Black feminist Moya Bailey); from trans and non-binary people writing about their day-to-day experiences; from disabled people who have had to work hard to put themselves on the map, as their stories have so often been overlooked; from clients I have treated and people I've met professionally and socially.

I have learned everything in this chapter from people who have been pushed to the fringes of society. For that reason, there is an extra reading list at the end of the next chapter to surface this important work that we can all learn from.

Dr Soph xx

4. Pride & Prejudice

Injustice is a virus, and we are all susceptible to being infected. We are all both victim and perpetrator, and none of us are immune.
—JAVHEED SUKERA

*Warning: please take care of yourself while you read this chapter as it includes references to: the murder of Black people and transgender people, and hate crimes against LGBTQ+ people, People of Colour, transgender people, disabled people.

It is commonly believed that therapists should only concern themselves with therapy and not with politics or social issues. This idea is problematic. Why?

Because emotional distress can be caused by being endangered, fearing for your safety, experiencing verbal and physical abuse, living in poverty and fearing how you will feed and support the people you know and love. And many of these examples arise in relation to racism, sexism, homophobia, transphobia, fatphobia, abuse, poverty, and many other forms of oppression and subjugation.

If therapists only focus on the emotional distress of a client, rather than acknowledging the underlying causes in society, then:

1. It denies there are very real problems in the world that need to be talked about and addressed.
2. It places the problem on the person experiencing distress, focusing on their need to change rather than the need for change at the level of the perpetrators and the systems that caused the distress.

Therefore, it is my view that psychology is both personal *and* political.

We have already touched on some forms of prejudice and where it arises – in the words of bullies in the playground and in advertising and media, which often shows positive portrayals of thin, white, non-disabled straight men, and stereotyped and negative portrayals of many other people.

Now we will go a little further into this issue that affects us all, because . . .

> *Until we are all free, we are none of us free.*
> —EMMA LAZARUS

This chapter will touch on three main areas that may shape who you are today and lead to you feeling distress: explicit prejudice from others, microaggressions and internalised prejudice. Whole books are written on each of these life experiences; this chapter should be viewed as a starting point to help you understand or discover where and how each of these experiences appear and affect your life. Further reading is suggested at the end of the chapter.

If you have a lived experience of prejudice, I hope this chapter will show you that you are not alone, that however you feel makes sense, and that often the best kind of support comes from being around people who share your experience, as well as through channelling your emotional energy (if you have some to spare) into campaigning for change.

If you don't experience prejudice, I hope this chapter will serve as a call to action. A just world can only be achieved if we all work together, and if the people who have privilege and power use both of these assets to make real, lasting change.

Explicit prejudice

In 2020, anti-racism protests in America spread worldwide due to the disproportionate murder of Black people at the hands of the police, something which horrifically was not new, yet was finally exposed as videos went viral.

Prejudice is real. And many people live in fear because of it.

In the first seven months of that same year, more transgender people were murdered in America than in the whole preceding year.

In the UK in 2019, two thirds of all hate crimes were linked to race, and the number of hate crimes increased compared with the previous year by:

- +37 per cent against people who are transgender or do not conform to the gender binary
- +25 per cent against people linked to their sexual orientation
- +18 per cent against Jewish people
- +14 per cent against disabled people

And in the week following the terror attacks on two mosques in Christchurch, New Zealand in 2019, anti-Muslim hate crimes in the UK increased by 692%.

Action point

If you are experiencing hate crimes or hate speech, please contact the police, a relevant organisation (such as Stop Hate UK, who have a 24-hour helpline) or someone you know and trust who can support you. If you are experiencing these problems at work and have access to support, speak to your manager, someone in your HR department or a trade union representative whose job it is to protect your interests.

But prejudice isn't just an idea or a belief system. It doesn't only exist in people. It is rooted in the structures that surround us – in our institutions, our policies, our employment, education and healthcare systems. This is what we call structural inequality.

And it is rife. A recent research study sent out job applications to numerous companies (over 2016–2018), each bearing identical qualifications and levels of experience but with different names and ethnicities of each fake job applicant.

They found that the fake applicants who were not white British had to send on average 60 per cent more applications to get the same level of positive replies as they did for people who identified themselves as white British – Nigerian and Pakistani applicants fared the worst, having to send 80 per cent and 70 per cent more applications respectively. I know people who are now naming their children white-British-sounding names to overcome this – a decision that may sound simple but erases a person's heritage and perpetuates the notion that hiding one's ethnicity is the only way to succeed.

Discrimination and bias during the interview process, and then during the pay-review process, has also been blamed as one of the main reasons women, disabled people and People of Colour are more likely to be paid less, and also to experience poverty in the UK.

Poverty and mental health

- Adults living in poverty face constant stress, not knowing where the next meal will come from, unstable housing and not being sure how they will pay the bills.
- On top of this they may have to navigate complex financial assistance systems, if there are any available, and figure out how to provide for their children or anyone else they are responsible for.

- Whatever the specific worries of someone living in poverty, the overload of stress can lead to emotional burnout, especially if someone is not receiving adequate nutrition.
- This can then start a vicious cycle: the person needs energy and motivation to manage their stresses but is so exhausted they are unable to do this, making it hard to engage in the tasks that are needed to get out of poverty.
- When children grow up in poverty, the ongoing strain can cause long-term effects on mental health. Disadvantaged kids experience a drain on emotional wellbeing and brain real estate that can lead to anxiety, low mood and a lack of concentration.

Sometimes I hear people speak as if earning money and succeeding is a choice – 'If you want it, you just need to work hard enough and you will be rewarded.' This simply isn't true for everyone.

Prejudice has real-world consequences that can lead to physical and/or emotional harm and can stop people from accessing the resources they need in life, such as money.

And for some people prejudice comes in multiple forms.

Psychology is personal. And it's political. How can it not be?

The layering of prejudice

Professor Kimberlé Williams Crenshaw coined the term

'intersectionality', a framework that makes sense of the way people's different social and political identities combine to create a unique mix of advantages and disadvantages.

Intersectionality helps us understand how each person may experience the world and be treated by the world because humans have so many aspects to who they are, including: gender identity, where you live, race, religion, age, ability, appearance, class, culture, education, employment, ethnicity, sexuality, sexual orientation, spirituality. And each one may be given more or less privilege and power by society.

If you belong to multiple marginalised groups, then you may experience a layering of prejudice, increasing the level of distress you experience. Like being a rock in a sea, buffeted and worn away from every side.

What makes understanding prejudice even more complex is that some aspects of our identity are visible to society, while others are not. Our skin colour, our height, whether we are able to walk without aids, and many other factors, such as our clothing, make some parts of our identity immediately clear to others. Some parts of our identity are less visible.

Some physical health conditions (such as renal failure, diabetes, chronic pain, chronic fatigue, fibromyalgia) and mental health conditions (all of them) are not visible to the eye, meaning that people may not be judged immediately based on this aspect of their lived experience.

Some people's sexuality may not be immediately visible either. For example, the stereotype of lesbians having short hair means that lesbian or bisexual 'femmes' (who present a traditionally feminine appearance) may be assumed to be straight.

If some aspects of people's identity have been hidden, this might have traditionally been regarded as useful, as it may have meant they were not targeted or discriminated against solely on the basis of their immediate appearance. However, some people with these lived experiences often do not feel that benefit. Why?

Because the people living with invisible health conditions are often not believed. And for those who do not outwardly appear non-straight, for example femmes, the assumption that they are straight may mean they're not seen as part of the LGBTQ+ community, again having to prove themselves as *queer enough* to be considered and included.

To anyone reading this and who needs to hear this, you don't need to *prove* your sexuality, your condition or any other part of your identity to others for them to be valid. They *are* valid. You are valid.

The deep harm of prejudice and hate

Have you experienced prejudice of any kind? If so, how has it made you feel? Have you experienced it in multiple areas or in one specific area? How has it made you feel about yourself and the world?

If you have lived these experiences, whatever you feel right now is normal and understandable. And maybe some of the descriptions below will resonate if you're feeling distressed. Prejudice of any kind can cause low self-esteem, fear and anxiety. If you are feeling this right now, Chapter 6 will help make sense of these emotions.

Prejudice can make people afraid to check the news or open their social media apps for fear of what they'll see has happened to people who share their identity – more hate crimes or another prejudiced story. Prejudice can even stop people from wanting to leave the house for fear of what may happen outside. Avoiding leaving the house is a common strategy people adopt after experiencing high levels of prejudice. While this helps soothe people in the short term, it stops people from accessing their other valued activities and community in the long, leading to a further decrease in wellbeing. For some groups of people, even home is not safe if they live with others who are prejudiced and could harm them. Meaning fear may be hard to escape.

The experience of prejudice will be different for everyone. However, it can lead to extremely high levels of stress and even thoughts of suicide. If you feel this last point resonates with you, please seek help from someone you know and love, your GP and/or a crisis line (such as the Samaritans or Shout Crisis Text Line if you are in the UK).

Knowing that these experiences are ongoing and have not disappeared can also cause people to feel a deep fatigue and sense of hopelessness. Especially when they're told that things will change, and they just need to be patient. Understandably, it can also lead to anger.

Unfortunately, when people show anger, wanting to discuss the prejudice they experience, their concerns are often dismissed.

> *I speak out of direct and particular anger at an academic conference, and a white woman says, 'Tell me how you feel but don't say it too harshly or I cannot hear you.'*
>
> —AUDRE LORDE

Accessing anger is helpful

A friend of mine sought therapy, as she was feeling numb and empty. She has used a wheelchair since childhood. She said she'd always been okay with her disability but had found other people's judgements and comments grating. People often *congratulated* her, as though she was a hero for simply getting out of bed. She felt patronised by this, as it seemed people didn't imagine she could do more than that. She noticed people rolling their eyes when she was getting on the bus, as the driver had to put the ramp down for her, which took time. She'd also had ableist slurs such as 'cripple' hurled at her many times. She learned that people were either amazed or annoyed (understatement) at her.

Initially she educated people who underestimated her, and would speak to the eye-rollers on the bus about the importance of accessible transport. Then she reached a point where standing up to people and for herself had simply worn her out. She had been told so many times 'No need to be so angry!' Being told she was angry had made her angry. As had the inequality she faced.

One day the anger disappeared. She started to feel numb. Like nothing mattered. Because this is what can happen when rage is not attended to, and when we feel we cannot make change – it can lead to a feeling of numbness and emptiness.

Her therapist recommended reconnecting with her anger. She made her journal to reconnect with her emotions, scream into her pillow when the emotions came back and felt too much (she found this genuinely helpful), and then suggested she connected with disability activists.

Now, when people called her angry, she agreed she *was* angry, as anger arises in the face of injustice, and there was so much injustice to face. Once she was able to access anger she used the energy it provided to make change in the world.

I learned so much from my friend. I learned the power of activism. I also learned that I was deeply unaware that society often 'disables' people. For example, someone with a wheelchair has a wonderful way to get around. Yet most cities are not made to support this. Even a single step can render a place inaccessible. One step can be the difference between someone being able, or not, to go into a shop, a cafe, a pub, bar, restaurant and, importantly, a public toilet. If you use a wheelchair or other mobility aid, you already know this. If you don't, spend the next 24 hours paying attention to each place you go into. Is there a step? I think you'll be surprised at how many barriers you find in that time.

If you feel upset, hurt, afraid, angry, numb, or any of the other emotions mentioned here, you are not only not alone, you are normal. Know that there are plenty of coping skills in the back of this book and, like my friend above, that there are groups of people organising themselves to challenge the prejudice in the world, and you can join them too.

Managing the effects of prejudice

- **Avoiding news and media around the time of a hate crime** or when you're feeling particularly sensitive is a smart way to manage this. Did you know you can 'mute' keywords and hashtags on your social media? Do this when you need to so you can focus on rest and self-care during these times.

- **Learn about anxiety and fear** (Chapter 7) so you can understand why you feel the effects of prejudice in your body.

- **Use the breathing exercises, grounding techniques and other coping skills (particularly self-compassion) found in Part Three of this book to ease your emotional distress.** While no amount of breathing exercises and self-compassion will change the prejudice that exists in society, it will help soothe your soul and ease some of your pain.

- **Join a group of people who share your identity and experiences either online or in real life.** You are not alone. And there are people who truly understand your experiences, as they live it too. If you are a disabled woman who experiences ableism and sexism, or a trans man experiencing transphobia, look for the people online already talking about these experiences. I know I have talked about Instagram's pitfalls, but it's a great place to start looking for a community. While no amount of support from another person can undo the wrongs and hurt you have experienced, being among people who truly understand how you feel can make the future seem more than a little brighter.

- **Allow anger to be present.** Anger and rage are normal feelings. They understandably arise when you see the injustice carried out in this world. My favourite writer on rage, Dr Jennifer Mullan, a clinical psychologist whose Instagram handle, @ *DecolonisingTherapy*, describes her work perfectly, says, 'Rage is the untranslated trauma of historical grief' and 'since rage is born in the face of trauma, marginalised Black, brown and indigenous bodies are frequently on the front line of this burden'. If this resonates with you, she says the rage needs to be honoured as it 'is frequently discarded, minimized and overlooked for far too long', causing, among other problems, 'brain fog, loss/increase in appetite, trouble sleeping, difficulty with planning and organization. And immune, digestive and nervous systems dysregulation'.

- **If you feel anger, allow it to arise.** Vent it into your journal. Express it when you need to. Recognise it may be concealing a deep grief. The next chapter will show you that anger is a normal part of grief, and Chapter 6 will show you one of many ways anger sometimes protects us from sadness and vulnerability. Chapter 14 will show you how to 'rage journal'.

- **Grieve as a community.** There is nothing more powerful than sharing a healing experience in a community setting. I once stood in a room of 1,000 women, everyone screaming at the top of their lungs, letting out their rage that was linked to the sexual violence they had experienced. It was raw, emotional and cathartic. The feeling of not being alone, but being one of many women, changed how I felt in an instant. People said they went into that room feeling afraid and small, and when they left they felt empowered.

- **Get political.** Use your voice and your voting power to make change. Chapter 17 discusses this in more detail.
- **Seek support if your emotional distress reaches a point where it feels overwhelming.** This can be professional support from a therapist, crisis line or from a friend you trust.

Social activism and voting are important coping skills and a form of preventative medicine. You have a chance to make change in the world, share your distress and channel it into something important. You have the power to stop future generations from struggling with the level of structural inequality we see today.

Microaggressions

'I feel a little mad. I feel like people at work are putting me down, making digs at me, but maybe I'm imagining it.' The first words of a new client I took on who came to therapy for anxiety, low mood and a pervasive feeling that she was 'less than' at her work.

Her colleagues were reportedly 'friendly and smiling' when they made requests of her and were 'never overtly unkind' in any obvious way.

Yet she couldn't shake the feeling they thought she was stupid in some way – everyone kept complimenting her, but in ways that seemed insulting.

She collected a selection of these comments. They included: 'You're so smart and so articulate, it's really amazing.' 'Your English is so good, wow!'

Her response: 'Why are people surprised I can speak?!'

Another two examples: 'It's funny, I don't see you as Indian' and 'What do your people think about the UK at the moment?' Her response – stunned silence, and then she asked, 'Who do you think my people are?' as it suddenly dawned on her that others were treating her differently because they didn't see her as British-Indian, they saw her as Indian, and as someone who was not only 'different', but who also shouldn't be able to speak English well. She had grown up in the same place as her colleagues but was being treated differently due to assumptions based on her skin colour.

In addition to this, she often noticed that in meetings men rephrased what she had just suggested – the experience commonly known as 'mansplaining'.

What my client was experiencing each day were microaggressions – subtle comments, often intended to be harmless or even complimentary, but which actually express prejudice towards people who are marginalised by society.

Professor Chester M. Pierce coined the term microaggressions to explain the subtle, eroding insults and dismissive language he saw being continuously used against African-Americans by non-Black Americans, and the term has now spread to now include discrimination of this kind against anyone from a marginalised group.

Here are some common examples of microaggressions:

'No, but really, where are you from?' – a question that can make people who are from the same country as the person asking, but who have a different heritage, feel like an alien in their own country.

'What are you?' – a question that can make someone seem even non-human.

'Wow, you are so articulate for a [insert identity here]!' – a comment that may be intended as a compliment but has the underlying message that people who 'look like you' (e.g. who are women, are gay, are People of Colour, are transgender, gender non-conforming, working class, or any other specific identity that is commonly prejudiced against) are usually inarticulate.

My client's colleagues made these comments, and others, daily, suggesting they didn't imagine English could be her first language, which it was.

'Wow, you are funny for a [insert identity here].' The underlying message: 'People like you aren't usually funny.'

'You aren't like other [insert identity here].' The underlying message: 'You are somehow better than the people I expect you to be like.'

'It's funny, I don't see you as [insert identity here].' The underlying message: see above.

Or, asking the one person who represents a group: 'So, what do [insert entire community of people here] people think?' The underlying message: 'You and your people are different from me, so you must all have the same experience.'

Let's be clear: the 'micro' in microaggressions doesn't refer to the level of harm done. It refers to the fact that these aggressions are usually covert, they happen under the radar, and they lead to those 'deer in the headlights' moments: *Hang on, did that person just say . . .?*

Each of these examples could, on the surface, be seen as a compliment. In fact, the people saying them often genuinely believe they *are* making a compliment, which leads to deep shock when the receiver suggests their comment was in fact offensive.

Microaggressions are so common that some friends of mine, and some of my therapy clients, say they now simply roll their eyes when they hear them, as they expect it to happen.

I cannot count how many times I've been told, 'Wow, you're funny for a woman', or 'You're not like the other women' by people who don't realise the implicit bias and judgement within their words. The message being that: 'People like you' (in this case, women) aren't usually so articulate, funny, impressive, and so on, basically implying: 'You're impressive for having transcended what is normal for people like you.'

Learning to recognise microaggressions is important and can be difficult, as microaggressions can also be non-verbal. For instance, that moment when someone clutches their purse a little tighter at the sight of someone previously construed in the media or in other prejudiced narratives as being 'dangerous'. This microaggression is commonly experienced by Black men, who, as I mentioned previously, have historically been shown in various media as playing the role of the criminal.

Like many people, my client felt not only upset by these constant comments, but she also started to doubt herself, and this is because microaggressions are often open to interpretation. Because of this, people on the receiving end often end up being subjected to gaslighting – the experience of someone denying your lived experience or telling you something isn't true when in fact it is.

'Hang on, did they just say something (racist/sexist/homo-phobic/transphobic/abelist/classist/fatphobic) to me?'

'No, they would have said that to anyone. It's not because you are [insert identity here]. You're so sensitive. Not everything is about that. Why do you always make it about that?'

Sometimes a response like this is made with the best intention. For example, as an attempt to minimise the hurt felt by the person who experienced the microaggression. Unfortunately, whatever the reason for this kind of response (ill will, ignorance or genuine care) the net effect is still gaslighting.

Gaslighting in this context means that the blame is effectively put back on the person the microaggression was made at. It keeps the problem alive and fails to acknowledge the impact on the person on the receiving end, and in some cases makes the receiver feel they are imagining things.

One microaggression may make someone feel confused, sad and/or worried, or even question themselves. Multiply this, and that confusion and emotion compounds; the message gets louder, likely diminishing their self-esteem and mood – death by a thousand cuts.

Psychology professor Derald Sue – who has carried out extensive research on the effects of microaggressions, specifically racist microaggressions – has found that anxiety, depression, loneliness and a diminishing of psychological wellbeing are common consequences.

He found that when microaggressions happen in the classroom, they can affect problem-solving skills and other cognitive (thinking) skills of schoolchildren. If it happens long-term, it can lead to high blood pressure, hypervigilance (a continuous state of high alert) and a dysregulated nervous system (a sensitive and highly active stress response and high levels of stress hormones).

What to do right now about microaggressions

1. If you experience microaggressions (and other forms of prejudice):

- **Know that you are not imagining it.** Microaggressions are real even when people tell you they aren't. Whatever emotions you experience in response to microaggressions are valid.
- **Talk to people you trust and share how you feel.** You could speak with one friend, or join a community of people who share part of your identity and who are already talking about prejudice. Whoever makes you feel most understood. Also, you could join with people who are working to campaign to make change as a collective.
- **Look for people who can give you a sign when microaggressions are occurring, so you don't doubt yourself.** For example, my friends and I have a facial expression that signals mansplaining

and sexist microaggression. And my client found a friend at work who gave her a subtle nod, and who would then step in (with my client's permission) saying, for example, 'She's British, why wouldn't she speak good English?' She also spoke to the management at her work and, with the support of this friend, the management team then addressed this issue across the business.

- **If you feel safe to, call out the comment.** You can choose to directly address a microaggression as a prejudiced statement – 'That was offensive to me because it suggests you think . . .' Or you could ask the person making the statement to elaborate for you – 'What do you mean it's surprising I speak good English/am articulate/am funny? Is there a reason this surprises you?' This latter approach may help the other person realise the preconceived ideas behind their comment, leading them to understand what has happened and apologise. If it doesn't feel safe to do this immediately, you can wait until a time that feels suitable and quietly have a word with the other person – 'I feel uncomfortable about something that was said earlier. Can we discuss it?' If the person seems genuinely confused about microaggressions, you could say, 'When people say _____ they often mean _____.' If this feels too uncomfortable, you could add, 'I'm sure that's not what you meant.' (You DO NOT have to add this, but I know many people who find adding this helps ease the conversation.)

- If someone tells you, 'I didn't mean it like that, I meant _____', you can, if you feel safe to, say: 'I hear that it wasn't your intention. I wanted to let you know the impact of the statement.'

2. If you see a microaggression or other form of prejudice occurring, stand by the person receiving the microaggression, show them they are not imagining it, and call out or call in the person making the comment or doing the action.

- It's important that it's not always left to the person on the receiving end of the microaggression (or any form of prejudice) to address the situation, so, if you witness this, and it's safe to do so, say something.

3. To people reading this thinking, *Uh oh, I've made microaggressions before,* learn about your biases and get comfortable with making mistakes.

- What makes microaggressions particularly tricky to manage is the fact that many of us are so concerned with 'being good'. Even thinking about the idea that we could make a microaggression can cause our defences to rise. When we get called on a potential microaggression, the defence may be even stronger, as we interpret the (public) call out or (in private) call in, as someone saying, 'You're bad', potentially sending us into battle or into a puddle of tears. If we consider that we may all have bias (as we grew up in a biased world) and all get it wrong sometimes, we could instead see these moments as an invitation. A moment to pause, apologise, question our own implicit biases, and learn.

- Learn about internalised dominance and unpick any prejudiced beliefs you might not even realise you carry. Internalised dominance is the theory that people who have the most access to power, or who are always talked about in the most favourable light, are unconsciously trained to believe they deserve this status, leading to microagressions and other forms of oppression that keep prejudice alive. *Me and White Supremacy* written by Layla F. Saad is an anti-racism workbook that walks you through this process.

Unfortunately, microaggressions can happen in therapy too. For example, if therapists make assumptions based on stereotypes, or if they avoid or minimise cultural issues. This obviously has implications for the outcomes of therapy. How can you feel close to and trusting of that therapist, or like there is any hope for change in the world, if prejudice finds you here as well?

If you have experienced this in therapy, please, if you feel comfortable enough, raise this with your therapist. If you do not feel comfortable to do this, and you do not want to continue with your therapist, you can end your work with them. Therapy is meant to be a safe-place for you.

Turning prejudice against yourself

It's obvious that explicit discrimination can cause emotional harm. However, what is not so obvious is how some people turn the prejudice they have heard against themselves. This is called *internalised prejudice* and it may make you:

- Believe stories that undermine your self-belief (like we discussed can happen following bullying or watching stereotyped TV and film).
- See yourself as one of those stereotypes.
- Start believing you should be talked about and treated as one of those stereotypes.

Here are a handful of statements made by clients and friends that show they have internalised the prejudice of the world. These are very common.

- 'I'm a woman. I don't deserve the same rights as men. I'm not as able as they are.'
- 'I'm not sexy enough or desirable enough for others.'
- 'My disability makes me less-than.'
- 'I'm a Person of Colour; white people are superior to me. I deserve to be treated poorly.'
- 'My skin is darker than theirs. People with lighter skin are better than me.'
- 'I'm gay. I won't be able to have a normal relationship as I'm not normal.'

- 'I'm transgender. There is something wrong with me.
  I shouldn't exist.'
- 'I'm fat. Shame on me.'

None of these statements are true. Everyone is worthy. Every identity is normal and deserving of love, respect and equal access to resources.

When we aren't aware of where these thoughts come from, or that we are even having them, thoughts like this are a one-way ticket to low self-esteem. And this can happen for any part of our identity. As we've heard many times so far, when we take on beliefs like these we may change our behaviour and make our own set of rules to make everything feel a little more manageable.

Having grown up in a world where women took on the side roles in TV and film, earned less than men, and did cleaning and other home-based tasks that were considered 'women's work' and were tasks generally looked down on, I learned early on that women were considered inferior to men. To manage this, I used to think it was okay to be a woman as long as I didn't act 'girly', and as long as I talked about and studied serious subjects. I never allowed myself to talk about who I fancied. I hid my emotions and disregarded anything that would be seen as overtly girly, such as fashion and make-up. I belittled those topics and distanced myself from anything that could be seen as 'feminine'.

Other common rules people make to manage prejudice are:

'It's okay to have a disability as long as I cover it up and hardly anyone knows.'

'It's okay if I'm a Person of Colour as long as I have light skin.' E. J. R. David PhD, author of *'Internalized Oppression: The Psychology of Marginalized Groups'*, believes that internalised racism and colourism is a major driving force behind People of Colour using skin-bleaching products.

'It's okay to be gay as long as I'm not camp.' I have heard this phrase more times than I can count, and met so many people who have pushed away any part of themselves that could be considered flamboyant.

'It's okay to be trans as long as I "pass" as cis-gender' or 'as long as I am fabulous'. If that latter point speaks to you, you may relate to this line from gender non-conforming writer Alok Vaid-Menon, who says, 'The only way that we [transfeminine people] matter to mainstream society is if we are fabulous and entertaining.'

'It's okay to be bigger, just not *that* big.'

The narrow rules we set ourselves lead us to alter our behaviour, and often result in high levels of self-criticism and emotional pain when we can't meet our self-imposed rules. What few people realise is that these rules also actively get in the way of one of the most healing things we can access – other people who share our experiences.

Internalised prejudice often leads people to:

- See other people with their shared identity as less-than too, and start treating them, as well as themselves, in such ways.
- Want to distance themselves from people who remind them of the harmful prejudice they've heard (not the people who made the hurtful comments, but the people who, like you, the comments were about).

- Act in ways that keep the prejudiced status quo alive rather than challenge it.

I used to push away parts of myself that were overtly feminine AND I used to criticise other women for their 'girly' ways: 'You're talking about dating AGAIN? God, you're such a girl! Stop being so emotional.' I was proud when the boys told me I 'wasn't like other girls', as it made me feel more powerful. I wanted to be 'one of the lads'. I had to work to unlearn this internalised prejudice and start knowing that being a woman meant so many more things than being the 'weaker sex'.

When I realised I was doing the work for the patriarchy (the structures that uphold the idea that there is one supreme gender – men) by belittling women and keeping them seeming small and less-than, I started to see many friends had swallowed the same ideas. Calling other women 'sluts' for being sexually free, or 'bossy' for having opinions or being strong-minded. Finding ways to undermine women's success – 'Who did she sleep with to get to the top?' – and enjoying watching them fail. Pointing out any moment a woman didn't appear as advertising told us women were meant to appear, for example: 'Did you see her? Did you see how she behaved? Did you see what she was wearing? Who does she think she is, wearing that? How about her hairy legs? Gross! And she's got old, wow!'

And this is happening all around us – to disabled people, People of Colour, LGBTQ+ people, people with fuller figures. Anyone who has internalised prejudice may notice they want to distance themselves from anyone else who shares aspects of their identity.

A gay Israeli colleague of mine who had migrated to the

Internalised prejudice can cause you to reject yourself and to reject the people who share your experiences, the people who could truly help make you feel seen, soothed and accepted.

UK as a teenager noted that for a long time he wanted to distance himself from his accent, any family members who didn't speak English and anything that could link him to his country of origin, such as food and customs. He laughed at people for being 'over the top', monitored his behaviour so it never equated to 'too much', and remembers shaming people for 'being camp'. For a long time he felt alone, like large parts of himself were missing. His journey to feeling whole again, recognising the prejudiced beliefs that were affecting him, and reconnecting with people with a shared experience to him, helped him reclaim pride in his culture. But before we get into how you can do this, should it resonate, we need to take a moment for a caveat.

Mirroring power

Changing our behaviour to match the dominant group is **not** always internalised prejudice.

It would be easy to assume that any time a woman makes herself seem more masculine it's a sign of internalised prejudice or any time someone who identifies as gay distances themselves from a pre-conceived idea of 'camp' or wants to "pass" as straight it's the same. However, this would be a blanket statement, an inaccurate one at that.

Some people alter their behaviours and physical selves as a style preference. And sometimes people mirror those in power *intentionally*, to ensure they will be seen or heard and/or to stay safe in an environment where they are either in the minority or experience prejudice.

The former British prime minister Margaret Thatcher lowered her voice with voice coaching so as to fit in, be heard and hold more sway. Her biographer, Charles Moore, said she did this to move beyond 'the hectoring tones of the housewife'. ('Hectoring tones'? 'Housewife'?)

Many women who reject the demands placed on them to dress, act and look the way magazines tell them to, often experience slurs and criticism from others they know, from people in the street and in hateful online comments.

Many LGBTQ+ people survived the COVID-19 lockdown by becoming more closeted around homophobic or transphobic family members. Many survive their lives in this way too.

Many People of Colour living in the UK (and many other countries too) have been taught, or have found out from their own lived experiences, that they need to be and act more like white people in order to be treated similarly – to get their CV looked at, the job they applied for or a pay rise, for example.

Likewise, while many research articles suggest that Black women opting to straighten their hair reflects internalised prejudice, again there are often other reasons too. Sometimes this is simply out of personal choice and sometimes out of necessity. Many young Black children are discriminated against for their natural hairstyles within school systems.

Adapting yourself to be more like those in power is therefore sometimes a survival strategy, making life anything from a little bit easier to actually bearable. If you are changing your behaviour in order to survive, that makes total sense.

Starting to work with internalised prejudice

- **Write down the aspects of your identity that you have tried to push away or change**, or that you have rules about, e.g. 'It's okay to be a woman as long as I'm not girly or emotional.' 'It's okay to have a disability as long as no one knows.' Write down any rules you have for other people who share your identity, or any reasons you might push someone away who shares your identity, e.g. 'They're too camp.' 'Their skin is too dark.' Ask yourself: *Do these rules suggest I have internalised prejudiced views, or do I do this so I can stay physically and emotionally safe?* If your response is, *Eek, I might have internalised prejudice*, it's not because you are doing something wrong. It's because you are human. It's because the structures we live within give us little choice to do anything else. All of the examples I have given in this chapter happen because prejudice is in our history and in the stories we learn every day. It exists, from the smallest whisper or suggestion of who is worthy and who is not, to the loudest shouts and acts of hate. When you swim in prejudiced waters, at some point you end up drinking that water.

- **Gently challenge these thoughts.** Start with your beliefs, then move to your rules for yourself and for others. Ask yourself when did this belief or rule start? Who taught you to feel this way? Are there other ways to think? What do you choose to believe? You can use mindfulness and journalling to raise your awareness of these thoughts if they do not come to you easily.

- **Look for opportunities to reconnect with the parts of yourself you have pushed away.** I decided to try making friends with more women. I used mindfulness to become aware of my negative thoughts about being female and allow myself to feel and show my emotions. My friends started reclaiming the words 'bossy' and 'slutty', to use them as terms of pride, saying, yes, I can be these things and call myself these things but without self-judgement, living these aspects on my own terms. My colleague slowly began to bring back his accent, asked his grandparents to share traditional recipes with him and started going to gay bars on his own, allowing himself to be less stereotypically masculine. My client slowly started finding out about her parents' heritage, and also about the history of Indian woman in the UK.

- **Read up on the histories and know there is pride to be found in your identity.** Many people have not been taught the full and beautiful histories of their identity, so I recommend looking up the people who share your heritage that you can feel proud of and hold as a role model. For example, did you know that Princess Sophia Duleep Singh, the daughter of the last maharaja of the Sikh empire, was one of many Indian women who campaigned for women's rights? Or that Rosa May Billinghurst, a disabled woman, was key to the suffragette movement? Or did you know Black trans women are often on the frontlines of political change? For example, activist and Black transgender woman Marsha P. Johnson was one of the driving forces in the gay rights movement and the Stonewall riots, yet this is often missed when people talk about gay rights or Pride. There are so many histories that have been erased but, thanks to Google, you can find them! And the people you find pride in don't have to be famous; they may be someone in your family who offers kindness every day to the people they love.

- **Connect to other people around you,** people who may share in your experiences and decide how you will build each other up. If you have pushed away people with similar identities to you due to internalised prejudice, recognise that they are a source of support, not a source of shame. When you find those people, if it feels right to, help each other notice moments where internalised prejudice may arise. My friends and I have talked openly about the times we noticed we had put ourselves down for our gender and put other women down too. We lovingly started pointing out these behaviours, and it was such a gift. We supported each other to feel proud of our gender identity. With the right support to show you that you can indeed be proud of who you are, and that there are already other people who believe you are worthy and deserving, you will find this too! Don't worry if you don't have friends to do this with right now. In Chapter 17 I will suggest ways to find a community.

- **If you are pushing away parts of your identity to stay safe,** this makes total sense too. Can you start a small (but safe) act of resistance today? For example, if you have been told you can't wear certain clothes, as they are not for your gender, could you design your dream outfit in your mind? If you have been told you are not allowed to wear your hair in its natural behaviour, show your natural skin tone, or act in certain ways, is there something you could do today that is the opposite of what you have been told?

An autobiographical note

I am someone who has access to many privileges. I am white, thin and middle class; these all mean I'm not discriminated against for any of these aspects of my identity.

I am a white woman who grew up in the UK. I have never had to think about whether the colour of my skin would affect my safety. I have been able to enter any space I wish and never worry about this.

While I worked my ass off to become a psychologist, I have to recognise that there were significant privileges I gained linked to how I look, the resources and education I had access to, and that I fit the bill for the role. I have to recognise the privilege I bring with me into the therapy room, the power I possess by having the title Dr in front of my name.

I have done my best to outline the issues above but I too am learning, which is why there is more recommended reading for this chapter than for others.

As a psychologist, I am also aware that mental health services have sometimes been the cause of prejudice and harm. For example, in the UK and the USA within the last 100 years there has been a consistent overrepresentation of People of Colour within mental health settings, involuntary sterilisation has been carried out on women considered to be 'mentally ill', and Conversion Therapy has been conducted on people due to their sexuality. In fact, homosexuality was a diagnosable mental illness until 1973. Many people do not trust mental health services, and for good reason.

No new rules

Psychology is political *and* personal. When thinking about your mental health, always consider the world you are living in. Connect with communities of people who have a shared experience to you. Campaign for change, and vote! Structural inequality, oppression and discrimination all have significant consequences on people's emotional wellbeing, and while coping skills such as breathing exercises and self-soothing may decrease some of the stress you feel, they will not change the societal structures that cause pain in the first place. The way to make real change in the world is by connecting with other humans to offer and share support, and to be politically active and use your voice where you can to make change.

Instead of new rules, here's a reading list you can peruse to learn more:

- *Microaggressions in Everyday Life* by Derald Wing Sue
- *Internalized Oppression: The Psychology of Marginalized Groups* by E. J. R. David, PhD
- *Disability Visibility: First-Person Stories from the Twenty-First Century* by Alice Wong
- *Me and White Supremacy* by Layla F. Saad
- *Men Who Hate Women* by Laura Bates
- *Beyond the Gender Binary* by Alok Vaid-Menon
- *Fattily Ever After* by Stephanie Yeboah
- *Queer: A Graphic History* and *Sexuality & Gender* by Meg-John Barker
- *Five Rules for Rebellion: Let's Change the World Ourselves* by Sophie Walker

If you enjoy reading, be sure to look up (fiction and non-fiction) books that include stories of people living full and joyful lives too, such as *Love in Colour* by Bolu Babalola and *Who's Loving You: Love Stories by Women of Colour* edited by Sareeta Domingo. Not just those that describe the fight against prejudice.

5. Life Events

The final topic I want to cover in the section 'How You Got Here' is life events.

Distressing experiences such as break–ups, the death of loved ones and loneliness are experiences few of us can avoid. When they happen, they cause an understandable cascade of emotions irrespective of how old you are. They can derail an otherwise ordinary life, giving you your first experiences of anxiety, deep sadness and emptiness.

This chapter will cover three common experiences that most of us will experience that cause extreme distress, grief and confusion, and may shatter our beliefs about the world.

Grief and life events

People think we only grieve death. However, any time we go through a transition period in our life or lose something dear to us, we may experience grief.

We can grieve a loss of a sense of safety, such as when we're bullied or hurt by others.

We can grieve any ending or change, such as a relationship break-up, a house, school or job move, or any change to our health or our financial security.

Many of us were collectively grieving the loss of our lives as we knew them during the COVID-19 pandemic, as well as, of course, the huge loss of life.

'Both/and'

'Both/and' is a useful phrase to hold in mind, as it helps us make sense of times when two things that are seemingly opposite co-exist.

When people have children, they may be BOTH overjoyed about the new addition to their family AND also grieving the loss of their previous life.

When their children grow up, they may be BOTH delighted that their child is becoming an adult AND also grieving the loss of childhood and the particular bond that existed at that time.

In therapy, grief can occur when people realise they are healing and making changes in their life. They may be BOTH excited about the future AND simultaneously grieving the period in their life that was deeply painful, recognising the effects that period had on their lives and how much pain they carried around with them on their own. You may even experience this while reading this book.

What is grief?

Grief shapes us. It tells us that something we treasure is now no longer with us.

It has physical symptoms that vary in severity depending on how strongly you feel it. When grief is strong it can cause:

- Fatigue.
- Nausea – I have vomited from the shock of grief before, so perhaps nausea doesn't quite cover it.
- Dizziness and physical aches and pains.
- Memory changes.
- Guilt.
- Fear.
- Panic attacks. They're normal and, while terrifying, can happen when what we previously thought to be stable, known, present and part of the fabric of our life (our safety net) is torn from us.

The stages of grief (based on a modified version of the Kubler-Ross 1969 model)

The following 7 stages explain the processes many of us experience following loss. These stages are not prescriptive and there is no time scale for each stage.

- **Shock:** this is the period directly after a life event

---

when we know something has happened but we can't really feel it yet. Numbness or a sense of unreality may be present.

- **Denial:** this psychological defence protects us by telling us, 'It can't be true. It's going to work out, surely?'
- **Anger:** this is when the initial shock and anxiety have worn off and you start to feel anything from mere frustration to rage. Who is to blame? Who CAN I blame? The anger may be aimed at the world, or at a person.
- **Bargaining:** this stage involves bargaining with yourself, others or a higher power. We say things like, 'If you could make it so that _____ didn't happen, I promise I will _____'.
- **Depression:** the sadness comes. The tears come. Getting out of bed can feel impossible. Hope is not lost, however, as the next stage is . . .
- **Initial acceptance**: some say this is more like surrender. Rather than accepting what is happening, it can feel like, 'I have nothing else I can do now, except surrender to the experience, the reality of this.'

The final stage is . . .

- **Hope:** the moment when you realise, even if just for a second, that you might be okay in the future.

A caveat: therapists love conceptualising stuff. We try to make sense of other people's experiences as neatly as we can, and many theorists have tried to do this with grief.

The reality is, humans and their experiences don't fit into boxes. Everyone grieves in their own way – there is no right or wrong and no timetable for the process. We don't necessarily move smoothly from one grief stage to the next. We may skip stages, or we may backpedal. We may feel it more as a rollercoaster.

I say this not to discourage you. I say this to give you a realistic and fair understanding of grief, and to say that some losses, like the death of a loved one, stay with us. But you will heal.

Can you think of some of the transitions and losses in your life? Did you feel any of these physical or emotional experiences? Did you allow yourself to? Were there any stages or feelings that you felt inside but weren't allowed to show? Were there any experiences you had that are not noted here?

Let's talk about some common experiences that cause us to grieve. As always, please take care of yourself while reading.

Heartache and break-ups

Break-ups are a very common experience once you hit your teens, onwards.

Sometimes we break up with people because they did something that we can't accept – they broke our trust and/or turned out to be completely different from who we thought they were.

Sometimes we break up with people purely because we aren't a good fit, or we're a great fit but we're better as friends. Or because we have simply grown apart.

Other times, people break up with us.

We like them but they don't feel the same way about us – this is the pain of unrequited love that has inspired so much music and literature. We don't even have to have been in a committed relationship to feel this way; we may have been dating only for a short time, or just loving them from afar. Whatever the reason for a break-up or heartache, it can be deeply painful.

When we head into our earliest relationships we are filled with hopes and dreams about how it will be. Our first break-ups can be shockingly painful. It can feel like we will never get over that person, ever.

However, break-ups can teach us many important life lessons, such as:

- Being single can be fantastic.
- What our red flags are in relationships (mine: people who text incessantly and then disappear, then start texting again the moment you give up; people who arrange a date and then don't message on the day).
- No matter how bad break-up pain gets, you always find a way through.
- No matter how hard you try, you cannot make someone love you if they don't want to, and this is survivable.
- How you wish to be treated in future relationships (the song *Thank U, Next* by Ariana Grande is a great example of this).

No matter how many life lessons we learn, or break-ups we experience, it can feel like rejection or loss of a relationship never gets easier or less painful for some of us.

Break-ups can feel physically painful and impossible to ignore. There's a good reason why. In 2010, American researcher Ethan Kross and colleagues found that people who were shown pictures of their significant ex had the same brain activity as people who were being burned on their forearm. Heartbreak is experienced in the body. It changes our brain activity and chemistry.

Another piece of research asked participants to pick potential suitors from a fake online dating site. They were then put in a PET scanner (a machine that looks at chemical processes in the brain) and told that some of the potential, but fake, suitors did not like them in return. When this happened, the brain released its own natural painkillers, opioids.

This doesn't mean that rejection and separation are exactly the same as a broken leg. It means your brain treats a break-up as if it's a threat to your physical safety.

But why?

As I mentioned, our earliest ancestors survived by existing in communities, and would have died if they were kicked out of the group. Our brain treats break-ups and rejection as threats to our existence – hence why we experience it so intensely. The stress response in our body is meant to notify us that something is wrong, and that we need to reconnect with the safety of the group.

After a long-term relationship, a break-up may even make us question our identity – *Who am I now, if not part of a couple?* Again, this is totally normal.

In a relationship, we incorporate our partner(s) into our sense of identity, that is, the representation we have of ourselves in our mind. When we break up with someone it's as if part of our identity has been removed. Suddenly there's a gap in our understanding of ourselves, leaving us feeling lost, confused and unsure of who we are.

How we move forward

Not everyone struggles with break-ups. Some people bounce back quickly, as they know their relationship status is no reflection of their worth (true), that break-ups do not reflect a failing on their part (also true) and because they have trusty coping skills at hand.

If you are struggling with a break-up right now, remember that when we break up with someone it can place stress on our body, make us confused about our identity, and can put us through the grief cycle. We may grieve the loss of the person, the future we had hoped for, and/or our ex's family and a myriad other things.

Use the grief cycle to understand how you feel and which stage you might be in. Use it to identify moments when you feel angry and use that energy to drive you out of bed and into the activities that will help you move forwards, and also to recognise that the bargaining phase is going to make you forget the bad times and remember only the good, potentially urging you to go backwards.

Most importantly, be kind to yourself and your body.

Tips for overcoming a break-up

Surround yourself with loved ones. Being around people you love releases oxytocin, a feel-good chemical, and we need as much of this as possible at this time.

Get active. Think about the times of day that are the most difficult and try to schedule something for that time. For example, if every morning is tough, go for a walk as soon as you are up. If evenings are the worst, arrange to call a friend or go out with someone. Exercise can help too. It breaks down stress hormones and increases endorphins (more feel-good chemicals).

Stop doing the things that make you feel worse but are oh-so-tempting. Stop checking your ex's Instagram. Stop walking past their house. Get a friend to support you through this to ensure you stick to it.

Instil boundaries. For example, if your ex is still in contact and it's making you more distressed, maybe it's time to say, 'I'm sorry, I can't do this. I need to stop contact until I'm feeling more stable.'

Build your identity. Chapter 16 will show you how to work out what your values are (what you truly believe to be important in life). Choose one valued activity to do each day and work towards the new you – the person you are, and will be, outside the relationship. I have clients and friends who can now salsa, or speak new languages, or who have moved abroad, due to learning what was important to them following a break-up.

Break-ups are hardest when the relationship is the central part of our identity – when we let go of our friends, work or hobbies to focus on the relationship. After you have built yourself back up, remember this. Head into future relationships remembering to nurture all the different areas of who you are. Chapter 10 talks about dating and revisits attachment styles, so don't worry, later in the book there's a whole section to prepare you for the next stage.

Use Part Three of the book to help with the emotions you feel. Feeling our emotions is healthy and helps us make sense of, and move through, our experiences. Chapter 6 will explain what your emotions are. Chapter 12 will teach you to soothe your stress response. Chapter 14 will give you the instructions for releasing your emotions through journalling. Chapter 15 will help you find the kind words you may need to speak to yourself, as self-criticism can be rife when we feel rejection – 'There's something wrong with me, of course they don't want me' – which only increases stress and prolongs our pain.

Repeat after me: '[your name], it makes total sense that you feel this way. Break-ups hurt, and it's okay to feel overwhelmed.' Make sure you say it in the third person, as speaking to yourself in this way increases the control you have over your thoughts, feelings and behaviours when stressed AND dampens down the stress response in your brain with relatively little effort.

Try not to add this break-up to the story of who you are. Break-ups shape us but can be a problem if we use them as evidence for something we previously feared to be true, such as: 'People always leave me', 'I'm unlovable', 'This was my last chance'. If you notice such thoughts, remind yourself that break-ups usually happen when a relationship has run its course, not because there is something wrong with you. There are people out there who would love to meet you, and to love you. Also, it's never too late. My nana, who was in her eighties at the time, met her last boyfriend at the cheese counter in Tesco! It's never too late.

To anyone who has had their heart broken: please don't let the actions of others harden you so much that you can no longer access the softer parts of yourself, the parts that dare to believe in possibility, wonder and the magic of human connection.

Death of a Loved One

> *Life changes fast. Life changes in the instant. You sit down*
> *to dinner and life as you know it ends.*
>
> —JOAN DIDION

You now know that the shock of loss and separation are felt physically in the body.

It's the same (although usually significantly intensified) when a loved one dies. Maybe you already know this. Maybe you were a child who lost a parent. A teenager who lost a grandparent or a sibling. Maybe you are an adult who has lost a parent, or a parent who has lost a child. Or maybe you lost a best friend, a confidante, or a partner.

If you have lost anyone dear to you, I am deeply sorry. Whenever we lose someone who had a significant impact on our lives, it can grind our lives to a halt. Loss can feel like it will tear you apart, like a massive hole has opened up inside you, and also in time and space.

Like I said at the beginning of the chapter, the grief of it can trigger panic attacks due to the shock of losing someone who represented safety and/or the shock of the fact that the world can change so suddenly. It can make us worry for the safety of the other people we love (if you are experiencing anxiety or panic attacks, Chapter 7 will teach you to understand these, and Chapters 11 and 12 will help you ground yourself and breathe through them). It can also lead to insomnia, confusion and appetite and/ or memory changes.

The grief cycle explains the shock, the bargaining phase

and depression phase, which are very common and perhaps unsurprising.

It also explains the anger phase that few people truly allow themselves to feel following someone's death. Anger at the world for taking someone we love from us. If we have faith, we may experience anger at God for doing so too. We may likely feel anger at our loved one for leaving us without them. And anger at everyone else because they are carrying on as if nothing has happened. After losing someone close to me, I remember feeling deep fury when I felt I was staring into the edge of the abyss and yet time hadn't stopped. The world had not stopped when this person died; it just kept going as if nothing had happened.

Yet it doesn't capture other stages and emotions you may experience, such as the guilt people are often left with. Guilt for surviving. Guilt for not having been more present in the other person's life. Guilt for not having done more to protect the other person from whatever harm might have befallen them. Guilt for the occasional relief we have if someone dies (this does happen) or if we notice we are starting to move on with our lives and feel this isn't okay because our loved one is no longer there to share our experiences.

We might ponder our own mortality after someone we love dies, wondering about our own death and what it will be like. We might start seeing the face of our loved one everywhere – in a crowded street, in shops and cafes. In our dreams too.

Sometimes you feel you're nearing the end of the cycle, and then a fresh wave hits: you wake up in the morning and, for a blissful moment, you've forgotten what's happened. You may hit a milestone, such as graduating, getting married, having a baby or doing something else you would so love to share with your loved one. And the ground suddenly slips from beneath your feet.

If you have experienced any of these things, then you are normal. And if the loss was in the past, you likely also know there's a point where you genuinely do start to feel like you can live your life again. Not because you are 'over it' but because the pain feels different, less horrendous, like something you live with.

How we experience the death of someone we love is affected by our age, the age of the person who has died, their relationship to us, the way they died, the knock-on effects of the death, what we understand about death and how we are supported during our loss.

Our age

While adults understand the permanence of death, children below the ages of six to ten years old rarely do.

They often believe loss is temporary, and sometimes believe it's their fault – *Did I do something wrong? Did my bad thought or action cause them to go away?* – meaning they need support to understand what has happened and to know it was nothing to do with them. They also can't understand or express their emotions well at this age, meaning they need support to get those mixed and messy emotions out.

Teenagers understand permanence but may face an additional challenge. As you learned in Chapter 2, teenagers are meant to spend this time figuring out who they are outside of their family. Therefore many people who were teens when their loved one died feel deep guilt for not having been more available (and often less argumentative) during that period. If this was you, you were not doing anything wrong; you were going through a normal stage of life, doing exactly what you were meant to do as a teenager in order to develop into the adult you were meant to be. I promise you.

In addition to this, teenagers are often unable to express their emotions, and the feelings manifest in other ways, such as withdrawal, anger, rebellion and other behaviours that may not immediately look like deep grief on the surface. This means they may need guidance to talk about their experiences.

If you lost someone you loved when you were growing up, know that it is never too late to process grief, and there's no specific recipe for doing so either. Some people don't get to truly work through the loss of a caregiver until they're adults. This can be because they were too young to make sense of it when it happened. It can also be that a person will wait until such time as they feel safe enough to look over the edge of the emotional abyss and take the risk of facing that pain, believing they will survive it, and not be consumed and annihilated by it.

Who we have lost and how they died

There is no hierarchy for loss; no death that I can tell you for sure will be easier than another.

However, we do have certain expectations about death. We expect it to come to the oldest people in our lives first. If a beloved grandparent dies and they have told you they're ready to go after a long, value-filled life, you may feel differently from losing someone younger, who has not yet reached that point.

The closeness of your relationship will have an impact too. If the person who died was extremely close to you, the shock of loss will be significant. And it may be further complicated if anything was left unsaid, or if your last interaction was left on a bitter note. This latter point can be a significant trigger for guilt, the fear that we didn't get a chance to make amends.

I had a client who didn't get a chance to say goodbye to her mum, so she started writing letters that she took to her mum's grave. At first, the letters only included her regrets about the recent arguments they'd had, and what she would've liked to say as her final words. Over time, the letters evolved to include how much she missed her, the secrets she'd never had a chance to share, and the many valuable life skills she learned from her. During one of these letters, my client realised a true skill she had learned from her mum was forgiveness, and suddenly she realised that her mum would forgive her.

To anyone who feels they didn't have a chance to say goodbye or to make amends, maybe you could write a letter and share the words you didn't have a chance to say. Or maybe you could do this on a visit to your loved one's grave, or at their favourite spot, or while looking at their photos. Whatever feels most comfortable to you.

Sudden or unexpected deaths

Sudden or unexpected death, due to medical complications during birth or life, or sudden illness, an accident, suicide or murder, can understandably trigger a sense of shock that shatters your belief in the safety of the world. We may be left asking ourselves, *Why? What could I have done?*

If it was an accident, suicide or murder, we may also have to be involved with the police, making the number of tasks we have to manage feel overwhelming. We may get stuck in our thoughts of their last few moments, wondering what it was like for them and if they were afraid. We may be furious at the situation that caused the death. And we may have to field curious questions from others – 'Do you know why it happened? Why they did it?' – which can feel simply too much to handle.

If someone you know is going through this right now, please offer practical support to help manage the tasks your friend is burdened with. And try not to press for information about what happened.

I must also clear up a myth here: people often believe that death following a long illness is easier, as we were 'prepared'. I had a client who came to therapy confused about the deep grief they were feeling.

'I knew it was coming. I don't know why I'm so upset but I am. I'm devastated and lost.'

Their parent had multiple sclerosis. My client had watched their parent change in front of their eyes over many years, seeing them become unwell, experience deep distress and then become dependent. They had spent the last year taking care of them, washing them, feeding them, putting them to bed and, in the end, being in the hospital making the final end-of-life decisions that, while guided by their parent (as they had made a plan a long time before), suddenly felt too much responsibility to bear.

While their mum had been alive, my client had kept up a brave face, busying themselves with the tasks of the day. After their mum died, there were no more distractions, so the pain of what they had witnessed over so many years suddenly surfaced.

They also felt lost, as their role had suddenly changed. They had previously been a carer, but what now?

And finally, they were deeply fearful and feeling guilty about the decisions they had made at the end of their mum's life.

If you ever wonder, *Did I make the right decisions?* My answer is always: 'You did your best with the information you were given at the time, and that is the best anyone can do.'

Lifestyle changes

As with my client above, the way we experience loss can be impacted by the knock-on effect it has on our lives. The more changes there are, the more complex the experience we have to manage.

For example, the young children who lose a parent may suddenly have to 'grow up'; they may suddenly need to parent their siblings, or even a distressed caregiver. They may also have to move home or school, meaning they have to make new friends and settle into a new home.

They may lose a role model too, someone who was going to teach them the ropes.

The adult who has lost a partner may have to manage financial issues, or to look after children. And they'll also have the responsibility of sharing the devastating news with others, which can be extremely difficult each time the topic arises.

What we understand about death

Some cultures talk about death as part of their lived experience.

Certain Buddhist teachings conceptualise life as the high-way to death, with every second we are alive counting as a second that we are closer to dying – a concept that is factual and also scares the pants off many of us.

In Mexico, the Day of the Dead festival, held each year in early November, means that people openly celebrate their connection with their ancestors who have lived and passed before them, meaning death is celebrated and talked about from a young age.

In the tradition I grew up in, in Britain, it wasn't like that. Death wasn't talked about. I went to church with my family, where it was taught that Jesus had died painfully. I watched *The Lion King*, and my family pet died when I was seven, so I had some inkling about loss. Yet the conversation was not on the table.

This is how it is for so many. This means that when someone dies, we don't have the language or framework to process our feelings. It means we struggle to process the enormity of the situation and who and what we have lost. Instead, we may throw ourselves into the practicalities, organising funerals, staying busy. But once it's over, what then?

Also, because of this, many people don't know how to support those who are bereaved – worrying they will say the wrong thing, making it worse, or that everyone will be crowding that person, so they will need space. This is how the bereaved often end up alone during a time when they have never needed others more.

A final note on losing a loved one

We don't move on from grief. We move forward with it.

—NORA MCINERNY

There is no good time for loss. Each age and stage comes with its own challenges – again, inadequate language for such a profound experience. And matters can be further complicated if there are any financial issues to resolve, or family conflict, or if there are ongoing criminal investigations or court cases or an inquest.

There is also no right or wrong way to move through grief. Everyone does it in their own way and in their own time. And the aim is not to 'get over' someone or forget them. Not at all.

If you are experiencing grief at the loss of a loved one right now, start with the grounding exercises (Chapter 11) and breathing exercises (Chapter 12). They will help to soothe your body and your mind. Ensure you have a place that feels safe to vent how you feel. Chapter 14 will help you set up a structure for journalling.

You can also write a letter to the person who has gone, or speak (possibly shout) out loud to them, telling them everything that is coming up for you.

To manage distress people often say … 'Just take it day by day.' Sometimes even day by day can feel too much when grief is at your door. It's OK to take it moment by moment, minute by minute, second by second.

If you feel able to think about a few more steps, here are some recommendations that many people I know report finding helpful at different points in their grief journey. However:

Expect the wave of emotion to return. Your grief is likely to re-emerge when you reach significant milestones that you would have loved to share with your loved one. Think of a way you could keep your loved one close in these moments. Maybe you could have their picture with you when you get married. You could mention them in the speeches. You could give your child your loved one's middle name, or display their photo in their nursery. You could write your loved one a letter telling them your news.

Helping others that are grieving loss

We often back away from people who have experienced loss, assuming they need space. If we all do this then that person ends up alone. If you know someone who is grieving, let them know you are available for them, thinking about them, and then see if they take you up on it.

It can be hard to know how to support someone going through loss, but here is some advice.

For children and teens:

Show them that all emotions are acceptable. Children need someone to co-regulate with. Show them how to release their emotions. For example, allow them to be angry. Maybe take them somewhere they can shout as loud as they want to – tell them that can be their angry place. Get them to jump up and down to let this emotion out. Show them the 54321 technique (Chapter 11) to ground them when they feel overwhelmed, and a breathing exercise (Chapter 12) to help them relax. Breathe with them. Make sure they know they can talk about anything they need to at any time they need to.

If you know a young person who has lost someone and they seem angry, cut off, or in any way different, please always hold in mind what is going on. Please do not assume their behaviour is because they are a 'bad kid' or a 'troubled teen'. Even if they tell you they're fine, please hold in mind what they may be feeling underneath.

Try to keep consistent. As I said before, a death can bring further losses. For children and teenagers, my clients often describe this as a loss of childhood, innocence, home, school and other previously dependable aspects of their lives. Try to minimise the amount of change they experience, as well as the burden of responsibility they may have to take on, as children and teenagers often have to parent their siblings and their struggling caregiver.

Find role models. Children and teens who lose a mother often report losing their female role model – someone who can show them the ropes of womanhood. This is equally true of fathers. Whoever a child loses, make sure they have role models for each aspect of their identity. Also, if you can, introduce them to people (in real life or in stories) who have been through loss and who are now living full lives, so they can show them we can be grieving now yet still be able to grow and have a future.

For everyone:
Acknowledge what they have lost. You can say the word 'died'. For example, 'I'm so sorry that your _____ died.' This symbolises that you can talk about this with them, that you can tolerate the conversation. Avoid phrases such as 'They are in a better place now', or 'It's time to move on' or

'Don't focus on the negative – think of all the things you still have to be grateful for.' You can do this even if the person is a child. Open conversation and support is important at any age.

Make yourself available to listen to how someone is. If it feels right, ask them, 'Would you like to talk about _____?', making it clear that it's okay if they *don't* want to talk, and that if you ask how they are you are not expecting them to say, 'I'm fine, thank you.' Be prepared to sit in silence with someone if that is what they wish, and also to be present to conversations about the person who died.

I know it sounds obvious, but if someone's relative dies by suicide, be led by them. People can end up fielding a million and one questions they're also asking themselves and are coming to terms with, so don't grill them.

Offer practical help. Make meals and drop them round. Offer to look after pets or children. Offer to stay with the bereaved person if this will help them feel safer. Sometimes people find it hard to answer the question, 'How can I help?' So, instead, you could say, 'I would like to make you supper – is this okay?' Or just cook something and drop it over.

If you can't be there to offer love and safety, you could send some items that would create a nurturing environment in their home. For example, you could make a care package with a cuddly blanket, something that smells and/or tastes nice, or a book that talks about grief. One I often recommend is *It's OK That You're Not OK* by Megan Devine.

Recognise this may take a long time. Be available for the long haul and remember significant dates such as anniversaries or any upcoming holiday that may be tricky, and remind your person that they are in your thoughts.

Don't be afraid to mention the person who has died in positive ways, such as, 'Do you remember when _____ taught me how to _____? When they did that _____. I loved that time.'

Do not judge the ways people grieve. Whether people choose to grieve publicly or privately, if they share pictures on their social media or keep everything to themselves, it is their grief and their choice. Our job is to support, not to judge.

Loneliness

What is humanity, really, but a family of families?
—DR VIVEK MURTHY

A common experience following break-ups, the death of loved ones and many of the other events I have addressed, such as bullying, feeling like we don't fit in or aren't accepted at home, in school, the community or the world in general, is loneliness.

Even before COVID-19, 9 million people were estimated to be often or always lonely in the UK. Loneliness is a normal part of being human, but it has now reached epic proportions.

In small doses loneliness may feel distressing. When chronic (part of your everyday life), research shows it is as dangerous for our health as smoking 15 cigarettes per day, and more dangerous than other factors constantly reported in research and the news as increasing our mortality rate, e.g. not exercising, alcohol use, abnormal blood pressure and obesity. It is also a causal factor for anxiety, depression, drug and alcohol addictions, and increases the risk of developing dementia.

Why?

Relationships protect us in many ways.

Being around people we feel connected to makes us feel good. It's a fact. Relationships offer BOTH emotional and practical support, which helps us manage stress, AND they make you more likely to behave in ways that prevent stress. For example, they may make you more likely to practise self-care and take more pride in looking after yourself and your body. They may also support you to exercise and point out times when you seem tired and in need of a break. And they offer you 'roles' that improve your self-esteem and give you a sense of purpose: 'I'm the helpful friend.' 'I'm the one who talks people through their problems.' 'I bring laughter and spontaneity. People like that.'

An absence of relationships means an absence of these protective factors.

When lonely, our threat response is activated (letting us know we need to get back to the group) and can also keep us awake at night. If our ancestors slept alone, they would sleep lightly, waking often to keep an eye out for danger.

Loneliness can be exhausting, leading us to be more vulnerable to other stressors in life, and also less motivated to try to change things. A vicious cycle can therefore start.

The important thing is, loneliness doesn't directly link to how many people are around you at any given moment.

Loneliness vs. solitude

Sometimes you can be totally isolated from others and feel deeply grateful for the solitude. Have you noticed that? You have a night to yourself, maybe your housemates are out, and you can finally get to read that book you've had next to your bed for a month without interruption. Bliss. Or you book a trip to a quiet location or a rural retreat with no phone reception and (if this is what you are into) you immediately start to relax.

Other times, you can be in a room full of people feeling like the loneliest person on earth. You have a worry, are surrounded by people you could potentially share with, but you're convinced they won't get it. Or you have a partner you'd like to share some exciting news or an interest with, but you know they won't be interested.

How being on your own feels is explained by choice (whether you have chosen to be alone), how long it will last (does it have an end in sight?) and connection (how connected you feel to others).

For example, the person with a night to themselves or in the rural getaway still feels connected to a web of relationships. They know there are people who value and understand them only a phone call away, who will be there for them the moment they are ready to connect.

They chose distance knowing they are still connected. However, the people who find themselves alone for extended periods, outside of their choice, may not have that safe and sustaining knowledge that there's a dependable safety net of humans thinking about them. Likewise, the person in a group may not feel connected either, feeling instead like a psychological island in a sea of people they are unable to reach.

People who live alone – and who have lost touch with their friends and family, or have health conditions and/or mobility issues that make accessing the community harder – are at increased risk of loneliness. Older people are therefore more vulnerable in this regard, as they are most likely to tick each of these boxes, as well as possibly losing their hearing and/or sight, all of which can significantly affect connection.

During lockdown in 2020, the conditions were ripe for people to feel lonely, as they were cut off from their usual daily activities and support networks. Did you know that, prior to COVID-19, the 'average' person in the UK spent 80 per cent of their waking hours with other people? Or that instead of the usual 14 per cent of people reporting loneliness, research showed during lockdown it increased to 35 per cent of the British population?

At that time, a dear friend and I spoke about this. We hadn't seen people's faces or hugged anyone in so long that there were moments when we started to wonder if we still existed (another common experience for the chronically lonely). Both of us had thought about a phrase we once heard: if a tree falls in the woods and no one hears it, does it make a sound? We then applied it to ourselves: if no one sees me, hears me or touches me, do I even exist?

We also realised that social media and video calls, while a lifeline, were a poor substitute for being with people in real life. The difference felt like fast food (instant gratification often followed by a slump) compared to a nourishing healthy meal (a slower burn that sustains you for longer). I am now surer than ever that digital contact does not offer the emotional nourishment we truly need, or the physical contact.

If you ever find yourself 'hungry for love' or feeling 'starved for attention', and you have access to people, please choose them. Social media is a means to an end – the connector to help you when you are away from others – but it is not a replacement.

What can we do about loneliness?

Identify if you feel lonely. Loneliness is a complex feeling. It can involve feelings of disconnection, emptiness, sadness, fear, worry, resentment and anger, and sometimes it can cause you to feel unreal, almost as if you don't exist. If you ever experience those feelings, could it be because you feel a little lonely?

Identify where the loneliness arises. Is your loneliness situational? Did you move town or did something (like lockdown) change your life in ways that mean you need to make new friends or a plan for how to connect with people? If this is you, what steps can you make to meet new people or connect with old friends today?

It saddens me how many of us walk around feeling like aliens.

Feeling like we don't fit in.

Not realising that the human sitting next to us feels exactly the same.

Is your loneliness social? Do you have a few close friends but feel you don't belong to any wider groups? Or do you have a partner but, outside of that person, feel there aren't others you can connect to? If this is you, what are your hobbies, passions and talents? What group could you sign up to today? A walking group? A book club?

Is your loneliness emotional? Do you have something you wish to share with others but can't? Does everyone you know have a partner except you, making you feel alone in your experiences? If this is you, you might be looking for deeper intimate friendships. Who can you message today, to say, 'Hi, can we chat?' or 'I'm struggling today'? Maybe you want to speak with a therapist?

Is your loneliness chronic? Has it become a way of life now? If so, planning the steps you will take to slowly reconnect with others may be very helpful for you.

Structure in at least 10–15 minutes per day of face-to-face conversation with another human. Initiating contact with others doesn't have to include you sharing your pain. 'Fancy a cuppa?' can be enough. Remember, if someone is busy, it doesn't mean they don't want to see you. Schedule to meet at a time to suit them.

Chapter 17 is dedicated to helping you find a group and connections that suit you. It also covers volunteer work, which is a beautiful way of finding meaning in your life and seeing the direct impact you have on the world.

I know that when you feel lonely it can be hard to motivate yourself to engage in these tasks. So, it's okay if it takes a while for you to get started with one of the ideas in that part of the book.

If you don't have anyone to talk to, join a group specifically designed to get people talking, such as Side By Side, an online platform run by the UK charity Mind, or, if you are over sixty, you can be partnered with a befriender through Age UK.

Look into local schemes near you that target loneliness. In the UK, 'chatty benches' are trialling in parks so that anyone wanting to have a chat can find one. There are some 'slow queues' in supermarkets, so people who don't wish to rush can talk to each other while they wait to pay. And The Chatty Cafe Scheme, which has 'have a chat' tables (similar to the chatty bench), is in over 900 cafes across the country.

Notice negative self-talk and social anxiety. So many people feel that admitting they're lonely is shameful in some way, like they must be to blame somehow: 'Why can't I social-ise or manage like others?' 'No one else seems to feel this way, they make everything look easy.' 'There must be something wrong with me.' 'It must be that others don't like me.'

If you've had these thoughts, I promise they're not unique to you and certainly not true. Loneliness is everywhere and, as people can't see it, they often don't know when to offer additional support.

If you have high levels of critical self-talk or anxiety, Chapters 6, 7 and 8 will talk you through these experiences, and Part Three will show you how to soothe yourself and distance yourself from your thoughts.

Get a massage. Physical touch can help soothe our threat response. If you can afford it, this is a lovely way to calm your body.

There is no shame in admitting you feel lonely.

If you aren't lonely right now . . .

. . . it's very likely you know someone who is. Possibly a friend, a quiet one you haven't heard from in a while, or equally the one who sent you an emoji-filled text recently telling you how 'fine' they felt, belying how they felt underneath. The person you sat next to on the bus recently might have been lonely, or the person who handed you your morning coffee, or who served you in the supermarket. We cannot see loneliness. But it is everywhere. And we cannot rely on other people telling us they feel this way.

Check in on the people you know. Message people, arrange times to meet up, make sure people know you're keen to connect and that you like them. Especially the people you know who might be at risk of feeling alone. Anyone with mobility issues, the elderly, people living alone, new parents, people who have a lot on their plate, anyone struggling with their mental health.

Connect to the people you don't (if it feels safe to). Start conversations on the bus, or in cafes, sit on the chatty benches, say hi to people, or simply smile at people in the street. If you're in a building with people who are elderly or isolated, offer to do their shopping, drop round something you've baked, say hi. Volunteer your time to charities that are addressing loneliness, such as the British Heart Foundation, Age UK or the British Red Cross. You never know who will benefit from that moment of connection.

Touch people! With their consent, and once everything is COVID-safe, of course. For example, hug people when you say hi and bye. If you know the person well enough, gently hold or stroke their hand if they're telling you they feel upset. If it feels right, and you have the kind of relationship where this would feel acceptable for both parties, offer massage too. I used to work with older adults with dementia; we would give them hand massages with lemon balm essential oil (which is meant to help cognition) and people reported feeling more connected and calm after this, knowing they were not alone.

No new rules

I'm not going to add any additional questions or rules at the end of this chapter, as I believe that what is required now is a moment of pause – a moment to do something grounding and soothing. A moment or more to reflect on what came up for you while reading this. Even writing these words brought up a physical response inside my body, and I have been studying and working in psychology and receiving my own therapy for quite some time. So, please be gentle with yourself right now.

This chapter brings to a close the first part of this book. You now have a pretty good understanding of the many layers that shape who we are. I hope I have made it clear that the earliest layers of our experience affect how we are able to cope with later life events, as well as how we understand the world and our place in it.

Okay, let's pause. Put the book down. Go and do something you enjoy. I recommend choosing one of the following:

- Jump up and down to get that energy moving and shake off some of the stuff that has come up for you.
- Blast some music or light a candle and breathe.
- Or, get a piece of paper and journal, getting your feelings out in words, then reread it or tear it up and then

Sometimes we are so determined to 'fix ourselves' that we gobble up all the advice we can find, working overtime without a break. This can be counterproductive. Take breaks. Put the self-help books down and breathe. Live life. Don't burn yourself out doing the thing that is meant to be making you feel calm, soothed and better about yourself and the world.

do something grounding or loud. Whatever you need.

A Note to You

Phew. That was quite a ride, wasn't it? It was a lot. I know. And being human is just that. A lot! We are continuously being shaped. Every moment of every day has an impact on who we are; every conversation you have outside of this book, in your real life, and every sentence you read here.

You could potentially read the first part of this book and think we are all in trouble. In some ways, that's true. I do believe that many of us are set up to fail, or to feel like we're failing. But in other ways, it isn't true. Struggling and worrying and adapting are very human experiences that need normalising.

I realise that when we read of the many things that can affect us, when we see them written in black and white, the reality of those words can be frightening. However, not everyone feels distressed about every single thing I've mentioned; we all have our unique mix of challenges and victories. Two people can live very similar lives and have quite different emotional reactions.

We are all a million and one things, and we are so much more than what I have written about in this section. These are simply guidelines explaining the main things that shape us, to normalise any coping strategies you have, any time you may have decided you are not enough but others are, or have turned the negative views of society against yourself.

And even when we do feel a total mess – guess what? We're human! And there's always something we can do to make things feel a little more manageable in the moment (even if this is just stopping punishing ourselves for feeling like crap in any given moment), and a lot more manageable in the long term – hence the rest of this book!

Even our brains can change. For example, meditation not only changes the way our brain processes information, making it easier for us to stay present and filter out distracting information, it changes the shape and structure of our brain too. Neurological studies have shown that it is possible to strengthen parts of the brain to be thicker and stronger, and turn down those we want to play less of an active role (e.g. the threat centres). These changes can be seen as quickly as two weeks after starting a daily practice, so know that your emotional reactions are not set in stone.

If I believed we were all in deep water without a paddle, I

wouldn't have written this book. But I *know* that humans are nuanced and deserve understanding, and that there is *always* hope.

My aim in Part One was not to set up the idea that we are all victims. When we feel like a victim, we are immediately disempowered. When we realise we are survivors of distressing life experiences, when we are given the information to understand ourselves and what has happened to us, and when we connect to the humans around us that have been through something similar – either to create a shared sense of compassion and resilience, or to create a collective that can actively make change – we become empowered.

We can find a steady footing from which to take either baby steps or great strides forwards to finding peace of mind or our chosen future. Both of which are equally valid, by the way; we all move at our own pace, and our own pace is ideal.

Before we move on to the next section of the book, 'What's Keeping You Here?' (in other words, what keeps you stuck), I want you to do something. This is important, as it will bridge the gap between Part One and Part Two. It will personalise it and ensure you know the specific beliefs and experiences you are dealing with in your day-to-day. Take some time to think about this. You don't have to have perfect answers, and you may not be able to access them easily, but do your best.

The beliefs that may be affecting how you see yourself, the world and others

While growing up, we are exposed to many different beliefs, whether we believe them or not. These beliefs may affect how we see ourselves, the world and others. I am going to list some topics and I want you to write the first things that come to mind, so please answer the following:

What was the main criticism you heard your closest family members make about other people's bodies? What was the worst thing you remember hearing or seeing about your own body? What judgemental comments did you hear? What did you learn while you were growing up about:

1. Bodies. What were you told about your body or other people's bodies and how a body 'should' look? What was deemed good/great and what was not?

_____

_____

_____

_____

_____

_____

_____

2. Gender. What were you told about gender? What were you told about the gender you were assigned and how were you told you should act? What were you told about other genders and how they might act and what was acceptable for them?

_____

_____

_____

_____

_____

_____

_____

_____

3. Love. How was love demonstrated at home? Who showed it? What words would you use to describe love? How was it described at home? Do you want that kind of love?

_____

_____

_____

_____

_____

_____

_____

4. Other people. How were other people described by your family and your family's friends when you were growing up? Were you told you could trust them? Or to avoid them?

_____

_____

_____

_____

_____

_____

_____

5. Friendships. How were friendships, growing up? Did they make you feel good? How were they talked about?

_____

_____

_____

_____

_____

_____

_____

6. Sexuality. How was sexuality described when you were growing up? How were you taught about it? What did you learn about what was 'good' or 'acceptable'? What were you taught that you were meant to do, or was okay for you? How about what others seemed to be allowed to do?

_____

_____

_____

_____

_____

_____

_____

7. Ability. What did you learn about which bodies were 'better' and who could be included (in activities, parties, games)? What did you hear about disabled people? Were there jokes? What were the messages you were hearing?

_____

_____

_____

_____

_____

_____

_____

_____

8. Race. How was race discussed when you were growing up? Was it ignored? Talked about a lot? Did you ever
hear jokes about race? What were the messages you were
hearing? Was any one race talked about as 'better'?

_____

_____

_____

_____

_____

_____

_____

9. Class. How was class and money talked about while
you were growing up? Were certain people seen to be
better because they had more money? Were they regarded
as 'higher' or 'lower' class?

_____

_____

_____

_____

_____
_____
_____
_____

10. What makes someone 'good enough' or 'worthy'? What messages did you receive about who is good? Who is worthy of love, friendship or admiration? Did these people look a certain way? Have certain things? Can you describe them?

_____
_____
_____
_____
_____
_____
_____
_____

I would now like you to finish these sentences:

I believe I am (choose three positive words to describe yourself):

_____
_____
_____

The three nicest things anyone ever said to me are:

_____
_____

_____

_____

_____

_____

_____

_____

Sometimes I fear I am (write another three):

_____

_____

_____

_____

_____

_____

_____

For me to feel like I'm good enough, I think I need to (write what you need to achieve or what you think you need to change. If you don't think you need to change anything, then write: 'Nothing. I already am.'):

_____

_____

_____

_____

_____

_____

_____

I got this idea from _____. (Did someone tell you this? Was it from one person or many sources?)

_____

_____

_____

_____

_____

_____

_____

Three of the nastiest things anyone ever said to me were:

_____

_____

_____

_____

_____

_____

_____

The three most important people or beings in my life are:

_____

_____

_____

_____

_____

_____

_____

These beings make me feel like I am:

_____

_____

_____

_____

_____

_____

_____

These lists will help you understand how the next few chapters relate to you specifically.

Having read Part One and listed your responses to the above questions, can you see why it's inevitable that we are all so concerned about what other people think of us? Why seeing that others appreciate us matters like hell?

Most of us have been taught to question ourselves and our worth, our uncertainty making the opinions of others important, a possible boon to life or the metaphorical thumbs-down of a Roman emperor.

My final task for you: please write down your personal timelines. I don't want you to do anything with your answers to these questions yet. I will explain why I asked you to do this exercise at the end of Chapter 9.

Circle the age bracket you're in. Where do you expect to be in life at the following ages? What do you think you should you have achieved, owned and/or been part of, or will achieve, own and be part of? These may link to expectations in work, who you should be and how you should act, healing, dating, family, property, how your body looks or feels, retirement, how much money you have, how confident you feel, and anything you hope for or expect.

At 20 years old I expected

_____

_____

At 30 years old

_____

_____

At 40 years old

_____

_____

At 50 years old

_____

_____

At 60 years old

_____

_____

At 70 years old

_____

_____

At 80 years old

_____

_____

At 90+ years old

_____

_____

Okay, so you now know how your *outside* world may have shaped your inside world. Are you now ready to learn how your *inside* world shapes your experiences of the outside world in return? If so, let's go!

Dr Soph xx

Part Two

What's Keeping You Here?

Part One hopefully showed you how family and societal conditioning shapes our emotional responses to the world. In this next part we are going to look at the things that keep most of us stuck, feeling anything from mildly insecure to downright anxious.

In my experience, the two main reasons people feel stuck are linked to a lack of education around emotions and thoughts, and difficulties in relationships.

The first four chapters of Part Two will aim to help you understand your inner world, teaching you what your emotions and thoughts are, what the fight–flight–freeze–fawn response is, which common coping skills make us feel worse, and how best to understand our inner critic.

The final chapter covers dating, love, and how our earliest attachment styles affect who we date and how we behave in relationships, and how modern technology increases our options in the dating world but may actually make choosing someone significantly more difficult.

Part Two will also show how the experiences we explored in Part One show up in our lives. How they infiltrate every thought and feeling. How they show themselves in our relationships and our behaviours, day in, day out, and how we cope with all of this.

Unlike Part One, the topics in this section are relatively separate ideas. Therefore, you can choose to read through in chronological order, or you can dip in and out, starting wherever you prefer. I recommend covering them all at some point. However, there's no rush!

6. Emotions, Thoughts and Predictions

What are emotions?

Emotions are physical feelings. They start in your body and arise outside of your conscious control. Sometimes they come on slowly and quietly, and you barely notice them. Other times they're instant and hit you so damn hard it's like a wrecking ball, dragging you from the present moment into a spiralling freefall.

Most people think emotions arise in response to the 'good' and 'bad' things that happen in life, as by-products of our experiences: happiness, excitement and interest when we experience something we enjoy; sadness, anger and anxiety occurring when we experience something we don't. This is partly true.

Few people realise emotions have a purpose.

Emotions create the energy inside us that we need in order to turn towards the things that keep us alive and avoid the things that might kill us.

When we aren't taught about emotions and thoughts, we often misinterpret the very normal experiences that happen within us.

The purpose of emotions

As we have learned, we are the product of millions of years of evolution.

We are here because our ancestors found ways to survive the almost constant threats from their environment. And also because they found enough rewards (things that feel good and enhance our survival).

For our early ancestors, threats and rewards were pretty clear: a nearby tiger, running out of food, being banished from the community . . . All of these threats were potentially deadly.

Rewards, on the other hand, pretty much amounted to safety, food, socialising and . . . well, sex.

When a threat crossed our ancestor's path, it will have been a form of what we call:

- **Anxiety** – which gave them the skills to worry about what could happen next.
- **Anger** – which gave them the energy and drive to turn towards a threat and fight to protect their resources, or whatever else might be taken from them.
- **Fear** – which had their legs moving faster than the speed of light out of harm's way (or would have frozen them to the spot, which has its uses too and will be talked about in the next chapter).

If our ancestors had acted in a way that could have had them exiled – maybe they weren't pulling their weight in their community, or had offended a clan leader with the power to exile them – what you and I call shame and guilt would have driven them to fix their behaviour and make amends. Yes, that mortifying feeling that I'm sure you've experienced at some point potentially saved our ancestors' lives.

When potential rewards appeared, happiness, interest and arousal will have ensured they pursued them.

While our ancestors might have been anxious, angry or fearful about the threats, and happy, excited or aroused about food, friendship and a spot of fornication, there is another layer to this.

To stay safe, our ancestors didn't wait until a tiger was at their door, the food was gone or they found themselves out in the cold before they reacted to the threats. That could be a lethal mistake. Instead, their brains developed to predict what would happen next, anticipating threats and rewards before they could occur, mounting a physical response that would ensure their survival.

Their survival depended on running at the first sound that might announce an oncoming predator, not sticking around long enough to find out if they were right or not.

Run for your life, ask questions later.

You and I may not face the threat of a tiger wandering into our midst. We may not worry that someone will break into our house, take all our food and leave us to starve. But we too have emotional reactions that arise in response to our predictions.

When we face a predicted threat – the rude stranger in the street who seems to be picking a fight, or the moment we receive a message at work or from a partner saying, 'We need to talk' – stress hormones such as cortisol and adren- aline arise, prepping us to fight or run. When we face a potential reward – the lover, the delicious meal, a promotion at work – feel-good brain chemicals and the hormones dopamine, serotonin and oxytocin arise, making us turn excitedly towards it.

Our brain prepares us for whatever our brain believes lies ahead.

What do I mean by predictions?

There have been many theories of emotions put forward to date. My favourite, however, is the theory of constructed emotions put forward by Professor Lisa Feldman Barrett from whom I learned the following ...

Your brain is not responding to the world right now. You are not responding to these words or your current environment. No, your brain is running ahead of you, predicting what's going to happen next. Predicting the words that will be in this sentence and what events are going to happen around you.

If I suddenly changed tack, wittering on about how the collective noun for owls is a 'parliament' (great fact), I imagine you would be surprised – the emotion that arises whenever our prediction is wrong.

Anger gives us energy to fight injustice. Anxiety gives us the ability to worry about an uncertain future, and to prepare for anything that may go wrong. Shame and guilt ensure we keep our relationships alive, avoiding rejection and the pain of being alone. All our emotions have a purpose – they drive us to take the action we need to stay alive and, also, thrive.

If someone burst through your window right now, smashing glass onto the ground, you would jump. A sudden threat-response would mount in your body, launching you off your seat. Again, because your brain did not predict it.

Wherever you are, whatever you're doing, your brain is making continuous predictions and your emotions arise in response to them. But how does it do this?

Let me give you an example.

Picture the scene: you are in your house, alone. It's night-time. You hear a noise outside.

Your brain is already ahead of you, predicting what's going to happen next. And here's the important part: **to make its predictions, it dives through its memory stores**, which are based on who you are, what has happened to you and the information you've been taught, and maybe even the magazine articles you've read or films you've seen recently. It looks for the information it has on houses, night-times and things that go bump in the night. Suddenly, it stumbles across a horror film you saw ages ago about break-ins.

'Ah! I predict a burglar,' your brain says.

This prediction causes a simulation (a mental image) to arise in your mind of a burglar in your house. Maybe it's a cartoon burglar with a striped top and an eye mask, or maybe it's a knife-wielding serial killer. This happens below your level of awareness, but the simulation causes all your senses to respond as if a burglar were really there.

Suddenly, you hear more noises. You may even see a movement. You may even believe you see someone – that's how strong the effect of the prediction and simulation is. Your body starts preparing to react – in this case to run or fight for your life.

While your heart pounds, the burglar either appears or he doesn't. If he does appear, you burst into action and more predictions, emotions and responses will follow.

If no one appears – maybe it was nothing, maybe a cat knocked something over – your brain processes the difference between the prediction and the event, updating your memory stores to reflect that not all noises are burglars; they are sometimes cats. Or wind or rain.

You feel relief but you're left with jittery feelings in your body.

Whatever happens, you feel fear. Fear not from the environment, but in response to your brain's prediction.

This example clearly outlines a situation where something physically dangerous could have occurred. If you swap the burglar in the house for walking in the forest at night and hearing a rustling sound in the bushes – *a snake!* – the outcome would have been the same: anxiety and fear.

I could have suggested a subtler scenario. I could have talked about what would happen if you had an important presentation coming up at work and, based on your previous experiences and fears, you jumped to a prediction that you were going to do something hideously embarrassing.

Or what would happen if you saw that your ex liked another person's picture (whom you always suspected they fancied), and your brain predicted this meant they've met someone new.

Or that moment when you realise your phone battery is about to die and your brain predicts you will be in immediate danger the moment you are without a phone – that you will be lost, and an emergency may occur. Anyone who has experienced this last one knows how powerful the prediction of danger linked to no phone can be, and how the prediction is almost always wrong.

I could have also given the same scenario of being in your house alone at night, hearing a noise, but with a totally different outcome. Maybe you heard the noise but, because you're expecting someone home – a friend, a partner or your new beau who hasn't been over before – when your brain runs through all the possible situations that may occur, it instead says, 'Yay, they're home!' Warm to hot, hot, HOT(!) feelings surge through you instead, as you dash to the door to let them in.

The point is:

- We do not experience the world exactly as it is.
- We experience it based on the predictions we make.
- Our predictions are based on our personal history.
- The predictions we make cause simulations, which cause physical responses, and we call these emotions.
- Our predictions are not always accurate and are sometimes exaggerated.
- Our brain will update the information it uses to make predictions when we gain new information.

And also, as shame and guilt show, we aren't just predicting what will go right or wrong in the future. We are predicting what our past actions and experiences mean too. This is why we can get stuck ruminating on past events – *Why did I do that? Everyone is going to hate me now.*

Shame vs. guilt

While shame and guilt may both arise following something that could cause harm to our relationships, there is a difference between the two.

Shame is accompanied by the thought 'I am bad', while guilt says, 'I did something bad'.

I believe shame is far less useful than guilt. Shame makes us see the world the same way as young children, who cannot hold good and bad in their mind at the same time. It makes us believe that one single moment in our life defines us, which is not the case. It can totally paralyse us.

That night when you got a little wild, and may or may not have said too much, and even that time you did indeed upset your friend, does not define who you are. You are made up of millions of moments, all of which come together to make the rich tapestry of who you are.

When you next feel shame and/or think 'I am bad', remember this and decide to see the specific moment or action where something went wrong as exactly that: one moment. Then decide how to make up for that one behaviour or moment. No single moment in time defines who you are, and all humans make mistakes; it's how we make up for them that matters.

Sometimes the threat is real

Are you reading this thinking, *But sometimes I'm not incorrectly predicting bad things are going to happen. Sometimes they really are happening!*

Learning we are prediction machines does not mean our experiences are not real. I'm not saying that every time you think something bad is happening that it's just in your head.

Horrendous things do happen in our lives. Bullying, sexism, racism, homophobia, fatphobia and other terrible prejudices exist. That boss who undermines you and micromanages your every move, ruining your day, that's real! And sometimes, the message that says 'We need to talk' really does mean that something bad is going to happen.

Sometimes we see these distressing moments coming, predicting that someone is going to slight or hurt us, and the confirmation we get in that moment proves we are absolutely correct.

Sometimes we don't see them coming, thinking instead that we are in a calm situation with someone, and then *bam!* They say or do something that we never predicted, shock flooding our system – remember, shock is the emotion we feel when there is a huge and sudden mismatch between what we expected and what happened.

But we sometimes overpredict the danger we face. Anxiety, anger, fear, shame and guilt arise when we aren't facing any danger at all.

And another thing: our brain updates its predictions when it has new information, but often we don't wait to gain new information. We make an assumption about what's going to happen, feel the emotion arise within us and react. We hear someone say something that sounds like a slight, but we don't pause to ask if our prediction is correct; we jump to a conclusion and maybe even launch an attack. We see someone look away or at their phone during a conversation and assume it means they're bored of us and what we are saying. We don't think about the million and one other reasons someone may look away for a moment – so, we feel boring and stop talking. Can you think of an occasion when you have done this recently? Is there a chance your prediction was wrong?

Overpredictions are most likely to occur when we already feel stressed out, because stress not only means we predict something bad is going to happen, it tells our brain that we are now in threat mode and need to be on guard for worse things to come.

Quick exercise: have you overpredicted threat?

Think about something that was worrying you a year ago – maybe a work or study assignment, and whether it would go okay. Maybe you thought a friend was mad at you? Or that your partner would end things? What happened? Did what you predict would happen, happen? If not, were you overpredicting the threat?

If what you predicted would happen did happen, was the outcome as bad as you thought? If the answer is no, this is an example of an overprediction.

If the answer is yes . . .

Now a year has passed, is the outcome of that event still affecting you as much as you thought it would? This latter point is important – we don't just overpredict threat, we often overpredict the impact of the event and underpredict our ability to cope and for time to pass. For example, when I think, *Oh my God, they're mad at me*, it can be easy for me to forget that even if this were true, I will have opportunities to make amends down the line.

Quick tip: how to check whether you are overpredicting threat

When a worrying thought or anger arises, do as author Brené Brown does: ask yourself, 'What is the story I'm telling myself right now?' For example, 'The story I'm telling myself right now is that this "We need to speak" email is the end of my career, this text the end of my relationship', or 'The wild night out and my bad behaviour is the end of my social life'. Remind yourself that this is a prediction. Then check for the evidence. What is the evidence for this fear? What is the evidence against it? If the worst outcome did happen, what is the evidence you would survive it? You can even check out your 'stories' with your friends. What evidence do they see that confirms your fears or goes against them? **When we are stressed or** worried it colours everything we see. **It shapes our predictions.** Friends who do not feel stressed may be able to offer different evidence.

We notice what we fear

The times when you and I overpredict danger might be quite different, as we have different information in our memory banks.

There are threats that can affect us all, like prejudice, bullying, break-ups, death, rejection and loneliness.

There are common experiences that make us feel good, like kindness, compassion, a delicious meal and a good night's sleep (reward).

Then there are the not-so-obvious ones, which are based on beliefs from our own histories: what we are told is 'good' and 'bad' by our parents, our friends, the media and society as a whole. And the uniquely pleasurable and painful experiences each of us have been through.

In Part One, we talked about perfection being revered by society and how there are many reasons people may adopt perfectionism.

Remember the examples: the kid who developed perfectionism to prevent punishment or abandonment in their family home and/or did this

We often feel so sure we know what others are thinking. Certain in the knowledge that they are judging or have judged us. But the reality is, we are guessing. Guessing what they think, based on our fears and what we worry may be true about ourselves.

to gain more of the loving looks and praise they wished for. They may predict that any time they act in a way that could be construed as imperfect, such as getting a bad grade or doing something embarrassing, they will be abandoned. So they spend their whole lives trying to be perfect.

The teen who learned to 'create a brand' – a 'perfect' exterior in order to prevent alienation or bullying and/or gain the acceptance and validation of others – may predict that any crack in their personal brand might lead to a resurgence of bullying and alienation. So they keep the façade up as if their life depends on it.

The person of any age who was conditioned by the media to believe they need to be perfect in order to be accepted by society, or by their friends and family, may predict they will be dumped if they don't look 'good', or that they will be publicly shamed like the people in the fatphobic and ageist articles we see in magazines if their cellulite, tummy rolls, or any signs of ageing are on show. They may predict others will think they're stupid (and alienate them) if they fail their exams, or don't get the promotion and the pay rise.

If we truly believe perfection is important, and that without it rejection or another pain may occur, our brain may start to treat imperfection in the same way as early man's brain interpreted a tiger at the cave entrance. It may try to anticipate imperfection as if our lives depend on it. It may predict and simulate catastrophic outcomes, continuously. This drive for perfection is why many of us feel so anxious, angry, fearful, shamed and guilty when we believe we're performing at any level that is not 100-per-cent perfection.

The more severe the consequence we predict, the more strongly we feel the emotion.

The flip side of this is why we may feel elated any time we feel we're getting close to what we deem to be 'perfect'. We predict this means 'good enough', 'lovable', even. That comment telling us we've lost weight, look like a movie star or will go far with our credentials may feel amazing – even when we truly believe these things don't matter anymore, we still often get a boost from such comments.

Just like our ancestors, when we make predictions about threats we often change our behaviour to try to prevent our feared outcome. We may never allow ourselves to be seen looking anything less than photo-shoot ready, or we may never hand in anything that could be imperfect – many people would rather fail a test and look like they were not trying than risk getting a poor grade for something they worked hard at.

Can you think of some painful past experiences that affect how you see the world now and cause you to feel threatened or rewarded?

For example: if you were bullied in school, it may be that, as an adult, any time you walk past a group of people laughing, your brain may predict and simulate the bullying experience. Suddenly, unconsciously, you are back there, feeling it. At the conscious level, it feels like they're laughing at you. Social anxiety and fear ensue, your thoughts telling you your worst fears are true, as you rush past, trying to get away from them as quickly as you can.

If you didn't feel safe around adults as a child, it may be that, as an adult, any time you're around someone who seems a little annoyed or has raised their voice, your brain may predict and simulate your early experiences. Suddenly you're responding as if the person in front of you is really angry. Maybe you shut down or respond in the way you would have as a child.

If a partner cheated on you, then, in subsequent relationships, any time you see they've made a new friend or don't text for a day or two, what do you think your brain would predict and simulate then? That it is happening again.

You see how this works. *What we fear is often what we see.*

If you have social anxiety, and left a previous social occasion feeling people thought poorly of you, you may enter the next event fearing that other people find you boring or might laugh at you. If this is you, you may notice that you see signs of boredom, or a flicker of laughter on their face, when maybe this is just their normal facial expression.

Or, if you feel particularly unhappy with your body or how you look one day, you may start interpreting other people's body language, mood or what wasn't said as a sign they're thinking about how you look.

Our past experiences can act like a personal virtual reality screen. If we were taught that something about us was unlovable or bad in some way, or if we feel something is dangerous, then on the days when we feel stressed, it will be like we are wearing a headset that shows us only the information and 'evidence' that proves our fears. This is how we carry our

> **The world shapes us, teaching us what to believe, what to fear and what to strive for. We then shape the world in return, interpreting our experiences and the actions of others based on what we have experienced in our past and what we believe and fear to be true.**

painful experiences with us, and how they play out suddenly and unexpectedly in our day-to-day lives.

This is why we all have different experiences of the world, and why two people could walk into the same situation, one of them slipping into paralysing anxiety if confronted with something that reminds them of a distressing event they faced in the past, while the other isn't bothered at all.

Exercise: what does your brain find threatening?

Think about the most recent time you had a strong emotional response and answer the following questions.

The most recent time I felt a strong emotion was:

_____

_____

_____

_____

_____

I think this emotion was:

_____

_____

_____

_____

_____

I think it arose because my brain predicted that the following was about to happen ...

_____

_____

_____

_____

_____

(If answering this question is hard, ask yourself: what does the situation I was in remind me of? Has something like this happened in the past?)

This tells me that I may find the following threatening:

_____

_____

_____

_____

Was the prediction correct? Or was it linked to a fear memory from the past? If it was an incorrect prediction, say to yourself: *I'm learning that my emotions link to predictions. My brain is predicting and simulating something that happened in my past. But it's okay. I'm not in my past. I am here. I'm okay.*

Predictions even happen for our internal experiences

The predictions our brain makes (about what will happen next) don't just happen for things in the outside world. They also happen for our internal world. Yep, your brain is also scanning *you*. Right now. It's looking at what's happening inside you and predicting what those things mean.

Did you notice that when COVID-19 first hit the news, any

time you had a tight chest or shortness of breath, there was a sudden moment of, *Uh oh, this is it*, as your brain predicted the feelings that signalled you had contracted the virus. Or have you ever met someone with a rash, then, when you next experienced tingling or itching, your body and brain filled with anxiety, and you thought, *I've caught it*?

The predictions our brain makes explain these experiences. And it goes further.

If you think certain emotions are good (happiness or excitement) and others are bad or dangerous (anger, anxiety or sadness) this is going to affect what you think you're feeling.

Few people realise that their internal body states are constantly changing and that it's totally normal. For example, your heart rate can suddenly ramp up and then go back down again; your muscles can tense and be relaxed again a little while later; your stomach can feel odd and then settle moments later for what seems no reason at all. Many times a day. Yet when we fear our emotional experiences, we may predict these normal internal fluctuations as something scary.

If you think anger is bad: your brain may predict that a racing heartbeat or tightness in your chest, which could happen for many non-worrying reasons, means *Aha, it's anger*. Suddenly you have a simulation of you being incredibly angry playing through your mind. Suddenly you feel it.

If you worry about anxiety: your brain may predict that the symptoms described above (a racing heartbeat and tight chest) mean something entirely different. Instead of predicting anger it predicts 'Eek, panic attack!' Suddenly you're simulating a panic attack and, oh my God, are you then feeling it!

You can bring on a panic attack simply by being afraid that

you're going to have one. This is one of the many reasons that panic attacks stick around, as people become hypervigilant for any sign one may occur. They then start to interpret every change in their body as being possible evidence that one is about to occur (some therapists call this 'catastrophic misinterpretation'), which causes panic to ensue, ramping up quickly.

Don't worry, this doesn't mean that anyone who has panic attacks is doomed to experience them for ever, or that you will always bring one on simply by thinking about them; it means we need to change our relationship to anxiety and panic so that we break this cycle. The next chapter talks about anxiety in more detail, so don't worry if you read that and thought, *Great, but seriously, how?*

So, the way you experience your bodily sensations and emotions depends on what you've been taught is normal, safe and to be welcomed.

There is no such thing as a good or bad emotion. We will experience many different emotions throughout the day, as we all have so many different experiences. Yet, right now, we are mainly taught that happiness is our only goal. The negative portrayal of mental illness in the media can mean that when you first experience a hint of distress, sadness or anxiety, your brain can feel overwhelmed, bringing forth the often inaccurate portrayals of people in news reports, TV dramas or in movies, whose lives are ruined by their mental illness, or who ruin other people's lives instead (this is why my 18-year-old self had such a terrifying fall from sanity following my first panic attack).

It wasn't always like this – in the sixteenth and seventeenth centuries, melancholy was the celebrated emotion, thought to make you more successful in life. So much so, a popular medical book for the masses called *The Castell of Health*, by Thomas Elyot in 1536, included a list of reasons to be disappointed, as it was thought that fostering sadness would cultivate resilience in the reader!

Secondary emotions

Primary emotions are the physical experiences we have talked about throughout most of this chapter. They are the emotions that arise first in response to whatever you are predicting, e.g. happiness arising in response to another person's smile, or anger in response to an injustice.

Secondary emotions, however, are the emotional reactions we have to the primary emotions.

Many people feel shame or fear when they feel anger. This is often because they've been taught growing up that anger is unacceptable. Conversely, many people feel anger whenever they feel vulnerability, sadness or anxiety.

I worked with a client who came to therapy to get support for his anger. We quickly realised that his issue wasn't anger. He had experienced a lot of rejection over the previous year and was feeling vulnerable and sad, but in his family, sadness and vulnerability were never shown. More than that, his dad, who he looked up to, was apparently well known and 'respected' in town because he was 'someone you wouldn't mess with'. He realised that his family saw sadness and vulnerability as signs of weakness, but that anger 'made you powerful'. Therefore, any time he felt vulnerable, anger sprang up in his defence, protecting him, stopping anyone else from seeing how he felt beneath.

In this case, anger was the guardian of sadness.

What we believe to be true about our emotions affects how we interpret our primary emotions, and then how we respond. This links to how we are taught about emotions by our caregivers, friends and society. How were you taught about your emotions? What did you learn about them? Fill in the blanks below to understand what may be affecting how you feel.

Exercise: investigating your beliefs about your emotions

The things we believe to be true about emotions usually link to what we learned about them when we were young. Take a moment to answer the following questions:

When I was young, I saw adults show the following emotions:

_____

_____

_____

_____

When I was young, the adults in my life managed anger and sadness by:

_____

_____

_____

_____

When I showed sadness and/or anger to the adults around me, they (write what they did in response to your emotions: did they support you, tell you how to work through it?):

_____

_____

_____

_____

When I was young, I didn't see the following emotions:

_____

_____

_____

_____

Now take a moment to think. What are your beliefs about emotions? Take a moment to answer the following:

I believe that emotions are (think about what you believed before you read this chapter):

_____

_____

_____

_____

The emotions I like having are:

_____

_____

_____

_____

I like them because (e.g. they make me feel energised; I was told this is what I should strive for):

_____

_____

_____

_____

When these emotions arise I feel (e.g. like I'm doing something right):

_____

_____

_____

_____

When they arise, I (e.g. I socialise, or do something else that is helped by this feeling):

_____

_____

_____

_____

The emotions I don't like are:

_____

_____

_____

_____

I don't like them because (e.g. women shouldn't feel these; when I was young I saw someone else displaying this emotion and it was terrifying):

_____

_____

_____

_____

When these emotions arise I feel (e.g. overwhelmed, like I want them to go away):

_____

_____

_____

_____

When they arise, I (e.g. I keep busy, avoid, let them in):

_____

_____

_____

_____

What do these answers suggest about what you believe to be true about your emotions? Do your answers suggest that you believe some are good and others are to be avoided? Do they suggest that you try to avoid how you feel?

Is there any overlap between the emotions you saw expressed well in your childhood and the ones you feel okay to show? Is there any overlap between the emotions you didn't see in childhood, or that were expressed in a way that felt unmanageable, and the ones you feel uncomfortable to show now? Is there any overlap between the emotions that you were supported/unsupported to feel as a child and the ones you feel good/bad about expressing as an adult? If your answer is yes to either of these questions, this will give you more insight into why you experience your emotions in a way that is unique to your life experience. It should also highlight some areas that may need further thought.

How others responded to our emotions when we were young affects whether we feel able to express our emotions as adults.

When I was young and showed anger or sadness, I remember my caregivers responding by (e.g. did they help soothe you? Did they tell you to get over it? Or that you were just tired?):

_____

_____

_____

_____

How does this feed into how you feel about expressing your emotions now? If you were shamed or silenced when you showed emotion as a child, it may be hard for you to feel safe showing emotions as an adult. Be gentle with yourself as you start relearning ways to share.

Emotions are meant to be fleeting

Emotions are meant to be fleeting. They arise to help you respond to a particular situation. However, our emotions can stick around.

Sometimes they stick around because the event causing the distress is still happening and needs addressing. The bullying, the prejudice or the asshole boss who's making your life miserable may all continue to make you feel distress while they are still around. These are the kinds of experiences that require action. In the case of bullying and prejudice, action may include knowing your emotions make sense, as well as finding support to stop the bullying and prejudice, sharing your experiences so you don't feel alone, and campaigning for change at the societal level that supports this kind of behaviour. In the case of the boss, action may include finding allies in your workplace to support you, taking your concerns up with your boss or HR department or . . . leaving your job.

Sometimes emotions stick around as the event was extremely distressing, and it will simply take time for you to recover – for example, if you're going through a break-up or are grieving. These experiences take time, and the kinds of emotional support we discussed in Chapter 5.

Other times our emotions stick around because we believe there's danger where there is none, and we get stuck ruminating on what might or might not be. These experiences require either the quick tip I described earlier in this chapter to test whether you are overpredicting threat (see p.195) or, and I prefer this, using mindfulness to become aware but not overly involved with your emotions and thoughts, allowing them to pass, whatever they are.

Other times, because we misinterpret the experiences inside of us, a single emotion spirals into a panic or rage attack. These require us to read the next chapter.

Most of us haven't been taught what we should do with our emotions when they arise. So, what do we do? We try to push the uncomfortable or overwhelming emotions away. We pretend not to have seen them; we keep busy, burying ourselves in work. Or we find something fun to temporarily distract ourselves – a quick scroll on a dating app, social media, or sweet treat such as a bag or three of Maltesers.

This is fine, from time to time. We don't have to feel all our emotions, all the time. However, if we do this all the time we tend to run into a problem – that problem is, pushing our emotions away is like trying to push a beach ball underwater. We can hold it under for a moment but it will inevitably pop back up, maybe moments or days later, maybe in a different location.

> *I drank to drown my sorrows, but the damned things learned*
> *how to swim.*
>
> —FRIDA KAHLO

This isn't because we are weak or faulty in any way. It's because emotions have played a part in our survival over millennia. They aren't meant to be ignored. They have a purpose. Ignore them and they just shout louder.

Ignore your emotions if you want them to stick around. Fight your emotions if you want them to fight you back. Welcome your emotions in if you want them to leave you alone.

Get in touch with your emotions

Right now: set a timer for 1 minute. Close (or lower) your eyes. Focus your attention on your breath. When you notice a thought arise, simply say 'thinking', and turn your attention back to the breath. When you notice a physical sensation, simply say 'feeling', and turn your attention back to the breath.

Afterwards: did you notice the difference between a thought and a feeling? Did you find labelling the experiences in this way, without judgement, helped them pass?

Noticing without judgment can help us gain distance from our thoughts and feelings. The more practice we have, the more easily we will learn to observe and let go of our internal experiences.

Moving forward: start a regular practice of noticing. Up to 5 minutes per day is sufficient. Scan your body from head to toe – when you find any kind of physical sensation, or something you might call an emotion, ask the following questions (there are no right answers; this is purely to get your curiosity going and to start your journey out of your head and back into your body):

- Where do I feel the sensation in my body?
- How big is the feeling? Are there edges to it (for

example, is it in my chest but stops at the shoulders)? Or does it fill my whole body?

- What shape would I say it is?
- How does it change (or not) when I pay attention to it?
- If I inhale and exhale slowly, what happens?
- What happens if I expand my awareness to include the sensation and the feeling of my feet on the floor?
- What would I call this feeling? It can have any name under the sun. You could also just label the part of your body where you feel it – you could choose a type of weather it reminds you of, or an emotion label.

If the emotion you find feels too much, identify somewhere that feels relaxed (or less intense) in your body and pay attention to that area until you feel grounded, then slowly turn your attention to a part of the feeling. Then go back to the safe-place on your body, slowly building up the time you can attend to the harder moments.

If you have spent most of your life pushing your emotions away, don't be surprised if at first you don't feel anything. Or if there's a moment when a feeling emerges but, just as you pay attention to it, it disappears. Acknowledge that it's now both safe and healthy to feel this or, conversely, that it's okay if you're not able to quite yet. When the feeling comes, just make space for whatever's there. When it disappears, don't look for it or berate yourself. Congratulate yourself for even considering making space for the emotion, knowing that one day, when you are ready, those emotions will come. And you will be able to welcome them in.

'Name it to tame it'

Research shows that labelling your emotions helps them to pass, as it decreases activity in emotion centres of your brain. Therefore, simply choosing a word to label how you feel in any moment – e.g. 'that feeling is anxiety', 'that feeling is shame' (or, if you don't have a specific word for how you feel, that's also okay, e.g. 'that feeling is icky') helps de-intensify your emotional experiences, allowing you to make choices about what you want to do next.

Start this today. Set a reminder on your phone that will pop up 2–3 times per day. When you see the reminder, scan your body and label whatever emotion is present. The more you do this, the more easily you'll remember to use labelling when an emotion arises: 'Ooh, I know you, you're anxiety! Welcome in!'

The new rules

You may need to revisit these new rules many times, as it will take a while for them to sink in.

- **There is no such thing as a good or bad emotion.** They have kept our species alive for millennia. While some feel better than others, they are all equally important.
- **Emotions usually start in the body,** as they are meant to galvanise us into action or stop us in our tracks.
- **Emotions arise outside of our conscious control.** Predictions, simulations and responses arise faster than you can consciously imagine. This is why it's okay if you suddenly feel overwhelmed but are unsure why. It also means emotions can be conjured purely from the thought of something scary in the future or the past.
- **The time in which you grew up, and the beliefs of the people around you, dictates what you learn about your emotions and therefore how you feel them.** If we are taught that certain emotions are good or something to be proud of, then when they arise we will feel them in a way that is more pleasurable. If we are taught that certain emotions are undesirable, socially unacceptable or even dangerous, then when we feel them they will be accompanied by a barrage of other, less pleasant (understatement) feelings, such as shame.
- **We all experience emotions differently.** Each of us has different life experiences and has learned different things about the world and about emotions. Therefore, we all differ in the way we predict what will happen next in any

given moment. Also, remember what I told you about brain development? As our brains developed in different environments, using different DNA, we really vary in terms of human emotion. It is important to remind yourself that the difference between people and their emotions is normal and has nothing to do with weakness, failure or any other negative thing you may be saying to yourself.

- **We can experience many emotions at once.** We may have mixed beliefs and memories about any given situation. This explains why our emotions can feel so complicated, as mixed simulations and responses may play out at any one time.
- **We may be primed to look for threat.** Being on high alert for threat may have helped our ancestors survive better than being on high alert for joyful and pleasant experiences. This may mean that we predict threat and focus on it more than we do on joy – hence why we often can't shake off the feeling we did something 'wrong', or the criticism we were given, while compliments and positive interactions can slip through our fingers like water. To manage this negative skew, write down three good things that happen to you each day (they can be very small moments, such as someone smiled at me in the street today), along with any compliments you receive. This will slowly train your brain to focus on the rewarding moments.
- **We need to acknowledge our emotions and thoughts and also recognise that they may on occasion be wrong.** Predictions are best guesses. Sometimes right, sometimes not. Your brain predicts with a heavily negative

skew and draws from past experiences, meaning it can get it wrong. Past experiences affect the predictions we make. But they may not be correct. This means that we must always attend to our emotional pain, soothing ourselves and our feelings, AND we must always ensure we check in on the reality of the present moment so our brain doesn't derail us with all of its worries about the future and the past.

This last point is why therapists are so obsessed with your childhood experiences. They know that your early years create the lenses through which you see the world and from which all your ongoing predictions will be made.

It is also why mindfulness is so important and effective, as this gives you the chance to slow your processes down, allowing you to observe what you are experiencing without immediately responding, giving you time to ground yourself in the present moment, check what's really happening and decide how to proceed.

Take a moment and check in with yourself. How much of this is new information to you? What is the response you have in your body when you read this? Or in your thoughts?

If you've grown up believing that emotions are dangerous, as they may overwhelm you, burden or hurt others, or get you into serious trouble, reading this may be very odd. You may strongly disagree with it. That's okay. These are new facts for you, and you won't start believing them overnight. Read them over and over and they will start to sink in.

Before you turn the page, repeat after me: 'I'm learning that all emotions are normal. Emotions are neither good nor bad. They are all important.'

7. The Fight-Flight-Freeze-Fawn Response

Stress, anxiety, panic (what people often describe as scary feelings) and horrendously debilitating thoughts: these are the main reasons people come to see me for therapy.

In the last chapter we learned that any time we detect a potential threat in our environment (or if any of our physical sensations scare us) we will feel anxiety, fear or anger. These feelings link to what psychologists call the 'fight-flight-freeze-fawn response'. This chapter will talk you through this response in more detail.

So . . . let's get right into it.

Scary feelings

Without anxiety our ancestors would not have survived. That constant worry about what might happen was good for our species, making them hypervigilant for anything that might wipe our species off the planet.

Anxiety sucks (understatement) but without it you, me, our species, we likely wouldn't have survived.

We inherited anxiety and hypervigilance for threat from our ancestors. But we need it now, as I showed you in the previous chapter, in case there really is a burglar in our house, or another real-life danger we need to pay attention to.

Mild stress (the experience that arises when we feel under pressure in some way) and anxiety is uncomfortable but also incredibly useful. The mobilising energy it brings can make us perform better, faster and quicker. There is an increased sense of 'I can' and 'I must'. There is a magic window where you have just the right amount of concern to snap you into action.

For the procrastinators and the 'last-minuters' out there (yes, I made up that label, and yes, I am one), you likely know this experience very well. It may even be your friend. How many times have you said, 'It'll be different this time. I'm going to get my work done ahead of schedule so the end isn't such a hideous rush', and then, the next time a deadline comes around, the Word document remains empty, the PowerPoint unmade, as the days tick by. Then, suddenly, you hit the sweet spot of anxiety, the exact amount you need to put an end to the procrastination, laser focus ensues and, like always, you click 'Send' with moments to go.

Yet if that magically productive threshold passes without you acting on it, it becomes less than pleasant. Tension rises in your muscles, you start to sweat, your hands shake, your thoughts turn to dread and feelings of panic can ensue.

For anyone who has experienced this, you might have noticed that when this happens, the 'I can' and 'I must' slips away as you plunge head first into 'I'll never get it done' or 'this is going very wrong, oh my God, oh my God, why is my chest getting tight now too?' The anxiety stops being useful, and you aren't able to function.

Suddenly the ability to think clearly has gone, replaced with overwhelming fear. Heat builds in your body, sweat beading on your forehead, your breathing starts to get harder (this is the moment in the movies where the person starts to anxiously loosen their tie, fumbling for their top button). Even writing what seemed like a simple sentence a moment ago, or making a simple verbal point, may seem borderline impossible now, as every feeling and thought signals impending doom. You want to run from your desk and give up.

For the person with a deadline, even thinking about the empty Word document or blank PowerPoint can seem overwhelming. But this doesn't happen only in work. These experiences can happen anywhere.

For the person who experiences overwhelming anxiety when they're out and about, for instance, while in a cafe or on the tube with a friend, the nervous energy that maybe had them chatting away one minute ago may suddenly escalate, the sudden change in feeling causing them to make hurried apologies – 'Something unexpectedly came up, got to go, sorry' – as they find themselves running towards the door, gasping for breath, even sobbing as they make it into the open air.

If panic hits a crescendo it can make you feel like you're having a heart attack, are going to die, or are losing your mind.

I have experienced each of these situations and many more like them. For people who haven't gone through this, it can be hard to understand quite how frightening and all-consuming anxiety and panic can be. It's hard to imagine that anxiety can make people feel like they are white-knuckling it through moments of life that other people take in their stride.

Each symptom we experience during anxiety and panic (and in fact during stress, anger, jealousy or any other feeling linked to a perceived threat) is a totally understandable aspect explained by the 'fight–flight' part of the fight–flight–freeze–fawn response.

For anyone who is going through anxiety right now: you are not dying, suffocating, having a heart attack or losing your mind.

I will show you what is happening instead.

Fight or flight?

Let's imagine what your body would need if it was going to fight or run hard.

For example, let's imagine what would happen if you stumbled into that tiger our ancestors were continuously trying to avoid.

Your body would become like a coiled spring, the tension increasing dramatically so you quickly become ready to respond like a bullet from a gun, sprinting to safety or fighting your way out. To make this possible, your heart beats faster, and your breathing gets quicker, gathering the oxygen and energy your body will need. Blood courses through your veins, sending this energy to your arms and legs in case you need to fight or run. Your muscles tense in preparation. Your vision changes. You lose peripheral vision so you can focus on the danger right in front of you.

Any area of your body not needed in the upcoming fight is shut down so that all energy is diverted to the necessary muscles. Blood is directed away from your skin towards major organs needed in the fight, and also to minimise blood loss should you be cut or harmed in any way. You are ready for one single purpose: to fight or run for your life.

When staring into the eyes of a tiger, this is very useful. In fact, in any life-or-death situation, this is useful.

When you step out into the road without looking and suddenly hear a car, your brain takes over and you respond by jumping out of the way without any conscious thought. When you see someone trapped under a car, your brain may also take over, giving you superhuman strength to save the day – such as happened to 22-year-old Lauren Kornacki, who lifted a BMW 525i off her trapped father in 2012, or Tom Boyle, who did the same with a Chevy Camaro (a huge American car) in 2005.

Once you fight, or run, and survive, this system shuts off and you go back to having control over your actions.

However, as I have shown you throughout the previous chapter, our brain can't tell the difference between real life-or-death situations and the things we *perceive* to be threats, meaning this response can occur at times when running or fighting are not necessary, e.g. when you have a work deadline, public speaking event, social occasion with strangers, or receive a rude comment.

If you never actually run or have a fight, there is no burst of activity to signal to your brain that the danger is over and you've survived, meaning the system doesn't switch off.

Instead, you have increasing muscle tension, shakiness and, to make things worse, the fight-or-flight response has left you feeling like you can't breathe – because your chest muscles are tense and at the same time are trying to put extra oxygen into your body. You are starting to sweat too – this happens because an efficient machine is a cool machine, so your body cools itself as another protective mechanism.

Your mind is churning out all the terrible possible future outcomes and bringing up memories of similar terrible times that resemble this one. This is meant to facilitate problem solving, as your brain looks for clues to the solution to your current predicament.

And what's more, your skin is cold and clammy (as the blood has been directed elsewhere) and your stomach feels weird – 'butterflies in your stomach' occurs because your stomach isn't needed when you fight or run, so the blood and oxygen leave that area to be used elsewhere, causing this weird feeling. Also, you often suddenly need the toilet.

Fun fact: your external anal sphincter isn't needed either when you fight or run, so it relaxes. Great – just what you needed!

It's hard to rationalise your way out of these feelings because, when in fight–flight mode, your frontal lobes – the front part of the brain, which are responsible for control and being in the moment – are not fully engaged. Your automatic pilot has control. Hence why it's so hard to 'snap out of it', as people often suggest to others who are angry, tense or anxious.

As not everyone is aware of these physical processes, we may interpret the bodily symptoms of the fight–flight response as signs of a heart attack or other illness, and the racing and terrifying thoughts that come with it as a sign of 'madness'. Our take-home message being: this feeling is unsurvivable. A threat to our very existence. The end is near. The belief that you are in danger then, you guessed it, results in a vicious circle, which increases the fight–or–flight response.

These experiences can be so terrifying that we understandably start to fear when another like it may occur. We may become fixated on trying to predict our next attack of panic, or checking to see if we are relaxed/not relaxed in any given moment. We may start checking our pulse, our blood pressure, and predicting that any change in our internal state signals 'it's happening'.

Unfortunately, checking and being hypervigilant in this way does not prevent anxiety; in fact, it makes it more likely. I described one reason for this in the last chapter, where I told you that when we fear certain emotions we may 'catastrophically misinterpret' normal experiences and predict anxiety is happening, *causing* it to happen. And the other reason is described in the next chapter, where we will talk about the coping strategies that often make things worse.

No judgement, if you have found yourself checking or being hypervigilant, by the way. Trying to anticipate danger and prevent it is exactly what our ancestors did to stay alive! It's what most people do when something scary happens. It's just another one of those tricky both/and things – there are BOTH times when checking and being hypervigilant for threat benefits us AND others where it hinders. Again, we will look at this in more detail in the next chapter.

Living with anxiety and panic is a bit like living with a faulty alarm system, one that goes off even when no danger is present.

One of the first parts of dealing with the fight-or-flight response is understanding what is happening and that your physiology is working correctly – learning that you are normal and that each of your experiences can be made sense of.

The next step is learning how to switch off the response when it arises. Part Three of this book, How To Move Forward, covers all the steps you need to start doing this. For people needing help with this *right now*: Grounding Exercises (Chapter 11), Breathing Exercises (Chapter 12) and Mindfulness (Chapter 13) will be your new best friends. But for now, practise these quick tips:

Anxiety and panic can you make you feel like you are having a heart attack or losing your mind. You aren't. You are physically safe, and once the feelings of anxiety and panic pass, you will know that too.

Technique 1: MOVE!

The fight–flight response is meant to be followed by a burst of activity. That is what would usually signal to the brain that the action has been completed, you've survived, and it can switch it off now. So, if you notice the tension rising, remember this: do something that gets your heart rate going and edges you towards sweating for 5 minutes. I have locked myself in many bathrooms to do star jumps to get my anxiety down. It works. I recommend it.

Technique 2: Know that you are safe

When anxiety (stress, anger, jealousy or any other threat-related emotion) causes your stomach to feel weird or your chest to feel tight, imagine telling yourself, 'I am medically safe. This is my body preparing to run or fight. That is all.'

Technique 3: Follow the 'What if . . . ?' thoughts all the way to the end

A typical thought linked to stress and anxiety is: *What if . . . ?*

What if I make a mess? What if I get laughed at? What if I get hurt? What if I look like a failure in front of everyone in the room or on the internet? What if I have a heart attack? What if I lose my mind?

When this happens, a surge of fear runs through our body and we fall into the hole that just metaphorically opened up in front of us, thinking: *Everyone will judge me, I can't cope, I'm going to die* or *My life will be over.* We don't pause and ask ourselves, *No, but seriously, what would I do if that happened?*

The next time your brain throws up a *What if . . .?*, don't just follow it down the rabbit hole. Pause, recognise it is an anxiety thought, and ask yourself, *Okay, what would I do if that was true? And then?*

An example (all parts of this example are one person):

What if I fail and everyone judges me (predicting horrendous outcome)?

Okay, what would I do if that were true?
I would feel horrendous and want to give up. It would confirm I was right to be afraid.

Okay, what would I do then?
Cry for a week, or maybe longer.

Then?
Probably get up and figure out what to do next? Ask someone for support? Maybe try again?

So it would be very scary?
Yes.

But you would survive it?
Yes.

Phew! Great.

Fight–flight tends to make us feel mobilised, adrenaline-fuelled, determined to find a way to safety through action. However, sometimes when we predict and/or experience something threatening, we slip into the freeze response.

Freeze

When we slip into *freeze*, we feel the opposite of flight-or-flight. This is where the 'I can' feeling often disappears, with 'I can't' taking its place. It's also where, in the more extreme cases, our body and mind feel slowed, to the point of (temporary) physical paralysis and psychological numbness. And there is a damn good reason for it.

When we face a life-or-death threat, we do not choose whether we will slip into freeze response or one of the other responses. Our brain dictates this. You could be trained in self-defence, a modern-day Bruce Lee, and still end up frozen to the spot if danger crosses your path.

The freeze response occurs (or is meant to) when your brain has assessed that the threat in front of you is inescapable, e.g. it's too close, too threatening, too dangerous, or you are trapped with an assailant or the tiger we've talked about so many times. If you were trapped with the tiger, the freeze response would help you in the following ways.

Your breathing would slow, or you may notice you are holding your breath. Your body temperature would drop. All movement stops. Have you ever seen an animal 'play dead' in order to put off a potential predator? Or hide still in fear? Freezing in this way can keep you alive for this very reason.

You would start to feel numb, everything might suddenly feel unreal; it may even feel like you're watching a film of someone trapped by a tiger. If playing dead doesn't stop the threat, you need a back-up plan, so your pain threshold increases and you start to dissociate (feel totally disconnected from the present moment), anaesthetising you to whatever might happen next. This is meant to happen only in real life-threatening situations. However, again, it can happen outside of those times – particularly if freeze mode has helped you to survive in the past.

I worked with a client who would 'go blank' any time we talked about their past, tried to discuss their emotions or anything they found stressful in their current life (such as the intense conflict they had with their partner, which they couldn't manage, as they 'went blank' every time this happened). They would be chatting away happily then, the moment any of these topics arose, they shut down. Their eyes glazed over and the speaking stopped. Yes or no answers only.

As a child, my client had witnessed domestic violence at home. He survived this period by freezing still to hide from, or not gain attention from, his dangerous caregiver, or freezing psychologically to survive any kind of harm he experienced. Now, as an adult, thinking about or facing anything that felt stressful sent him back into the freeze response.

If you survived by using the freeze response early in your life, you may notice this response now happens any time stress arises. Also, anyone who has experienced anxiety or panic attacks for a while may notice that the freeze response starts to creep in, adding a new dimension to their experience.

Outside of a life-threatening situation, the freeze response may not physically paralyse you. It may instead feel like you are shutting down and your mind has gone blank. You may find it hard to speak or make sense of the words of others. You may start to feel unreal, as if the world is foggy or lifeless (therapists call this derealisation). You may feel numb, hope-less, helpless, depressed or even ashamed. This experience can last moments and never return, or it can come and go.

The symptoms associated with the freeze response were the parts of anxiety that I hated the most. So, if you've been through this, I feel for you. It's scary, but know that you are safe and you can use all the tips and tricks in this book to help you.

The fawn response

Most people have heard of the fight–flight–freeze response, yet few people have heard of the fawn response. Fawning means displaying flattery or affection in order to please.

Most of us want to please others and make them happy; this is normal. When the fawn part of the threat response is activated it means more than that, however. It means pleasing, appeasing and possibly flattering another person so that they will not harm you.

I'm sure you'll have seen this in films. A character's life is threatened, and at first they fight back. When this doesn't work, they try to escape. When this doesn't work, they start pleading with or fawning over the assailant: 'Please, I'll do whatever it takes, whatever you say!' Or, more subtly, they may try to befriend and compliment the person who is threatening them.

This also helps explain something we talked about in Chapter 1.

Remember I told you that children may learn to please people as a way to adapt to stay safe and close to their caregivers during childhood? Well, the fawn response is one of the reasons behind this.

If there are high levels of stress or danger at home, a child may learn that fighting against their caregivers' behaviour, or running and hiding from it, doesn't work to keep them safe or out of trouble, but find that fawning (or freezing) does. If the fawn response works for the child, they may keep using this strategy to stay safe throughout life, even if the danger associated with home life is no longer present.

Each of these examples links to high levels of danger, but the fawn response can arise at any time. So, if you've noticed you have the overwhelming urge to 'please' when anxiety arises, now you know why. It is one of our primary defences and is totally normal.

You are now well versed in the fight–flight–freeze–fawn response.

If you're going through any of the experiences described so far, I know it feels unpleasant, but know that it is a survival response, and that the grounding exercises in Part Three will help get you back to the here and now. However, if you suddenly experience new symptoms, please speak with your doctor to rule out anything else that may be happening, and/ or if they go on for a long period of time, please speak to a therapist to give you peace of mind and the right support to get you feeling calm and centred again.

Thoughts

Even though I haven't explicitly taught you what thoughts are yet, I have been implicitly teaching you across the last chapter and a half.

Thoughts are the words and stories your brain puts together to make sense of the predictions your brain makes, the emotions you feel and the experiences you live through. They are the words and images your brain assembles in response to everything you see and come across in your life.

These can be thoughts about the past, present, who you like, who you love, what makes you

Our thoughts are stories, not truths.

feel good, what makes you feel bad, what you will have for dinner and, more often than not, what will go wrong in the future. In the last chapter they were the *Aha, it's a burglar/Oh my God, they hate me now* moments. In this chapter they were the *Oh my God, I'm going crazy/I can/I can't* moments.

Sometimes we choose our thoughts. For example, when you intentionally think, *What will I have for lunch? What do I like about Amy? How do I fix this bike tyre?* Sometimes, we don't choose them at all. They pop up in line with our predictions. This is why we learned 'How to check whether you are over-predicting threat' in Chapter 6, and why I've given you a box below with some of the most common thinking errors that we all engage in but need to keep an eye on.

Common thinking styles that make us miserable

Black and white thinking: we think of everything in absolutes – *If everything isn't perfect, then everything is terrible* – when the reality is, most things are grey (somewhere in between).

Filtering: we ignore all of the positive aspects of situations and focus solely on the negative.

Jumping to conclusions: we take a small amount of information and assume we know what's going to happen – *It's going to go badly* – even though the world is unpredictable.

Mind-reading: we assume we know what someone else is thinking – *They looked at me funny, they hate me* – when we can't know this to be true unless someone tells us. People may look at you funny for many reasons. They may be having a bad day, or might be squinting because they don't have their glasses on!

Emotional reasoning: we assume because we feel something it must be true: *I feel stupid so I must be stupid.* Nope!

Overgeneralisation: we take one event and apply it to everything – *This always happens to me. No one ever likes me.*

Personalisation: when we make everything personal – *Everything is my fault* – even in situations where events are out of our control. We can do this to other people too – *It's all their fault.*

Catastrophisation: we escalate a worry to the worst possible outcome – *The world is going to end!*

Discounting the positive: when something goes well, we minimise our success – *I did well by chance, it was a fluke.*

Do any of these resonate? Spend the next 24 hours paying attention to your thoughts. Notice the negative thoughts and come back to this list. Ask yourself which thinking style you might be engaging in. Then decide to look for the evidence you might be missing. Look for a more balanced thought. For instance, instead of a black and white thought, you could instead say to yourself, *This experience isn't perfect, there were challenges and learning points, and, overall, I did the best I could.* Instead of over-generalisation, you could say, *This time didn't go well but this doesn't mean every time I do this activity it'll be this way.*

Sometimes our thoughts are fleeting. Other times we get totally stuck in them, ruminating about what will happen. As you know, thoughts can be deeply upsetting. And sometimes, our thoughts can be utterly, life-changingly terrifying.

Have you ever had a thought that you might do something horrible? A thought that *says* you might want to do something very dangerous? To yourself? Or to someone else? Have you ever had a thought that made you question whether you were a good or safe person to be around?

Learning that our thoughts are not facts does not take away the validity of our experiences. Instead it shows us that the thoughts that plague us, undermine us and derail us need to be examined, challenged and reworded in order for them to reflect the actuality of the world.

I have. Many people have.

Many people standing

234

on train platforms have had out-of-the-blue thoughts (or flashes of images, as thoughts can come in picture as well as word format) such as, *What if I jump? What if I'm pushed? What if I push someone onto the tracks?!*

Many people holding knives have had out-of-the-blue thoughts (or flashes of images) such as, *What if I stabbed myself with this knife? What if I stabbed someone else?*

Many people holding babies have had out-of-the-blue thoughts (or flashes of images) such as, *What if I drop this baby? What if I throw it?*

And it's not because these are bad people, or dangerous in some way, or because they want to do any of these things – in fact, it's the opposite.

As you know, the human brain continuously scans the environment predicting what will happen next, coming up with a million and one possible outcomes every single day. While much of this happens below the level of our awareness, on occasion the brain hits on a prediction that causes a significant emotional response and so ... your brain shoves it into your awareness.

Think of the person holding the baby. Let's imagine it's a new parent or caregiver. Most new caregivers feel they must protect their baby at all costs. It therefore isn't too big a leap to see that when their brain is predicting and simulating all the stuff that could get in the way of that, one of the many things it comes across is, *What if I harmed it?*

Think of the person holding the knife. If they are conscientious about safety (which most people are) and their brain scans the environment looking for danger, a knife could feel pretty dangerous. Knives can cut, knives can stab ... *What if I ... ?*

Think of the person on the train platform too. There are so many obvious dangers around trains that our brain could pick up on, so it isn't at all surprising that our brain sometimes generates: *What if I jump/push/am pushed?*

If we are already feeling a little anxious or vulnerable, our brain is *even more* likely to find something terrifying for us to muse over, as its threat detectors are working even more keenly to keep you safe during those times.

Newsflash: you are not your thoughts. You can have any thought under the sun. Seriously. Any thought on earth. And even if that thought involves the most hideous criminal act, it means nothing at all about you. The thing that makes us who we are as people is how we act – not the thoughts that pop up now and again, terrifying the life out of us.

It can be helpful to think of our intrusive thoughts like those pesky boxes that pop up on internet browsers, warning something has gone wrong – *security alert!* Sometimes they're genuinely useful, warning us to check our security settings. Other times they're spam and can be ignored.

Brain spam

Every person on the planet has odd thoughts from time to time. Some people don't even notice them; they arise, and are shrugged off. Some find them annoying. Some find them comical.

When I was a newly qualified psychologist, my career ahead of me, I spotted one of my clients in a public place. Suddenly the thought popped into my head, *What if I shouted their secrets out loud, to all of these people?*

Even therapists can have anxiety, panic attacks and scary thoughts!

I know that thoughts are just thoughts, so, when this happened, I didn't panic. I chuckled at my new worry and the image of me bellowing confidential secrets at the top of my lungs to the rush-hour human traffic of Oxford Circus, and then I moved on. If I didn't know the truth about thoughts I might have worried about it, predicting I was about to do something potentially career-destroying, panic building in my body.

The difference between these two possible responses is extremely important. If a thought pops up that makes you feel afraid, but you realise it's just that, a thought – a random piece of information that was shown to you because your brain hit upon something scary – then you will notice it and let it go . . . and probably forget about it two minutes later.

Unfortunately, that isn't usually what happens, especially for the *really* terrifying thoughts – the violent ones, the sexual ones, the sexually violent ones. And this is where people get into difficulty.

From a single thought to a real problem
Few people know that thoughts are fallible or often based on predictions. Instead they believe they *choose* each of their thoughts. Therefore, when an alarming thought or image intrudes into their day, they panic.

Let's go back to the example of the new caregiver with the baby. Let's imagine they've never had a scary thought before (or at least never realised they've had one). Can you imagine how they might feel when that thought of harming the baby they love and cherish enters their mind? I have treated many people who have been through this exact experience, so I can tell you. It usually goes a little bit like this:

The thought or image flashes up. Within seconds, cold-sweat-inducing panic ensues (the fight-flight-freeze-fawn response ramps up) as they feel overwhelming responsibility for the thought. *Did I just think that? What?! Oh my! If I thought that, it must mean I want to do it.* Guilt, utter terror and shame then follows. It's not just that they believe their thoughts could quickly lead to action, or that they must want to do it – there's another issue at play here. Many people believe that thinking something 'bad' is as morally reprehensible as doing the thing, which, just to be clear, it's not.

The next step that can shift this single scary thought into an actual problem is: they then make an appraisal about themselves, such as 'Something is wrong with me' or 'I'm dangerous'. This conclusion isn't surprising, considering the only reference point many people have of situations like this are 'the mad' and 'the bad' shown in the news, on TV and in films.

There are two more actions that many people take that ensure this thinking not only sticks around but that it grows in intensity, and spreads to other areas.

1) They decide to never tell anyone, not a soul on earth. Ever. For fear the person they tell will see the dark truth about them and possibly have them imprisoned. In therapy people often tell me they are genuinely afraid that if they tell me their intrusive thoughts, I will immediately call the police.

2) They push the thought away (therapists call this 'thought suppression'). If you've been through an experience like this, you'll know that every time you push an intrusive or even upsetting thought away it just comes right back, a fresh wave of panic and fear arising every time. This makes the new caregiver even more convinced there must be something wrong with them: *If I didn't want to do it, why would it keep coming back?*

Want to know one reason why it keeps coming back? Have you ever tried NOT to think about something? Let's try it now. Whatever you do, do not think about your favourite dog . . .

Have you brought that dog to mind?

DO NOT THINK ABOUT YOUR FAVOURITE DOG.

Don't.

No dogs here, please.

How did that go?

I imagine it was pretty impossible to avoid thinking about dogs.

For me that experience was lovely. I love dogs. But for most of us, the thoughts we are trying not to think about are the most troubling. These are called *intrusive thoughts*.

Avoiding thoughts makes us think those thoughts more. Metaphorically it's as though you tag that thought as dangerous, so your brain says, *Eek, look at this! Danger! Look! Solve this situation now!* For anyone reading this who has had intrusive thoughts or is experiencing them right now, this is why it feels like the thoughts get worse. It is NOT because you really want to do whatever your thoughts have suggested.

There is no link between the number of times a scary thought arises and your intention to act on that thought.

It's also not because you are secretly dangerous. It is because suppressing thoughts makes them bounce back.

Also, think about it: what was your response when you had the intrusive thought the first time? Most likely it was anything ranging from worry to all-out fear – the opposite of desire and motivation to do the act!

I am going to reiterate this, as I work with so many people who live with intrusive thoughts, who have lived with them for many years, never telling a soul, who feel scared stiff and utterly alone. If you have troubling thoughts, they do not mean anything about you as a person. They do not signify anything about how good you are, or how safe you are to be around, or anything else, in fact. You have not changed as a person. You are not suddenly bad or dangerous. The thoughts were random. But they made you feel (more than) worried, and (deeply) responsible for the thought, so they stuck around.

If you have had thoughts like this and have been carrying the burden of fear and shame, you have not changed as a person; you are not bad or dangerous.

Start separating from your thoughts

Create distance from your thoughts, whether they are scary or not. These are the tips recommended in Acceptance and Commitment Therapy and written about in *The Happiness Trap* by Russ Harris.

1. Repeat the thought and add, 'I notice I am having the thought that . . .' to the beginning.
2. Sing that thought to the tune of a song that makes you laugh. See how this changes how attached you feel to the thought.
3. Repeat the thought in a silly voice.

In fact, give it a go right now. What thought just crossed your mind? Was it . . . *What? That's so silly*. If so, repeat after me: 'I notice I'm having the thought that that's so silly! But now, sing it to the tune of 'Jingle Bells'. The more you practise this, the better. Set an alarm on your phone to practise this multiple times a day. Over time this will seriously help. This exercise is not to make light of whatever you're feeling or thinking. It's to enable you to distance yourself from the thought.

For people who are in the thick of intrusive thoughts:

1. **Do not avoid the thoughts.** Use the tips above when they arise. Chapter 8 will describe the effects of avoidance in more detail and the Appendix will help you make a plan to overcome it.

2. **Repeat this mantra:** 'Hi there, thought, I see you. I am learning that you are just a thought. I know it feels tempting to believe you mean something about me, but you don't. I am good. I am safe. I am exactly the way I have always been.'

3. **Learn to ground yourself, trigger the relaxation response and practise mindfulness** – in Part Three.

4. **If it gets too much, seek support.** Therapists work with this all the time and with great success.

When intrusive thoughts become Obsessive Compulsive Disorder (OCD)

When people have intrusive thoughts that go from being an annoyance to something they're fixated upon and feel overwhelmed by, therapists call this Obsessive Compulsive Disorder (OCD).

Don't let the thought 'It feels silly' get in the way of you trying out a coping skill that may truly work for you.

I haven't talked about many diagnoses in this book, but this deserves a special mention as when people think about OCD they usually think of someone who compulsively washes their hands, checks the door is locked, or the lights are off, or tidies things obsessively. While rituals like cleaning, checking and making everything 'just so' can be part of OCD, there are many other forms it can take.

In the case of intrusive thoughts and OCD, the thought is the 'obsession' and the compulsions are any action that involves:

- Pushing away the thought.
- Neutralising it by repeating a special word or prayer, for example.
- Distracting yourself any time it arises.
- Avoiding anything that could trigger the thought. For example, people may start to avoid holding their baby if they fear they could harm them. They may lock their knife drawer, or only keep blunt knives in the house. They may avoid any train platform where the 'pusher' or the 'jumper' thoughts arise.

People sometimes call this kind of OCD 'pure O', as you cannot see the compulsions with the naked eye. However, they are compulsions: they're just in the mind.

The treatment for this is generally Cognitive Behavioural Therapy (see Chapter 18 for more information). It involves managing the anxiety, using the grounding techniques and breathing techniques you can find in Chapters 11 and 12, and slowly introducing you to your scary thoughts in ways that allow you to feel increasingly safe over time, slowly dropping the compulsions. You will reach a point where you can purposefully or accidentally have the scariest thought in the world and recognise 'It's okay!', and watch the thought pass on by.

Common themes in thoughts linked to this kind of OCD are:

- Harming yourself or others.
- Not being able to trust your sexuality.
- Sexual thoughts towards others – babies, children and adults. This is the one people tend to feel the most scared to talk about.

If you experience this, and it's getting in the way of your life, please seek help from someone with expertise in this. It's amazing what a relief it will be when you're finally able to tell someone what you've been thinking and feeling and they say, 'You're normal, you're safe and this is what we are going to do about it.' In fact, OCD is well understood and responds very well to treatment.

The new rules

- **All emotional experiences can be understood.** They can be scary and, when they feel out of control, terrifying. But anxiety doesn't mean you are crazy or 'going to die'. Every feeling you have associated with anxiety, anger, jealousy, fear and anything else that makes you feel threatened makes total sense.
- **The fight-flight-freeze-fawn response will be activated any time your brain believes it has found a threat in your environment.** The strength of the response you feel will depend on what kind of threat

has been predicted, how imminent the threat appears to be, whether it seems to be surmountable, and how you have successfully responded to threatening events like this in the past. If the threat appears imminent your brain will react without giving you a moment to even notice something has happened, like when your hand flinches from a hot surface – but if it is far away, or there are things in the environment that keep you feeling grounded and safe, the process will be slower. You will be in a state of high alert or anxiety until the threat disappears, the fight–flight response has completed, or until you trigger the relaxation response or breathe through it. The problem is, the perceived threat may not be a physical threat; it may be something we worry about happening, or even the feelings of anxiety themselves.

- **Follow the fight–flight response with exercise.** This is a high priority for managing stress. It's not just that the fight-or-flight response is meant to be followed by a burst of activity. It's that exercise is a simple and effective way to calm the nervous system, burning away the nervous energy created in the body, metabolising (breaking down) excess stress hormones. Lower levels of stress hormones mean a calmer body and mind.

- **Your thoughts are still valid and real but ...** we need to find a way to separate from them so they have less control over our lives, particularly as they are sometimes absolutely terrifying.

- **Scary thoughts do not mean you are a scary or bad person.** I need to reiterate this. I would not be doing this job if I were not 100 per cent sure that scary thoughts do not mean bad people. I sometimes sit for hours seeing client after client who experiences these things, singing violent thoughts such as, *What if I stabbed my sister with a kitchen knife?* or *I want to stab my sister with a kitchen knife* to the tune of Rihanna's, 'Umbrella' or, the Bee Gees' 'Staying Alive', then switching to saying the thought in the voice of any celebrity that my client and I can get remotely close to. Sometimes, I'm actually standing in their kitchen while they have a sharp knife in their hand, doing the very same thing. It sounds like a weird thing to do, but the more we do it, the more exposure the person has to the thought and the fear, the more they can see the thought is merely a string of words. And that the anxiety it caused will rise and finally fall, when the fear is faced.

- **If you have worried about this for a long time and want to know more,** read the book *Pure* by Rose Cartwright or watch the Channel 4 adaptation of the book. For people who have gone through these kinds of experiences, reading about it and finding out why it's happening can change your life. As can seeing someone else who has been through it and is surviving and thriving. *Pure* gives a first-hand experience of intrusive thoughts, written by someone who lived with OCD. The first line of the trailer is: 'There's something wrong with me. It's like the *Sixth Sense*, but I don't see dead people, I see naked ones', which is brilliantly accompanied by the image of a bus driver pulling up alongside the narrator, and, when the doors of the bus open, he's naked. As this is what intrusive thoughts and images can do.

- **Share your thoughts with someone you trust.** If you're unsure how they will react, you could give them this chapter first and talk about it hypothetically – 'Isn't this interesting? Did you know this? Wow, it makes a lot of sense to me, what do you think?' If that goes well, share your thoughts and fears with them, or with a therapist.

- **If someone tells you that they have intrusive thoughts or images, please support them.** Please listen and tell them you know they have not changed. Then maybe give them this chapter, show them the grounding techniques and breathing exercises, and, if they are ready to, gently suggest singing some of the thoughts out loud, repeating them over and over, or support them to find a therapist who can do this with them.

- **Remember, the way you act tells you who you are,** and most people who have scary thoughts know they would rather hurt themselves than someone else, which tells us that even if you fear you are bad, you are not.

- **You are a human.** This means we have a ton of emotional experiences and all of them are okay. You do not have to pretend to be happy all the time.

- **At the same time, if you are not feeling okay for a long period, or are feeling frightened at all, please seek help.** Know that when I say this, this is not code for 'I think you're a bit mad' and 'You need help'. It's because I know that therapists are trained to work with these exact issues. They can help get you back on your feet and to feel safe much faster than if you shoulder this burden alone. And because I know how bad this can feel. I've been there, and therefore, even though I don't know you, I know that you deserve somewhere you can talk and be truly listened to.

A Note to You

Hello!

How's the reading going?

Do you have a sense now that being human means experiencing a mixture of emotions and having thoughts that sometimes get us worried in advance of there being something to worry about?

Can you see that the world shapes us and we shape the world in return because we see it and interpret it through our own lens?

We are finally onto the stuff we *do* to cope.

Everything you did from the moment you came into the world was a form of coping. Crying out as a baby, coping with the new and daunting experiences in life, calling someone to make it a little easier. Adapting yourself to stay close to the people you loved, so that they could keep you safe and help you stay alive. Shaping yourself in line with the standards and ideas shown to us in the media, about what is 'good enough' so you can feel like you belong.

People come to therapy when their coping skills no longer

work. When they can no longer keep distress or another emotion at bay. When they can see through their defence to the thing they have tried to protect themselves against for so long. So, the thing that keeps most people stuck is not that they don't have any coping skills. It's that their coping skills no longer serve them and they are ready for an upgrade.

I want to help you identify this and show you the way forward.

Dr Soph xx

8. Coping Strategies
That Make Things Worse

Coping strategies are any behaviour or action we engage in to regulate our emotional state. They are every action we take in our life to feel grounded, more 'normal', and to be safe, especially in periods of stress.

Think about some of the things you do in the day to keep yourself feeling centred:

- The pause you take to get a coffee between pieces of work – a break for your brain and your body, and possibly some relief from monotony.
- The times you scroll Instagram or check text messages as an attempt to alleviate loneliness or boredom.
- When you put on your favourite playlist, dancing around your room, shaking off the stresses and strains of the day. Or do yoga, moving your body in time with your breath, moving and meditating.
- Or ... any time you use movies, booze or drugs to numb or avoid your anxieties. These are all common forms of coping, and everyone has their own.

Unlike most magazine and online articles written about coping skills, I will not tell you there's a clear, cut-and-dried distinction between unhealthy vs. healthy coping mechanisms. I don't think it works like that. There is no such thing as perfect coping.

Sometimes coping is that moment you burst into tears, slide onto the floor, sobbing into your hands, tears soaking your shirt. Sometimes it's pulling the duvet over your head, switching off the lights or deciding to end your day at lunchtime so you can zone out until the following morning. Other times it's a breathing exercise and a structured meditation regime. This last coping mechanism is 'officially' approved but the others are fine – I do them too – so long as they're not happening every day.

In my experience, most people's coping strategies that end up failing them fall into two categories:

1) **Preventing** distress from arising in the first place. For example, someone may try to take control of every situation they face, or by avoiding places or people that have made them feel distressed in the past, or by lying about something they did or didn't do, or by being defensive – 'I'm not the problem, you're the problem.'

2) **Avoiding** distress once it has arisen. For example, someone may try to numb themselves with booze or drugs, distract themselves with TV or another engaging activity, or flat-out deny the pain they feel inside.

The problem is that when our coping mechanisms rely solely on preventing or avoiding our emotions and the

situations that cause them, they usually come back and bite us on the bum.

Here are some of the common methods of preventing or avoiding distress that I see in my clinic.

Control

Feeling we have control over our lives is imperative for our wellbeing. Feeling as if we are passengers in our own lives, not knowing what'll affect us next, can be overwhelming.

When we feel confident we can take action that will directly impact and improve our future – e.g. *If I work hard I can get the outcome I hope for. If things get tough I can persevere, and I will get there* – we not only feel empowered and in the driving seat of our lives, research shows we will bounce back from shocking events much more quickly than people who do not have a sense of control over their lives.

I'm sure you can think of moments where taking control of a situation that felt chaotic and distressing helped immensely. Something as simple as writing a to-do list can provide immediate benefits during overwhelming and uncertain times. Something as hard as choosing to leave the person you've been dating, who has been coming in and out of your life but not committing to you or answering your requests to talk, saying, 'I'm not sure' for far too long, giving you no sign they'll change, can be the exact thing you need to regain a sense of control over this area of your life, feel empowered and move forward – bittersweet relief.

This whole book is an attempt to give you a little more control over your life, giving you the tips and tricks you need to understand yourself and what you need to make the most of who you are and who you want to be. Control is a good thing ... to a point.

When people take control of every minute of their day, their schedule, their environment and their life, as a way to feel safe in this world, or simply as a way to feel calm – which many people have been taught to do – problems arise the moment something unpredictable happens. And, I am sorry to say, the unpredictable will happen. The world is unpredictable. People are unpredictable. We simply cannot be in control of every aspect of our lives.

2020 was a clear example of how unpredictable the world can be. One moment we were all getting on with our lives, able to leave the house, grab a coffee, go to work, go to concerts, dine in busy restaurants, get trains, fly, hug, snog (great word, even better pastime), and live what we knew to be our lives. Then COVID-19 arrived.

People started dying around the globe, and panic and uncertainty was everywhere. Life as we knew it changed in ways we could not have imagined. People weren't allowed to visit ill relatives or say goodbye to those who were dying, let alone leave the house, go to work or do any of their usual day-to-day activities.

2020 destabilised most people's lives – it took away our sense of certainty and control.

Did you feel exhausted during 2020? Most of us did. Uncertainty triggers our threat response, meaning we burn through our emotional resources quickly, leaving us drained. For people whose main coping strategy was control, it may have felt like a wildfire was spreading through their nervous system.

When your main coping strategy is removed, whatever the strategy, it can feel like there's no safety net (when someone takes away the water, how do you put out the fire?). The emotions you've been trying to avoid or have never experienced before tend to rush right in ... and suddenly anxiety is now everywhere, in every thought, every breath and every (now racing) heartbeat. This is why having multiple coping strategies to hand is always a good idea.

While it can be very annoying to have someone tell you to 'go with the flow', they do have a point. If we can find ways to accept and adapt to the things life throws at us, we will ultimately feel much happier. Easier said than done, I realise.

If you feel like you cope solely through control, and are looking for a way forward, I recommend that:

- **Today:** Choose one small area of your life that you would usually take control of and decide to not do it. See what happens. If you are the primary homemaker in your house, maybe ask someone else to cook for once. Maybe don't tidy; leave whatever room's a mess exactly that, a mess. This isn't meant to feel good, by the way. It may even feel daunting to let that responsibility go. But I need to show you ... it is survivable! I want to show your brain that whatever it predicts will happen if you don't take control is manageable, and you don't need to use your old strategy in the same way in the future. You need to update your memory stores!
- **Going forward:** Add mindfulness (Chapter 13) to your coping skills, as this will help you practise acceptance and letting go. Keep practising relinquishing control,

one small area of your life at a time. **You are not trying to get rid of control**, you are just trying to create flexibility and a sense that you have many ways to cope when life gets unpredictable.

Perfectionism

Perfectionism is a common control strategy. It is also one of the coping skills people feel quite proud of: 'I'm such a perfectionist, honestly.' It's a coping skill that society approves of, and that some people wear as a badge of honour.

We struggle when we feel like the stress of the world outweighs the number of coping skills we have to manage. The more coping skills you have to manage, the less you will struggle with the stress of the world.

Perfectionists tend to think that if they can control everything they care about – their work, their plans, their Instagram, their physical appearance and how they appear at all times – they will prevent scary things (e.g. rejection by loved ones) from happening and/or ensure something rewarding will happen (e.g. they will gain respect, favour and potentially love).

There are many kinds of perfectionism:

- **Self-oriented perfectionism** – holding yourself to exceptionally high standards, judging and criticising yourself any time you fail to meet them.
- **Other-oriented perfectionism** – holding others to exceptionally high standards, judging and criticising them instead.

- **Socially prescribed perfectionism** – believing you are being held to exceptionally high standards by others and society. Maybe you feel that people in your life expect exceptionally high standards from you, or maybe it's what we talked about in Chapter 3, and your self-worth is tied up in the societal expectations set out by the media.

Do any of these resonate with you?

If our perfectionism is oriented towards ourselves (self-orientated or socially prescribed) then we may feel 'in control' as long as we are able to 'be perfect'. Problems start to arise when we cannot maintain the level we expect of ourselves.

Perfectionists are extremely driven. They may become very good at things because they apply unwavering focus to reach 'perfection'. However, this drive may leave them anxious and exhausted if they realise they can never quite reach 'perfect', because it doesn't exist.

Unfortunately, life and all things are imperfect. And perfectionists have exceptional 'error-detection systems'. They can spot a potential flaw a mile off! They can even find a flaw in something that, to others' standards, would be flawless. If you are a perfectionist, or you know one, then you already know this.

'The essay that got ninety per cent was still ten per cent imperfect.'

'The beautiful meal cooked for a table full of guests, well, the pasta wasn't al dente.'

'That outfit, stunning, yes, but did you see the crease on my hem?'

You know how hard it can be to feel content with your work or with yourself, as there is always something more that could have been done. Even when perfectionists achieve an award or a pay rise, or some other milestone of success, the bar they set for themselves simply moves higher and higher.

Therefore, burnout can be extremely likely for the person who can never stop what they're doing and simply say, 'You know what? This is fine just as it is.' Once burnout happens, it can become almost impossible to keep the perfectionist work alive, meaning that even more anxiety ensues.

Work hard to achieve perfection

↓

Fear work isn't enough, so you work harder

↓

Fatigue builds, making it impossible to work as hard

↓

Fear of imperfection increases

↓

Keep trying as giving up would be unacceptable

↓

Burnout

If this is you, it has been me and many other people too, so no judgement – please rest.

Not only is perfection unattainable and unnecessary – you are already bloody marvellous – but pushing yourself harder and harder to achieve more and more is a false economy. Taking breaks, looking after our minds and our bodies, that is how people gain the energy to push forwards.

If our perfectionism extends to others, we may end up pushing people away who achieve anything less than 100 per cent. Or we may find ourselves taking over other people's tasks, thinking, *I know best, I'll just show them how it's done.* Hard truth: we may think this is us being helpful, and in small doses this can be the case. However, when we do this continuously, we rarely show people a 'better way'; we often just end up showing them that we don't trust their ability, or worse, them. Over time this will undermine not only our relationships, it will undermine other people's abilities as we slowly erode their confidence in themselves. Eek!

Fun fact: Many self-oriented perfectionists describe themselves as contradictions. They say, 'It's funny, in some areas I'm all about perfection. I throw myself into the task and give it my all. Then, at other times, I try something and I just give up. Immediately. Never trying it again.'

This is not a contradiction – not at all. Most perfectionists cannot tolerate being bad at something. It feels too threatening. So, when they try something new that doesn't come naturally to them, the experience can be so uncomfortable (understatement – it can feel extremely threatening) they immediately give up. This can be the same for change. If we can't be sure that we can navigate the change perfectly, we may avoid it at all costs.

I have a friend who runs an extremely successful business and is a master at everything he turns his hand to. I took him to a salsa class once. Within minutes he was pouting. The pouting turned to frustration, which turned to (mildly hilarious) hostility. 'This is stupid,' he muttered, stomping off the dance floor (vulnerability thinly masked by a veil of anger). He never danced salsa again.

He has done the same with cooking, languages and other skills where someone else in the room makes it look easy but he feels he is right at the beginning, having to work through the laboriously difficult early stages. This is not selective perfectionism. This is intolerance for imperfectionism!

Again, no judgement, as the threatening feelings are not arising out of choice. They likely mean his brain is predicting and simulating danger and has him reliving upsetting or shaming experiences from the time in his life when he first developed his perfectionism.

If you feel like perfectionism is getting you down and are looking for a way forward, I recommend that:

- **Today**: choose one thing to do imperfectly and see what happens. As with all other suggestions in this chapter, this is to show you that you can indeed survive without your perfectionism, and to teach your brain that whatever it predicts will happen if you aren't 'perfect' is manageable, and that you don't need to use this strategy in the same way in future. Maybe you're a perfectionist in the kitchen – if so, burn the bacon a little and serve it anyway (without telling the person you're feeding that you did it on purpose). If you're a perfectionist at work, leave a typo in something you send to a colleague. If you're a perfectionist about your appearance, maybe wear your less good outfit today, or only put mascara on one eye. If you require perfection in others, intentionally share something you did imperfectly with someone you usually criticise for their imperfect ways.

- **Going forward:** mindfulness (Chapter 13) and self-compassion (Chapter 15) will be your friend, as will regularly picking something each day to do imperfectly. In fact, speaking of friends, top tip: surround yourself with people who are not afraid to be flawed, who are open and willing to admit, 'I am imperfectly human, and I think it's great.'

People-pleasing

Being a people pleaser – the person who does everything in their power to meet the needs of others – does not come with the same recognition as being a perfectionist.

Few feel proud to say they are a people pleaser. Yet many people adopt people-pleasing as a safety strategy in the same way as others adopt perfectionism and control, which makes them equally resourceful and equally smart. Making other people feel good, showing them you care and nurturing relationships is a wonderful thing. People who please others bring kindness and energy to the world.

We are meant to exist in a community, so wanting to please people is not a bad thing, and almost everyone cares what other people think; we are hardwired to do so. If you think of yourself as a people pleaser, you can do it with a sense of pride.

However, people-pleasing can be problematic if it reaches the point where we are willing to do *anything* to ensure someone else likes us, and if our emotional state is totally overwhelmed and feels like it's in all-out collapse if someone doesn't.

Because this feeling can be so overwhelming, people who use pleasing as a way to cope may learn to never say no, saying yes even to things they don't like. Even to things they don't have time to do. They believe that saying no would cause upset, leading to abandonment or another worst fear.

Saying yes may minimise anxiety but can lead to situations that are at best tiring (filling up your diary with other people's priorities) and kind of boring (having to do activities you loathe) and, at worst, could be devastatingly dangerous (if you are unable to say no to a request to be involved in something illegal, for example, or something sexual that you don't want to do).

Another way people avoid the fear of displeasing others is by assuming total responsibility for the other person's emotional experience, feeling guilty if they see that person isn't having a good time and doing everything in their power to fix it.

Have you ever done this? Have you ever been to a party but can't relax as you are overly consumed by the experience of the person you're with – *Are they having fun?* Have you noticed it can leave a night anything from slightly marred to totally ruined by your preoccupation with others? And/or can have you apologising for, and taking the blame for, things that are not your responsibility and that you have likely blown out of all proportion?

Over time, the constant prioritisation of others' needs can lead people pleasers to feel unsure of what they want in life, as they have ignored their own emotions and desires for so long. It can also leave them exhausted, as they've given away all their time and energy, leaving nothing to sustain themselves with. And it can leave them feeling resentful: *Why don't they ever ask me about me? How I feel? Or what I want?* – a lesser-known side of people pleasing.

To the people pleasers reading this, does this resonate?

Constantly playing second fiddle can wear thin over time. It can start to feel like we are being taken for granted. The tricky thing here is that when we constantly prioritise others – asking them what they want and they need – when we deflect conversations away from ourselves, we may teach others that we don't ever want or need to talk about ourselves.

If we don't realise this, we may predict that other people don't care what we want or need. What we really need to do is start speaking up more frequently, so others know we have wants and needs just like them: 'I had a really bad day – can we talk about it?' is a great place to start. Scary but great!

Time for a hard truth: the irony is, constantly pleasing others rarely makes us more likeable. Think about the people you like most in the world. Are they the ones who conform to your every wish, or are they the sassy individuals who know their own minds? Maybe it's time to turn down the people-pleasing and try a new boundary or two. If you feel like people-pleasing is getting you down, and are looking for a way forward, I recommend that:

- **Today:** decide on one thing you will say no to this week. A small thing. Maybe get your friends together and start a 'no' club (or a 'no, thank you' club if no doesn't feel safe enough to use yet!). Agree to say no as many times as you can this week and next. Hold each other accountable. See what happens.
- **Going forward:** I recommend a strong dose of self-compassion (Chapter 15) and some time working out what you value in life (Chapter 16) so that you know

what YOU want to do and are able to be kind to yourself while you do it.

Avoiding triggering places and activities

We cannot control every aspect of our lives. We cannot be perfect at all times. We cannot please everyone we meet. The good news is, we don't have to.

Sometimes, when we haven't managed to stop an emotion or feeling from occurring in another way, we start avoiding the places and events that caused the distress in the first place. Another smart move.

The person bitten by a lion or a snake should indeed stop going to the lion's den and the snake pit. Likewise, the person treated cruelly by another human is making an excellent decision if they start avoiding that person at all costs. And sometimes, avoidance seems like a good idea but, as we discussed in Chapter 7 when we learned about intrusive thoughts, it can prove a rather unsustainable strategy.

If you panicked or felt something else equally unpleasant while public-speaking, socialising or when out and about, you may notice yourself opting out of career or social opportunities (predicting the worst will happen again), and may even notice you don't want to leave the house anymore, for fear of what'll happen if you do, and thus find yourself missing out on fun and joyful events.

The problem is, the more you avoid something, the more dangerous it feels. Have you ever felt this? Trying another public-speaking gig, taking new opportunities, facing your fears (with the right coping skills to hand) is how you eliminate them.

Have you ever put off a piece of work because it feels too challenging and difficult, or a household chore because it seems boring – your reluctance to do it increasing every second you get closer to the moment where you simply cannot put it off anymore – then you do it and it seems fine?

A big example: when I was eighteen, I had a panic attack on the London Underground. After that, whenever I thought about the Underground, I (my brain) predicted I would have another attack should I go down there. So, I stopped using the Underground.

Panic attacks feel like the world is ending, so avoiding the place that made me feel like that seemed a smart move, right?

Yes!

And no.

Avoiding the Underground meant I didn't have panic attacks anymore – *woo hoo!* That felt better in the moment but there was a problem. I was now walking or riding my bike to places I used to get to by train, which sometimes added hours to my journey. But there was a bigger problem: my anxiety didn't go away; it got worse and started spreading to other areas. Why?

Avoiding the place that caused panic taught my brain that the reason I survived this scenario – remember, our brain thinks in terms of life and death, anxiety occurring when a life threat has been identified – was only because I avoided the situation and the feeling.

My brain *did not learn* whether there was any real life–death danger on the Underground, or whether I could have survived a panic attack should it have happened, or if I'd allowed it to happen with the right coping skills in place.

Suddenly the Underground was tagged in my brain as being the everyday equivalent of an open war zone – a place to be avoided at all costs. And worse than that, it upped the level of danger my brain now associated with anxiety and panic, increasing its fear of any potential symptom related to anxiety that cropped up in my body.

Soon, any whiff of a raised heartbeat or new bodily sensation (which could have been down to any normal, moment-to-moment bodily change) or talk of a train journey started the panic.

As with most people who have gone down this route, as my anxiety increased and my avoidance strategy started to expand, my life shrank until I could hardly go anywhere. Everywhere seemed to come with the threat of anxiety, and therefore needed to be avoided. Panic spread like wildfire. My brain was screaming 'constant danger!' as I screamed, some-times literally, 'I CAN'T COPE!'

To overcome this, I started therapy. My therapist showed me how to ground myself and build my way back into feeling safe in my body and in places I'd come to associate with panic. I gradually exposed myself to the fear I was avoiding, and now I can go anywhere I please.

Remember: the common negative consequences of avoid-ance are that they may make our worst fears seem like they are actually happening.

For example, if you feel socially anxious and worried people won't like you, you may turn down party invitations, gatherings and other social events to manage how you feel. This may make you feel temporarily better, but when you do this enough times it can send a message to the other person: 'I'm not interested in your parties', so they (thinking they are doing the right thing) stop inviting you to future events. How does your brain then interpret their radio silence? As proof that people don't like you; otherwise, surely, they would still be inviting you to things.

I told you our coping strategies can bite us on the bum!

If you feel that avoiding things is getting you down, and you're looking for a way forward, I recommend that:

- **Today:** decide on one thing you can do that turns you towards the thing you have been avoiding. One small thing, nothing big. If you've been putting something off, make it the first thing you do today after putting this book down. If it's late, decide to do it tomorrow morning. Get it out of the way. Decide to test your brain's prediction and find out if it's as bad as your brain would have you think it is. If you feel socially anxious, text a friend, ask how they are, initiate conversation. If you've been having panic attacks and are now avoiding somewhere that is not an actual snake pit or lion's den, and there is no one physically dangerous there, your task for today is to just practise the 54321 technique in Chapter 11, and the breathing exercise in Chapter 12, without going to the place you've been avoiding. Then think of the smallest step you could take towards that place with these skills in your pocket.

- **Going forward:** grounding, breathing and self-compassion, covered in Part Three, will help you feel your way through avoidance. Take it

Slowly exposing ourselves to the things we fear in life is the fastest way to learn that we can cope with the things we are afraid of.

slow and be kind to yourself. For the people avoiding the big stuff, if it's taking over your life, please seek the support of a therapist (see Chapter 18 for recommendations). If you don't feel able to do this, there is a step-by-step plan for you in the Appendix.

Seeking reassurance

When something happens that makes us anxious, we may be compelled to ask someone else for reassurance – those anxious questions like: 'What do you think?' 'Is this right?' 'Is it wrong?' 'Do you like my outfit?' 'My new date?' 'My new job?' 'How I acted?' 'The food I made?' 'Do you like me?' 'Love me?' 'Will you stay?' 'Are you sure?' 'No, seriously, are you sure?' 'Will I/everything be okay?'

Have you done something like this? Of course you have. We all have. And it's smart. We're meant to exist in relationships, so asking people for advice and support is deeply human and something we should all do.

However, when reassurance-seeking is our go-to coping strategy, it can be something we engage in with more and more panic. Over time we may notice that, ironically, the more we ask for reassurance or check something, the more unsure we become.

And again, it's because of what we teach our brain when we do this.

When we ask for reassurance, the brain learns that the reason we stayed safe was only because someone else helped and gave us advice. It did not learn whether there was any real danger in the first place, or whether we could've survived it on our own. When we do this all the time, our brain learns that other people are needed to make us safe, and that we cannot cope with anxious feelings or trust ourselves to make decisions.

When uncertainty arises again, which it will because our brain now thinks we can't cope with the world alone, our brain switches into alert mode: *Alert! Alert! Something bad is happening. I need someone else to help. I can't cope with this on my own. DANGER!* The wave of emotion comes again and, if no one is around to check with, it surges hard and fast. The need to check becomes doubled, tripled, increasing exponentially.

A similar coping mechanism to seeking reassurance is checking.

Checking the door to see if you've locked it, or if the gas and the lights are off, even though you've already checked them and know you've never forgotten this. Checking in on your loved ones to see if they're safe, even though they left the house only a few minutes ago or you've already spoken to them many times today. Checking every sentence of your work to ensure perfection, in case you can be called out and judged as imperfect. And for the people who have had panic attacks, a common one is checking to see if your pulse is racing or your blood pressure is up, two fingers to your pulse points.

The more we check, the more we feel we need to:

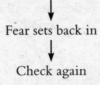

Worry about something

↓

Check the thing

↓

Feel temporarily better (so your brain learns you only
stayed safe due to the reassurance of checking)

↓

Fear sets back in

↓

Check again

The cycle continues. Until you end up having to check the
door several times before leaving the house.

When we check or ask for reassurance, we may be doing
it because we learned early on not to trust ourselves, or that
we had to defer to others. We may simply do it because anxiety and the pattern of needing reassurance took on a life of
its own. We may check things because we're worried about
making mistakes and being seen as bad.

If you feel like checking or reassurance-seeking is getting
you down and are looking for a way forward, I recommend
that:

- **Today:** pick one thing you won't check on. Maybe
  you're worried about your outfit? A choice you made?
  How someone feels about you? Don't ask anyone about
  it. It can sound scary, I know, but we just want to
  introduce you to this slowly. Decide to rely on your
  own judgement and see how it goes!

- **Going forward:** grounding, breathing and self-compassion will help you manage the anxiety that arises as you keep resisting the urge to ask for reassurance or to check something that you feel anxious about. If you notice that it is taking over your life, i.e. you are spending hours checking the doors are locked and/or the gas is off, and you are unable to let go of these behaviours, a therapist will be able to support you with this (see Chapter 22 for recommendations).

Numbing

We all numb out from time to time – watching Netflix, eating something soothing, diving into our work so that we can't feel any of the other stresses of our lives. Sometimes we grab a drink, go on a bender. Sometimes our brain does it for us – when we are in shock, or in the freeze response, for example. Contrary to popular belief, when we feel emotionally numb, it is rarely that we have no emotion. It's the opposite. It's precisely because we feel so much that we feel numb. It's a response. Not an absence.

Sometimes, however, numbing can go from temporary relief to coping strategies that at one point in time felt good but have become problematic.

Booze and drugs numb your emotional state quickly. They diminish anxiety, shame and loneliness, then send you towards feeling like the person you may wish you were: disinhibited, relaxed, free maybe. The world suddenly feels bearable, exciting even. If you have lost someone important to you, thought something frightening, feel socially anxious or are experiencing something generally upsetting, this can be the relief you are looking for.

The problem is this relief is fleeting. It's no more than a window in time where everything feels better. Then it passes and you're left with a hangover or a comedown. The world seems greyer, possibly tinged with a sense of impending doom. If this downward spiral feels too intense then you may suddenly need more and more of your chosen numbing agent.

A cycle may start, a psychological reliance, another thing you need to cope with. If this goes on long enough, your brain will alter itself so that it needs that substance just to feel normal – this is what we call addiction.

How we become 'addicted'

Our brain always wants to stay the same. It doesn't want big spikes of activity happening day-to-day.

When we drink or put other substances into our body (coffee, booze, nicotine or drugs), it can cause a spike of neurochemical activity (usually either a strong buzz or a relaxing feeling), then a crash. The high, then the low. If you use these substances consistently enough, your brain will change so you stop having these spikes.

If you use something that gives you a buzz (nicotine, caffeine, some form of upper like Ecstasy or cocaine) your brain will decrease the amount of chemicals it would usually produce to make you feel awake, buzzy and feeling good, as it doesn't want the big spikes of

---

activity. When this happens you need the cigs, coffee or party pills just to feel normal. If you keep going even further, your brain will continue to adapt, making you need more and more over time. This is why I am now almost continuously glued to my coffee cup.

Likewise, if you use something that is considered a relaxant (e.g. alcohol or some form of 'downer', like Valium) your brain will decrease the amount of chemicals it would usually produce to make you feel calm. And again, you will need more and more booze or downers to get you through.

If this goes on long enough, and the drinking is heavy, when you don't drink, anxiety, the shakes or worse can set in, as your brain isn't making enough 'relaxant' naturally to stop this. This is why people should never quit a long-term habit without consulting a doctor.

Whatever you are dependent on, withdrawing is a process. Whether it's caffeine, booze or even your social media apps, you are going to need time. And possibly support. There is no shame in that.

The reason I'm telling you this is not to scare you. I'm telling you this because people assume that drinking or other forms of numbing are 'a problem'. They treat them as though they're a stand-alone issue. They often aren't. They often started out as coping mechanisms that then took on a life of their own.

We need to know this so we can stop the shaming narratives

surrounding drinking and other forms of numbing. And so that people get the right support when they want to move forwards from these behaviours.

If you strip away a person's coping skill, what happens? The stuff beneath comes flooding in. Therefore, if you want to move away from a numbing behaviour (or any other behaviour, to be honest) and ensure you don't end up relapsing or replacing one escape hatch with another, you need to know what fears lie beneath.

With the right support to reduce or stop excessive drinking, or other numbing behaviour, AND the right tools to address the underlying distress, you will move forwards.

Always ask what is underneath your coping mechanism

Are you numbing to avoid the pain of grief? Are you avoiding somewhere to stave off a panic attack? Are you checking doors to avoid the incessant feeling you didn't lock them, even though you do this each day? Are you making sure everything is perfect to avoid your fear that someone will see you are flawed? Are you taking control of everything because it feels as if the world will collapse on top of you if you don't?

Or are you simply doing these things because you enjoy doing these things?

Your answers to these questions matter.

Before we remove a coping strategy, if the emotion you're avoiding is a big one, we need to know you have something else in its place to help you manage.

Some of the things we do to cope don't fit into one single category put forward in this chapter. Some of them are a little bit of all of them. Food is a great example of this.

Few people realise this, but food isn't just food anymore. Nope, many of us aren't eating solely to manage hunger; we are eating to manage our emotions too.

People often change the way they eat in order to feel a sense of control during times of chaos, or to nourish themselves during times of neglect, or to swallow and distract themselves from pain. And it's smart.

Food is often associated with love, joy, celebration, tradition and lots of other beautiful moments and memories from our lives. It is a place where we can relive our earliest moments of joy and safety, that feeling we had as a baby when we were held and fed by a precious caregiver. That time we cooked Grandma's recipes together, laughing and feeling connected as a group. That birthday meal, just for us, that came with cake and a giant helping of attention. That family ritual of grabbing food after school each day, or spending hard-earned pocket money on penny sweets.

Even if we didn't have these experiences we may still associate food with love, as we may have seen our friends or characters in movies live out these moments and yearn for that for ourselves too.

Food also fills our tummies, giving us a sense of being in our body, out of our heads and away from the hellish thoughts, grounded back into this present moment, making it an understandable go-to any time we feel dysregulated.

The problem is that food has been so villainised by diet culture that, unfortunately, food often also equals shame, sin and punishment. This means we grow up with a complicated (to say the least) relationship with food. We may eat to soothe, but then feel shame, so we eat more, or restrict our food intake to punish ourselves. This is a cycle that can feel so hard to stop: soothe, punish, soothe, punish. Especially if your inner critic then gets loud, fighting with you, shaming you further.

When people are in my clinic, talking about how they hate the way they eat, shaming themselves for the way they consume food, shaming themselves for eating when they aren't hungry, we draw out their relationship with food, their body, and what they saw around food and bodies growing up.

We write down all the meanings food has for them, including all the best memories and worst times linked to eating and their bodies. We map out how this pattern creates safety. How it helps, and also how it hinders. You can do this too, by the way, for any coping strategy you realise you use. Write all of it on a big piece of paper. We also talk about emotions, how and where they feel them, or don't. We work on the origins of any deep distress and/or trauma, and we work on this, not the food.

Slowly, over time, people realise they were doing something incredibly smart in the absence of other ways to look after themselves. The shame starts to lift, and we think about ways in which we could, if they still wish to, break the cycle by meeting the emotional needs they have in each moment in a way that suits them. And, if eating has helped them protect themselves following trauma, we focus on that.

We need to address the underlying fear. We need to address the grief, the panic, the uncertainty, your belief you aren't enough (when you most certainly are). There are ways to do this – through the suggestions in this chapter, the coping strategies in the back of the book, through sharing our distress with our loved ones, and possibly through therapy.

If you try to stop a behaviour that turns out to be a coping

Many of the behaviours I often hear people judge to be 'bad lifestyle choices', such as emotional eating, addiction to alcohol or drugs, are not 'bad lifestyle choices' at all. They are actions that started out as coping skills in the absence of another way to manage.

skill, you will be left vulnerable to your old emotions and traumas, in need of something even stronger to keep you afloat. So, always ask yourself what your coping strategy is doing for you.

Then, if you want to, find a new way to address that need – slowly, one step at a time, trying something new.

A final note: expect your old coping strategies to return

If you successfully replace your coping skills, don't be surprised or worried if the urges and drives to repeat these strategies suddenly come flooding back during times of stress. This is normal. In times that feel dangerous, your brain will revert to what it knows helped you 'survive' in the past.

COVID-19 was a great example of this. So many people who had moved on from old coping patterns of eating, drinking, taking control of every situation, suddenly found themselves reaching for their old ways. This was not because people were relapsing; it was because the world had changed. And their brains went back to look for what worked in the past.

So, if this happens to you, don't worry. Offer yourself a kind word, tell yourself it's totally normal and a sign that times are stressful, and do whatever you did in the first place to look after yourself and move away from that behaviour. And if you don't know how you did it the first time, delve into Part Three of this book and find something that works for you.

You did it before; you can do it again. I believe in you.

The new rules

- **Emotions are like waves.** They come and go, they ebb and flow. Even the most troubling emotions, which feel like they'll reach fever pitch, will eventually die away. When we try to block those emotions, it can be like blocking a wave. This doesn't stop the wave or disperse its power. It sends it back temporarily, ensuring its return. This doesn't mean you have to face every emotion all the time, but it does mean that dropping your barriers and allowing the emotions in (through the coping skills at the end of this book) will help you manage even the stuff that feels like a tsunami, making it more likely that the wave passes.
- **There is no such thing as perfect coping.** Allow the mess to be messy from time to time.
- **Understand what you do to cope.** Ask what you might be trying to avoid or protect yourself from.
- **Take baby steps if you are going to move away from a previous way of coping.** Don't go cold turkey. Make bite-size, manageable steps – chicken-nugget-size steps that get larger only when you know you have a bucket load of other ways to cope in your metaphorical arsenal.

- **Know that your old coping skills will always return.** This is not a problem. If your brain believes you're in danger it will dig into what it knows has worked in the past, irrespective of whether it will work for you now. So even when you make changes, expect the old stuff to arise.

- **Make a coping jar!** We don't always need a 'scientifically-backed coping skill' to get us through. Most of our moment-to-moment stresses can be managed with a small action that simply makes you feel good, held, active, or just shakes you out of the funk you may have slipped into. I canvassed my pals and my family to see what small actions they take each day to make everything feel a little better, the kinds of actions you don't find in psychology books. I have summarised them here for you. But better than that, I have put them into little boxes you can cut out. Cut them out, fold them up, throw them into a jar and, whenever you need a little pick me up, shove your hand in and see what you pull out. Then do that thing! Add in anything that you already know helps you too, and ask your friends to contribute surprise notes. If you're using the audio version of this book, or a reading aid, and writing or reading visually is not an option for you, you could record this list as a voice note on your phone or other device, and when you want to use it, you could fast forward through the voice note, stopping and playing it at a time that feels good. Then get to it!

Shout really loud! You can shout into a pillow if you can't do this loudly.	Go for a slow walk around your block or nearest park. Try to move as slowly as you can, pay attention to your body and listen for what is around you.	Do 10 star jumps. If these are inaccessible to you, do any form of movement that gets your heart rate going.	Make a music playlist to reflect your mood, or what you would like to feel.
Ask someone for help	Put on the loudest music you know of and shake along to it. Or . . . The quietest music you can find, and sway to it.	Send someone a text telling them, 'Hi! I was just thinking about you, and how great I think you are, and how my absolute favourite thing about you is _____ (insert favourite thing here).	Vent your feelings into a journal. Even if you only write one sentence. Reread, re-listen, tear it up, delete.

Wrap yourself in something and lie down for 5 minutes. Make the wrap quite tight so that you feel held. It could be a duvet, a blanket, a towel.	Look for something blue, green or flowering. What can you find? The sky, the sea, a tree, a plant?	Play with soil, garden or walk barefoot on grass – when our skin makes contact with the earth, the bacteria in the soil makes us release serotonin – the feel-good hormone. WILD!	Focus on one single sound in the room, or wherever you are today. Maybe you can hear a child laugh? Or you can pick out one specific layer of a song on the radio.
Draw something or colour something in – it doesn't have to be pretty!	Plan a lazy night in, but only do the things you associate with taking it very easy. Make sure you have snacks and your favourite book, Netflix series or old movie to hand.	Cook or eat something that reminds you of someone you love. Do you have a recipe a grandparent or other beloved person used to make for you?	Plan a get-together with people you like and/or love.

9. The Inner Critic and Negative Self-Talk

A tree doesn't grow any faster when you sit there and criticize it. Neither do you.

—DR JENN HARDY

'You aren't good enough.'

'Look at you, trying to do that thing.'

'What a joke.'

'Things might seem like they're going well now, but just you wait.'

Sound familiar?

What makes the inner critic so painful is that it is with us 24/7, our own personal heckler that follows us around all day, and it sounds just like our own voice, meaning most of us believe every word it says.

Can you think of some of the times when your inner critic has been loud recently? What was it saying to you? Was it focused on only one aspect of your life, or did it comment on many things? Is it sometimes about how you look, other times about what you said, or how you behaved, or how people seem to be responding to you? Is it sometimes about your work?

Are you thinking, *What even is my inner critic?*

How to Recognise Your Inner Critic

Some people know their inner critic better than they would like to. Others, however, have only heard of the inner critic, and aren't sure how to recognise theirs.

In case that's you, here are the telltale signs that your inner critic is around.

The inner critic usually speaks in absolutes. No grey areas. You are 'a loser', 'an idiot', 'a pig', 'boring', 'thick'. There is no balance, no nuance, no curiosity and no exception.

It is always negative.

It really likes to use the word 'should'. You 'should be better/smarter/richer/hotter. Why aren't you?'

It dishes out punishments that almost never fit the crime. For example, if you fail an exam – you failed. It's a fact. But this is not proof you are *a failure*. It's just one instant where you did not pass. Yet your inner critic is likely to tell you're always going to fail, that this failure is no surprise whatsoever, and that your whole future is doomed.

Our inner critic usually devalues us, pointing out everything that's wrong, and it never offers a suggestion of how to move forward, or what you could do to improve in the future.

Tara Mohr, in her book *Playing Big*, offers another aspect of the inner critic: the 'one–two punch':

1) It insults you and THEN 2) shames you for having those thoughts in the first place. For example, 'I'm such a failure' is followed by 'I should be better than this, bigger than this, why am I doing this? I bet other people don't worry about stuff like this, what's wrong with me? There are people starving and I am worrying about . . .'

Shame upon shame. Being a human can be exhausting sometimes, can't it? We are held hostage by our need to reach an inhuman standard.

Where the words of the inner critic come from

Like all thoughts, some of the things our inner critic says are made up of:

How we have made sense of other people's behaviours or attitudes towards us. Common examples of this are: *They are good, so I must be bad. If I was better I would be treated better. If I was better they wouldn't have left.* For many people, their first experience of the inner critic might have been thinking, as a child, *If I was different, they would love me more.*

What other people told us, especially if it was negative or critical. Common examples of this: *Don't do that. You can't. Bad! Lazy! Why would you do that? What's wrong with you? Shameful.* If you were bullied, or have experienced any form of abuse, the words from that time may be in there too. Continuing the abuse even in the absence of the abuser.

Society, the media, your faith and other power structures that broadcast messages about how we should be, act, live and look. Common examples of this are: *Those people in the pictures are the ones who are worthy and lovable. I don't look like that so I'm a failure. Masturbation is a sin, and the fact I'm thinking about it makes me a sinner. Fat and cellulite are shameful; my body is therefore disgusting.* **None of these things are true.**

Overall, our inner critic is an amalgamation of all the words and messages we've heard, or, rather, interpreted as being said. They are a mishmash of every moment our brain registered an *Uh oh, something is wrong with me!*

You don't have to grow up in a cruel environment to take in messages like this.

If you grew up around people who were caring and compassionate to you, but hypercritical about themselves, their negative self-talk and self-critical attitudes may have rubbed off on you. For example, many people who saw their caregivers panic about ageing or putting on weight may notice their inner critic starts attacking them about this if and when they start to age or put on weight too. Or even before that.

It's common for people to try to motivate children with statements such as 'Work harder', 'You're only going to let yourself down', 'Don't slack', 'Don't do that, just focus'. These words are meant for our common good, but can, for some of us, end up becoming another part of our negative self-talk – 'Stop slacking – what's wrong with you?'

Children commonly experience peer pressure growing up: 'Don't be a wuss', 'Only chickens are scared', 'I'll like you more if you do [xyz] for me' – leading many of us to have inner critics that shame us any time we want to resist other people's suggested activities, worrying others won't like us if we don't comply.

In his TED Talk 'Who Decides What You Think? Not You . . .', Staffan Ehde says that the average child will have heard the words 'No', 'You can't' or 'Don't', and other negative statements like this, approximately 148,000 times before they turn eighteen. That's an average of 23 times per day. Even when we grow up in a warm and loving environment, that negative skew and immediate 'No', 'Don't', 'Can't' may be there to stop us, even as adults.

This doesn't mean we are all screwed. It's actually the opposite. It means we can all start to see that our inner critic may not reflect the here and now, what we genuinely believe to be true, or a reality we should listen to. It means we can start to say, 'Hey, I see you, critic! And I don't know if I agree with you!'

Quick exercise: learning about your own inner critic

Spend the next 48 hours paying attention to your own self-talk. Notice the positive comments and the negative comments you make towards yourself. Keep a pad of paper and a pen with you, or type them into a notes app on your phone. After 48 hours, come back and write them down here.

The positive comments I made about myself were:

_____
_____
_____
_____
_____
_____
_____
_____
_____
_____
_____
_____

The negative comments I made about myself were:

_____
_____
_____
_____
_____
_____
_____
_____
_____
_____
_____

Was there a big difference? Were there more positive or negative thoughts that arose over the 48 hours? Are you surprised by the outcome?

Next, go through the negative comments. What are the main themes? Are they 'You are not good enough'? 'You need to change'? 'You are bad' in some way? 'Do more'? Whose words do they sound like? Is there someone who has said these things to you in the past? When was the first time you thought this? Think specifically if any of these thoughts link to something your caregivers said, or anyone else who you felt had more power than you.

Go back to the page between Part One and Part Two of this book and your list of beliefs about who you should be, and the 3 nastiest things anyone said to you. Is there an overlap? If so, it's very normal, and proof that our inner critics are personalised.

Why is this happening?

Even though each of us will have inner critics that focus on different themes in our lives, the common themes of most people's inner critics are: 'You are not good enough', 'You are unlovable' or 'You are bad in some way'.

Why is this happening?

No one likes it when I say this, but, just like shame, the inner critic may actually be something we develop to keep us safe.

If your response is, 'What? *Protect* me? All my inner critic does is harm!', I hear you! But bear with me. Think about your inner critic ... when does it get louder? When is it at its loudest? Is it when you've gone out of your comfort zone? Or when you are about to do so – either in a relationship, at work or in another area of your life? Is it when you've taken a risk or are about to take a risk? For instance, *Don't do it, you'll just do a bad job. It's going to go wrong. That mistake you made proves you're gonna mess this whole thing up.*

Is it when you've noticed something about yourself that may affect how others will judge you? Is it when you've been around people and said something you're now second-guessing? *They think you're an idiot. Why did you even bother saying anything? They probably hate you now!*

Or when you've been doing something that wasn't approved of when you were a child – even if the person who may judge you isn't even there? *Only lazy people lie in bed all morning; you're lazy and will amount to nothing.*

Our inner critic usually gets loud any time it thinks we are in danger. We are now talking about the kind of danger we discussed in Chapter 1 – the danger of doing something that'll cause us to end up out of favour with our caregivers or the people we love.

While we are growing up our brain internalises and sum-marises all the messages that tell us who the 'ideal' child is. This creates a blueprint of who we think we 'should' be and what moral standards we must enact if we are to be seen as the 'perfect' or 'good' child in the eyes of our caregivers, community, faith and the world around us.

Every time we deviate from the perfect 'cookie cutter'

mould, it pipes up, potentially using the words of the most abusive people you have ever come across to whip you back into shape. This is one of the many reasons why people who have really suffered at the hands of others – or have been neglected by others – have such ruthless inner critics.

The inner critic is like an all-seeing eye – police officer, judge, jury and executioner all rolled into one. It wants to guarantee that you gain approval. It acts as if other people are watching at all times, giving you the information it thinks you need to protect you from their judgement.

It actually wants to protect you from shame, from the belief that 'I am bad'. The problem is, the inner critic doesn't go for a gentle, 'Oh, by the way, that thing ... maybe don't do it because you could get in trouble or you could fail, and the people we love won't be happy.' This is because it's more effective to use strong language to shape our behaviour or inhibit our impulses, especially when we are young.

Think about it: you might reach for that forbidden treat (the one your caregivers said will make you fat and have called you 'fatty' when they've previously seen you eating it), or you might start to cry and share your distress with them (when your caregivers have distinctly told you crying is for 'sissies') and hear the voice and say, 'Nah, it's gonna be fine. I'll do it anyway.'

So instead it attacks. It judges. It punishes.

The verdict: you are bad. YOU ARE BAD! BAD KID! BAAAADDDD KID. It uses shame-based language that can become actual torment.

As we hate these feelings, and rarely know how to manage them, we tend to avoid the situation that caused them, or try desperately to change the thing about us that the inner critic speaks of. Inner critic 1: you 0.

You might start avoiding the cookies or feel shame when you think of how much you want one. You might avoid crying or feel shame any time emotions like that arise.

Once we learned what our ideal self was meant to be like, and acquired our own set of personal police officers, something else happened. We likely pushed away many of the parts of ourselves that were outside of what was acceptable, jettisoning them into the dark, and this carries on into our adult lives.

For example, if you were trained to be the 'good girl', you may have tried to push away any parts of yourself that could be considered 'bad'. As an adult, you may have moments where you think, *Fuck it, I'm going to let loose.* You have an amazing time. Then, the next day, the judgement gets loud: *There you go again; good girls don't do that. Shame on you – what were you thinking? You're an adult. You're such a failure; now everyone else knows it too.* You vow not to have a night like that again.

Until, you do.

A cycle may start that looks a little something like this:

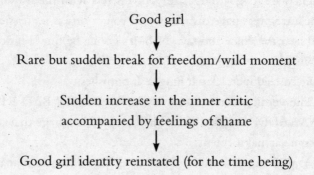

Good girl
↓
Rare but sudden break for freedom/wild moment
↓
Sudden increase in the inner critic
accompanied by feelings of shame
↓
Good girl identity reinstated (for the time being)

The reality is, for many 'good girls' who experience this cycle, they secretly want to be more free, more themselves, and have done so their whole lives, but any time they allow themselves to be who they are, their inner critic gets louder (and often sounds suspiciously like a family member or other authority figure from their childhood – no coincidence).

They don't realise that trying to comply with the inner critic (or in this case, likely their inner caregiver) and avoiding these free or 'wild' behaviours and urges only increases the likelihood of rebellious outbursts happening again.

If this section speaks to you, to get out of this cycle the answer is not to stop having wild times. It is to recognise that your inner critic may actually be an internalised version of your caregivers (or whoever else trained you to 'be good') and that incessant voice is still trying to make you impress them. You are still trying to be a 'good girl' in their eyes.

But you are more than just a 'good girl'; you are now an adult, and have many more sides to you that demand to be explored. EXCITING! This is direct permission to allow yourself to stop behaving for the caregivers or other voices you carry in your head, who are very likely not even around to watch you anymore! Bring on the 'bad' times!

If you were raised religiously, you may have been taught to be 'chaste' and not to 'sin'. The inner critic in this case developed to keep you 'good' in the eyes of your family and/or your religious leaders and/or your god. You may always want to adhere to your faith and its beliefs around sex and/or masturbation and/or the necessity of being straight – so you may try to push those parts of yourself away. But then you 'slip up'. You have sex, or engage in another form of intimacy, maybe with yourself or someone you 'aren't meant to'. Shame rushes in, as you rush to the shower, feeling you can't get yourself clean enough quick enough, your inner critic piping up the whole time: *You're a sinner, you're going straight to hell, water isn't enough to wash away your sins.* So, you promise never to do it again. Until, well, you know what's next.

Again, if this is you, masturbation, intimacy and sex are not shameful; neither is whether you identify as straight or as LGBTQ+. You are a wonderful and deserving human. And you don't need to clean yourself, because you are not unclean – unless you actually got really messy, but that's a different thing entirely.

If you were raised to be a 'real man', an 'alpha male', someone who doesn't show emotion, always knows best, is the leader, you may push away the emotional and uncertain parts of yourself. When sadness or fear arises, your inner critic pipes up: *You're weak. Get a grip.* The emotion is pushed away, deeper down – repressed for a later date.

When someone else shows knowledge or skills that possibly outstrip yours, your inner critic warns you – *What kind of man are you? A beta male?* So you reassert yourself, showing your power and prowess in other ways, getting competitive about who knows more.

This may be particularly true if you were raised to believe men are the stronger sex, who must stay dominant. Any time a woman speaks knowingly about a topic, you must reassert yourself and possibly re-explain exactly what they just said! The inner critic is one supporter of toxic masculinity, which, once recognised, can be overcome.

So, in its own messed-up way, our inner critic evolved to help us. To keep us, metaphorically, glowing in Mummy's/

Daddy's/another authority's eyes. But damn, nowadays it can really mess with us!

Finding out what your inner critic wants for you

Ask yourself, *What does my inner critic want for me?* I know most people's knee-jerk response will be, *It wants to destroy me,* so below I have given the '7 Styles of Inner Critic' set out by Jay Earley, PhD and Bonnie Weiss, LCSW in their book *Activating Your Inner Champion Instead of Your Inner Critic.*

Circle any of the styles of critic that resonate with you. Pay attention to the reasons they do this, and then ask yourself: but does it work?

The Perfectionist: fearing you will be judged, rejected or abandoned if you are imperfect. This type of inner critic never lets you believe your work or any task is complete exactly as it is. It will keep finding flaws, thinking striving of this kind will keep you safe.

The Inner Controller: fearing you may get out of control, overindulge and therefore be shunned by society. This type of inner critic tries to control your impulses so you fit into society, e.g. drinking, eating, sex. It believes it is up against an inner indulger that cannot be managed without strict reprimand.

The Taskmaster: fearing you may be seen as lazy, unacceptably average or a failure, this inner critic pushes and pushes at you to keep going, no matter what, shaming you the moment you consider stopping or resting.

The Underminer: fearing you'll fail, or will succeed and be 'seen', judged and not be able to cope with this, this inner critic attacks your self-worth, so you won't take any risks.

The Guilt-tripper: fearing you'll repeat past mistakes, this inner critic tends to live in the past, dragging you back there, reminding you of everything you did wrong, never forgiving you.

The Conformist: fearing you may become too free, too rebellious, too yourself, and not what your family ordered, this inner critic whips you into shape any time you try to express something that feels truly you and not what was prescribed.

The Destroyer: experts say this is the 'most debilitating critic' and it often comes from early-life trauma and neglect. This one, fearing it is 'safer not to exist', continuously attacks your self-worth, telling you you're broken and not worthy of respect or an ounce of understanding. If you resonate with this, please get support outside of this book, because living with the pain of the Destroyer is devastating. You deserve support from someone who can hold your experiences and help you separate from this, helping you to know that you deserve to exist and that the world benefits from your presence.

Which of these resonated with you? Was there a lightbulb moment? Did it clarify the ways in which your critic may be trying to be helpful? We may have one or a few, depending on the views we have internalised.

Can it change?

Yes!

As we age, the inner critic may not seem to mature or update its views about us. It may continue to personalise everything, making it seem that everything that happens to us is our fault, and it continues to think in good/bad terms.

However, we CAN change. We can get better at:

- Observing and not getting caught up in our thoughts, using mindfulness and the distancing techniques on page 304.
- Noticing what might be missing from our inner critic's black and white views.
- Recognising we are now in control of our lives and do not need to keep pleasing the internalised voices of others.

- Believing in our own voice – the one that doesn't belong to our inner critic – and what we believe to be true about the world and ourselves (Chapter 16 is dedicated to helping you to work out what your values are).
- Offering ourselves self-compassion, which is the antidote to the inner critic and is explained in Chapter 15.

When we can do this, we can learn to honour what is important to us in our lives. We can have a lie-in, or take the day off, and when our inner critic says we are lazy, instead of saying, 'Oh shit, you're right', we can pause, breathe, remember why we're doing what we're doing, and say, 'Hang on, I need a rest. I'm allowed a break.'

We can start a new hobby, make mistakes, and, when it says we're stupid, we can say, 'Actually, making mistakes is one of the best ways to learn.'

When someone who thought of themselves as a 'good girl' hears their inner critic pop up on their way to have fun, they can observe it and say, 'Thanks, I hear you, but I'm doing what works for me right now', as they head into the bar.

When a religious person who finds a way to make their faith and their personal values align hears their inner critic pop up on their way to a date, they can acknowledge and thank those words, knowing they're trying to make them 'good' while also knowing they're doing what is right for both them and their faith, as they greet their date with a confident smile.

When the man raised to avoid emotions and to show dominance and leadership at all times realises he doesn't agree with these outdated ideas, he can hear his inner critic arise, and say, 'I hear you, and I know my masculinity is not challenged or defined by my emotions, knowledge, ability or dominance. I am already a real man.'

I would love to end this chapter there. However, we need to cover one more thing.

Being kinder to yourself

I am ...	
~~Imperfect~~	Human
~~Failing~~	Human
~~Struggling~~	Human
~~Inconsistent~~	Human
~~Broken~~	Human

I had a client who was doing really well with their mindfulness practice. They were able to observe their emotions as they surfaced and then faded (watching them as one might watch the clouds passing over the sky, knowing they were only temporary). Yet when it came to their critical thoughts, there was no change whatsoever. When we examined this, we found a sneaky belief was getting in the way.

My client, like so many people I've met, believed they needed their self-critical voice so they could criticise themselves before other people did, and in order to motivate themselves to be the best they could be.

They thought that letting go of self-criticism meant stagnating, and increased the risk that others would see the 'real them', the one that wasn't good enough or worthy of their attention.

Do you feel like that? Do you feel like self-criticism stops you from behaving in a way that would allow others to see how flawed you really are? Do you feel that without criticism you will, at best, stagnate and, at worst, truly fail?

I used to believe this. I whipped myself into perfection, into exhaustion,into misery, believing I was doing myself some kind of favour.

If we ever want to overcome the pain of our inner critic, we must address, challenge and replace these beliefs. If we don't, I could teach you all the best ways to separate from and overcome the inner critic and it wouldn't make a jot of difference as, even though you hate your inner critic, deep down you believe you need to keep it around.

So, let's test out this belief. Does self-criticism work?

Imagine a child learning to ride a bike. At first, they don't have a clue how to do it. They get on the bike and start trying. Now, imagine that every time they make a mistake you shout at them, 'No, you idiot, not like that. Of course you're getting it wrong. Typical. Stupid, stupid, stupid. What made you think you could do it in the first place?'

What do you think will happen? Do you think all this shouting and undermining is going to help this child learn how to ride said bike? No, of course it won't.

One: all you're doing is pointing out what's wrong. You are not explaining what they actually need to do. Two: the ongoing criticism will create a growing anxiety in the child that will arise every time they think or do anything associated with riding a bike. This anxiety will make them want to run from the situation, fight against it, or may paralyse them, making thought and action impossible.

Now imagine the situation again.

Instead of criticising them, this time you notice that the child is going to need to learn many steps before they can ride safely. You notice the areas that are going to need improvement first. You offer a smiling face, encouragement and praise for the bits that are going well, then you offer advice and reassurance for the bits that need to change. How do you think this will be different from the previous scenario?

When you criticise yourself, you are the adult in the first example. You aren't encouragingly looking for the areas that need improvement and then constructively offering ways to move forward. You are sending yourself down a path of anxiety, so you shut down.

Need more convincing? Don't worry, I was ready for it. No one shifts lifelong-held beliefs following a single example.

Imagine you are at work. You make a mistake. A big one. One that causes problems for others in the organisation. Something needs to be done to fix the problem. You are extremely concerned about what you did and what's going to happen.

Now, imagine you have two bosses, both very good at their jobs. One of them gets easily angry and critical. The other is very boundaried and takes no nonsense; however, this one is more constructive.

You know that if you go to Boss 1, they'll shout at you. They will shout out loud all the things you've already said to yourself: 'You idiot, how did you let this happen? Of course it was you who messed it up. Typical! Fix it. Fix it now!' etc.

You know that you'll leave this exchange feeling overwhelmed with anxiety, sadness and shame, and will have no idea how to progress. Even if you wanted to be productive after the meeting, you know there is no way you'll be able to focus.

You also know you have the option of going to Boss 2. You know they'll also be pretty damn cross. You did mess up, after all. However, you know they'll say something like, 'Now, that was quite the fuck up. This is really bad. However, we need to get it sorted. We have a few minutes to figure out what went wrong and fix it. Let's figure this out so it won't happen again.'

Boss 2 is clearly the boss to turn to if you want to overcome the problem. Boss 2 has been able to notice flaws, have emotion about that, and still be constructive. Even though you may still feel anxious, sad and ashamed, speaking to Boss 2 will be less distressing than speaking to Boss 1, and you would leave with a plan, and support.

A new attitude to self-criticism

Self-criticism stops us from growing. It gets in the way of the goals we think we need it for. Maybe you already know this. Maybe you've noticed you avoid going for jobs or to new places if your inner critic has said, 'Not for you – what are you thinking?'

Maybe you've noticed that even though you want to go to the gym, the more you criticise yourself for not going – 'Why aren't you there yet? God, what's wrong with you?' – the less inclined you are to go?

What are your alternatives?

Generally, people think that if they aren't critical then they won't achieve their desired goals. This is a perfect example of all-or-nothing thinking, something we all engage in, much like good vs. bad.

All-or-nothing thinking is the idea that there are only two positions that you can take in a situation. In this situation those positions are 1) critical as fuck, versus 2) mollycoddling, being overly protective or indulgent of yourself. However, there are so many more positions available.

I purposefully made Boss 2 sit outside of those two positions. Boss 2 was able to be firm, honest about the mistake, and yet see it for what it is: a mistake – something all humans are capable of. Then Boss 2 managed to accept the mistake had happened and found a way forward.

What could you now choose for your new belief about self-criticism? Take some time to think about this. It's never as simple as deciding on a new belief and the brain just agreeing with it. It will take time and it will take practice.

Being kind to yourself and working towards self-acceptance does not equal giving up or stagnating. Quite the opposite, it offers a chance to step away from the burden of self-flagellation and into a life lived to the full.

Here is a possible new mantra you could trial, and one I frequently share with my clients (and have used many times myself):

'I am learning that although it feels like being critical to myself at all times will be helpful, it may actually be causing me to become anxious and unable to engage in the tasks I want/need to complete. Therefore, maybe self-criticism isn't as important as I think. Maybe it's more important to catch myself while being critical and decide to take a moment, say something calming to myself, and then make a plan on how to move forward.'

Have a go. Write this down somewhere you can access it over and over. Read it as often as you can. Test it out. See what happens when you say this to yourself. See what happens when you take the steps outlined in the new belief. Do you feel different?

Quick tips for overcoming the inner critic

1. **When you notice your inner critic pipe up, ask,** 'Would you speak to your friends the way you speak to yourself?' If the answer is 'No!' (which it usually is, plus 'I wouldn't have any friends left if I spoke to them the way I spoke to myself') then ... visualise your friend experiencing what you are experiencing, worrying about what you are worrying about. What do you want to say to your friend? How would you like to treat them? Would you like to make them a cup of tea? Give them a hug? Tell them that it makes total and utter sense that they feel the way they do? Once you have decided what you would say and do, say those words to yourself. Do those things for yourself.

2. **Give your inner critic a name.** To create distance between yourself and your inner critic, ask yourself what it would be called, what it would look like, what it would sound like, what shape or form it would take if it was a three-dimensional thing outside of you. I know many people whose inner critics are like Regina George from *Mean Girls*, a scathing, bitchy teenager whose own insecurity and shame drives them to bully and harm. I know others who think of theirs as the drill sergeant from the Stanley Kubrick movie *Full Metal Jacket*, who shouts, 'What is your major malfunction, numbnuts?' And some consider theirs a mist or a shadow whose depth increases as its voice or effects get

louder. I have always imagined mine as the nastiest version of my own self. She looks like me, sounds like me, but lacks nuance and any kind of empathy or curiosity. I call her 'that girl'. When your inner critic pops up, imagine this version of the inner critic. Then (as with the techniques from the page before) say the thoughts out loud but in the voice you create for the inner critic.

3. **Who is your inner cheerleader?** On p.39, I asked you to name someone (or a pet or a place) that makes you feel supported and safe, someone or something that helped you survive. And between Part One and Part Two, I asked you to write down the three nicest things anyone ever said to you, and the three most important people (or beings) in your life and how they made you feel. Is your inner cheerleader one of these beings? Is it a mix of them? Do they say the supportive words of these people? Or is it a character? You can choose. When your inner critic pops up, turn your attention to what your inner cheerleader would say in response. An advanced tip: also choose who your inner coach would be, the voice that isn't just supportive but is wise too. Use the inner coach to help you see things in a balanced way, and the inner cheerleader to spur you on.

If you have beaten yourself up for years, negative self-talk will feel safe, predictable, like home. Changing this can be scary, alien and unknown.

Milestones and self-criticism

We are often at our most vulnerable to the inner critic any time we miss a 'milestone' in life: *I'm twenty, I should know what I'm doing with my life. I'm twenty-five, I should have my shit together. I'm thirty, I should have a house and a stack of cash,* etc. (By the way, I'm in my thirties and do not feel I have managed any of these things fully yet!)

On page 179 I asked you to write down where you think you should be at certain points in your life. Timelines and goals are important, right? They allow us to focus our energy towards the things that are important to us.

However ...

We cannot control many of the things we are striving for

We are often taught that the things we aim for are easy to attain, that if we focus our energy we will surely achieve what we hope to achieve. However, this is not the case.

We can't control when we will meet others or who we will mesh well with, yet it is assumed we will date and find love, and most of us expect that this will happen in our twenties or thirties.

We can't control or know whether we will be fertile or whether we will be able to carry a baby to term. Yet many of us are taught that we will have children and/or that we must have them.

When it comes to work, we can do our best, but we cannot control other people's opinions of us when we apply for jobs, or what will happen financially in the world.

Sometimes people will choose us, sometimes they won't. Sometimes the odds will be stacked in our favour, sometimes they won't. And so much of what happens in our life is down to luck and privilege, yet we beat ourselves up for things that are outside of our control, especially considering the number of unforeseen events such as illnesses, accidents and world events that can happen out of the blue, throwing us off course.

Lots of our timelines are ageist

We've all heard expressions such as 'on the shelf', 'cougar', 'mutton dressed as lamb'. These comments lead people to believe there is a certain point by which they must be coupled and behaving differently. I realise this last point is heavily gendered, and there's a reason for that: a lot of our most ageist timelines ARE heavily gendered and favour men, who get to become 'silver foxes', 'bachelors' and remain eternally fuckable. Just look at the casting in films.

Ageism is damaging. It hurts us and, coupled with our internalised timelines, makes a lot of people feel they are failing constantly.

While it's true that certain parts of our lives do have time limits – e.g. fertility does diminish as our egg count and quality decreases, which can make the race to find a potential partner feel stronger (hence why many more people with wombs are taking back control, freezing their eggs early so they can use them at any time) – lots of people assume that doors have closed to them much earlier than is true.

Yuichiro Miura, a Japanese climber, summitted Mount Everest at the age of eighty. Charles Betty, a British D-Day veteran, completed a PhD in history at ninety-five. George (103) and Doreen Kirby (91), an incredible British twosome, were the 'oldest newlyweds' on record at the time of writing.

And Patricia Davis, another D–Day vet, who had not felt safe to express her wish to transition genders earlier in life, transitioned in her nineties! Go, Patricia!

So many of us are striving for ideals that are not actually ours
Whenever I hear someone say, 'I should be doing . . .' I always ask, 'Who says you should?' because often, they were told by the media that they should be going to the gym to lose weight; by society that they should be achieving a new milestone every week.

One of my clients spent six years trying to get accepted to study medicine, berating themselves for the yearly failure when they didn't pass the interview, before realising they weren't chasing their own dream, they were following their dad's ambition. It's quite possible it was because this dream was their father's, rather than theirs, that they never fully applied themselves to the application process.

When we buy into our timelines, basing our goals and our worth on our achievements, our wellbeing is always at risk. We base our sanity on life events that may or may not ever happen. This is why I have personally taken a couple of years off from having any timelines at all. The only timelines I have at present are the deadlines set by the people and companies I work with.

How does one organise one's time and energy without personal

> **Getting married, buying a house, having an impressive job title, a boat load of money, or even a boat, may be nice, but they don't make you a better person. These things do not reflect your worth.**

timelines? By working towards a value-driven life, which I can't wait to discuss with you in Chapter 16.

Quick exercise

Return to page 179, to your timelines.

1. Do you feel your worth is based on achieving any of these milestones?
2. Are there any milestones you have missed? If so, have you criticised yourself about them?
3. Are there any milestones you have gained by criticising yourself into getting them?
4. Which milestones may be affected by factors outside of your control?
5. Working through each milestone, who told you that you 'should' achieve these things? Whose ideas were they? If they weren't yours, do you still want to do them?
6. Do you believe that past a certain age it will be too late to achieve these milestones or that it will be too late to try something new? Who told you it'll be too late?

Quick tip: to explore a different way of thinking about timelines, go to Chapter 16 to work on your values.

The new rules

- **Your inner critic arose as a way to make you 'behave' and be perceived as good when you were a child.** Its ideas are outdated, and as an adult you do not need to listen to it. Decide who you want to be, and who you would be if this voice wasn't trying to stop you. Would you apply for a different job? Audition for a play? Would you be more wild? Would you have more sex? Try an adventurous activity? What would YOU do?

- **Each time you notice your inner critic arise, come back to this page,** visualise your inner critic in full, repeat its words but in the voice you have assigned to it (preferably a silly voice). Say 'Hi', nod your head at them, thank them for trying to keep you safe, then visualise walking away from them. Let them fade out. Or visualise letting them sit down next to you as you turn your attention back to the task. Or, and this really is my favourite, visualise your inner cheerleader, their words, the kind things they would say. Hold them in mind.

- **In the immediate term, if you feel overwhelmed by your inner critic, connect with your friends,** share how you are feeling, ground yourself, do a breathing exercise or a mindfulness practice – anything that works for you from Part Three of this book.

- **In the long term, you need to create the antidote to the pain caused by the inner critic.** You need to cultivate your compassionate voice and create an inner cheerleader. If self-compassion is a struggle for you, see the exercises on pp.304–5 to find a place to start.

- **Expect that, for a short while at least, the inner critic may get louder.** When we start to find our own voice, our own value system, and act in the ways that we want to, we may notice our inner critic attacks more frequently. When this happens, it's okay. We just need to continue practising separating from our thoughts – use the silly voice or the song suggestions from Chapter 7.

- **Whatever you do, don't fight with the inner critic.** When we fight it tends to get louder. Remember that fighting probably does not constitute 'good behaviour', so it becomes all the more ruthless.

- **Know that whatever your inner critic says, you are a multifaceted and incredible human who is more than it will admit.** Start to trust your friends when they pay you compliments. They are the ones who know you better than anyone now. You can listen to them.

- **If your inner critic sounds like someone who abused you, please speak to a therapist or someone you really trust.** For people who have suffered at the hands of others, it can feel as if the abuser is still with them in their heads. If this is you, please speak about it with someone else who can support you through it – maybe a therapist, as they know how to help people with these experiences. See Chapter 18 ('Get Therapy') for more information on this. The 'Internal

Family Systems' approach described in that chapter may suit you.

- **Whenever you believe you 'should' be somewhere in life, ask, 'Who said I should?' and then replace the word 'should' with 'could'.** When we use the word 'could', we switch to a position of choice. It feels automatically more empowering. Rather than 'I should go to the gym', 'I could go to the gym' gives you more choice over your actions and ensures you do the things you wish to do rather than what you feel others think you should do.

- **Many of us criticise ourselves for not 'constantly growing'**, yet, as Jenny Odell so wisely says in her book *How to Do Nothing: Resisting the Attention Economy*: 'In the context of health and ecology, things that grow unchecked are often considered parasitic or cancerous. Yet we inhabit a culture that privileges novelty and growth over the cyclical and the regenerative. Our very idea of productivity is premised on the idea of producing something new, whereas we do not tend to see maintenance and care as productive in the same way.' You do not need to change to be enough. Whether you reach your milestones or not.

- **The antidote to negative self-talk and the inner critic is self-compassion.** Chapter 15 addresses this in Part Three. If the word self-compassion feels too fluffy for you, you can choose another title for it. The title I made up that helped me actually give it a go was 'How not to be a total dick to yourself'.

A Note to You

Hello!

We are nearly at the end of Part Two of this book.

In Chapter 1 we talked about relationships – the ones we didn't choose but that set us on our life path. Now we have come full circle, to talk about relationships once more.

This time, however, these relationships are the ones we choose – in dating and love.

The next chapter will start with the modern dating experience and will finish with the shared factors that affect us whether we are single, dating or in a relationship.

This feels like a fitting place to end this journey.

Dr Soph xx

10. Modern Love

Love, and the hope for connection, are perhaps the most human experiences of all. In my clinic, people say they feel stuck in their search for love.

'Dating is so painful. What's going wrong?'

'My relationships keep collapsing. I lean in, they pull away.'

'Am I too independent to be in a relationship?'

'What even is love, anyway?'

These questions come from everyone – those who are dating or have temporarily sworn against it, and also people in relationships either newly started or as old as a favourite jumper, worn soft and to your shape by your years together.

This chapter will help demystify some of the most common stumbling blocks in dating and love by talking you through the pitfalls of dating apps, how our attachment styles affect our romantic relationships and how to find out what love truly means to you.

Dating apps

Dating has never been more accessible. Decide you want to start dating at lunchtime, download an app and you can be dining with your date that evening.

Dating is a chance to connect with others. To see how

you might bring joy into each other's lives. Yet, have you ever headed into a date excited to find out about the other(s) and, a few moments (or a few dates) in, notice you suddenly switch from, *What do I think about this person?* to *Am I enough? Are they interested in me? Am I attractive to them? What do I need to do or demonstrate to make sure I am 'the one'?*

Dating apps can lead you to the love of your life. They can also lead you to feel anxious, disposable, and overwhelmed. Take care!

Have you ever forgotten to get to know your date(s) properly, instead focusing entirely on whether they will choose you? If so, you are not alone.

It isn't because we are all 'insecure and neurotic', which is what many of my friends unkindly (and inaccurately) describe themselves as.

How we feel when we date (and when we are in a long-term relationship) is due to a complex mix of factors, such as the previous experiences we had while dating (if someone cheats on you or hurts you, you are likely to be wary the next time you start dating); the timelines we talked about in the previous chapter, which leave people panicking that they only have a limited time to find the right person; whether we equate our relationship status with our worth (if this is you, remember your worth is not based on your relationship status, you are already incredible), as well as all the other information in this chapter, such as dating apps.

Modern dating apps have added ease but also complexity to dating.

You log on, the lights flash, and hopefully the matches flash up too. On 'swipe to like' dating apps, swiping and matching is the dating app equivalent to the likes and shares on social media; another peer-rating system, like Instagram, that leaves some people feeling miserable, where it's easy to believe that the 'score' we get is our self-worth. Hence more potential dopamine peaks and slumps that are likely to get us hooked in ways we discussed in Chapter 3.

Dating apps are brilliant, but not something you want to get addicted to.

Increased use of dating apps has been linked to decreased body satisfaction and increased body monitoring (continual awareness of your body), social comparison and beliefs that you are meant to match the societal beauty ideal set out in the media.

Apps have also, counter-intuitively, made some people less likely to find the suitor they are looking for, by providing a 'paradox of choice' – *Maybe the person for me is one swipe away! Maybe there's someone even better on the next swipe, or three.*

Unlike what we might imagine, increased choice isn't always a good thing.

Whenever I go to a restaurant where there are a hundred things on the menu, I suddenly have no idea where to start. I decide tentatively to have the spaghetti, then someone else at the table says they'll have the steak, and suddenly I'm stumped – *Oh God, what if that's the better option? What if I make the wrong choice?*

It can be hard enough to decide about food when there are too many options – a decision whose impact will affect less than one hour of one day of our whole life. Imagine, therefore, how the endless choice offered by dating apps can affect a decision we believe could affect the rest of our lives.

When there are seemingly so many fish in the sea, if you meet someone and there isn't an instant connection, why stick around to see if you can build one when the next person may set your heart on fire? If there's conflict, why work through it, when the next person may be instantly more aligned with your values?

The thing is, connection isn't instantaneous for everyone and sometimes takes work or a conscious decision to build something together.

The paradox of choice also risks devaluing each human on the app, as they are instantly replaceable. And many people do report feeling disposable while dating, assuming that the high turnover rate is to do with their looks, personality and social skills, rather than the complex mix of it being normal that not everyone meshes with the people they meet. This, compounded with the modern paradox of choice, means many people find it hard to settle.

Dating apps also mean we can have a tick list, and shop for someone who measures up: 'I want a redhead who's out-doorsy.' 'I want a petite blonde who's into politics.' Yet what we think we want may not be what we do want or even need.

It isn't always obvious who will light your fire. You may meet someone who doesn't fit your blonde-and-curvaceous, or tall-dark-and-handsome, criteria, but for some inexplicable reason you want to run straight into bed with them, or into your future life with them. You may meet someone who ticks all your criteria, looks perfect on paper, and feel nothing. Maybe outdoorsy or political is preferred, but what if connection and joy are awaiting you in someone who has interests that lie elsewhere?

Also, many of us don't realise that we are unconsciously drawn to what we know.

Don't be surprised if the person who really lights your fire is the one who re-enacts some of your early life experiences. This is a normal, by the way, and great for people who had positive childhood relationships. For those of us who had rejecting, chaotic or abusive childhood relationships, we need to be aware that we might on occasion be attracted to people who at first seemed nothing like our caregivers, and then, down the line, suddenly seem to be making us feel like we did when we were children. If this is you, ask yourself if you've noticed any patterns in how you date. If you identify any, ask yourself what were the first signs that your partners were rejecting, chaotic or abusive. Add those to your list of red flags. Keep an eye out for this when you date and ask your friends to support you, so they can keep an eye out for it too. This is a pattern some of us need to quit, and it can take the support of others for that to happen.

> **Dating is not like shopping. You can see a picture of a pair of shoes, know you love them in an instant and as long as they fit when you slide your toes in, hey presto their yours. You can't do this with people. True connection is about putting in the time and the effort to get to know someone and learning to accept the things that would usually put you off.**

When I work with people looking for love right now, I

318

don't just teach them about their attachment style (which we are about to revisit) or the common experience of dating people who make us feel like our caregivers did. I teach them about the paradox of choice, and how feeling disposable while dating isn't due to their 'failing'. I help them understand they will benefit from knowing in advance:

- How you want to be treated, so you can look for this when you date.
- What your red flags are, so you know when to leave.
- That apps require strong boundaries, such as plans around what time you will check the app and when you will ignore it (a survey showed people spend up to 90 minutes per day on the app, meaning it eats up your time and your attention span).
- How to practise self-compassion when dealing with the ups and downs of dating (see Chapter 15).

But also, what you hope for in a partner in terms of looks, shared hobbies and life goals etc. is important to know, and can be kept slightly flexible. Opening yourself up to dating people who could surprise you can be an important way forward.

When we date, we time-travel

Wherever you meet the person you date, there is another thing to watch out for.

When we like someone, our brain takes the smallest amount of information about the person in front of us and fills in the gaps. It creates a fantasy.

Have you ever met someone once or twice, felt you had a connection with them, then they mentioned they had some similar interests to you and suddenly you were lost in the idea of them? *Oh my God, I love camping/nature/drinking cider on park benches* (a previous prerequisite of mine – don't judge me!)/*totally niche German minimalist techno too! We have so much potential!*

Have you noticed how quickly you started dating the *idea* of the person you had in your head, rather than the person in front of you, and how quickly you got caught up in fantasies of the future? Fantasising what you will do together, where you will go, imagining your future trips abroad, that time you'll share a plate of pasta, slurping on the same strand of spaghetti and meeting for a kiss in the middle à la *Lady and the Tramp*, or whatever else you're into and hope for?

If so, this is normal! But we must try to be aware of it, as it's easy for us to get hooked on the *idea* of people and the *idea* of the future, rather than the reality of the moment and of the person we're with.

It can mean we lose sight of what is happening right now, making it even more likely that we'll forget we need to find out more about this person rather than relying on our projection.

It means we can feel distraught when that person doesn't fit the bill of the expectation and hope, or doesn't see the dream with you, or even when they just take a little longer than usual to text back.

If the relationship ends, we not only feel the hurt of an ending, we grieve the loss of a hoped-for future. The pain is less about them and more about the fantasy.

I have been both the projector and the projectee. I have

dated people and forgotten they are strangers. I have been emotionally whisked off my feet, got lost in the vision, seriously overestimated our connection and how we were 'meant for each other'. I blame the cider and park benches!

I have also dated people's *potential*. I have tried to mould them into the person and relationship I saw in our future – a terrible move. Miserable for me and really unfair on them. I barely knew these people, yet I kept trying to change them, thinking I was being helpful. I wasn't.

I've also had someone date an idea of *me*. They got so lost in their projection of hope that I was put on a pedestal early on, and from that point onwards I was a constant disappointment to them. That sucked.

It's easy for us to assume we know people when we don't. Remembering that someone is a stranger is a simple but important step for some of us while we date.

Quick tip: date the person in front of you, not their potential

- When you date, BOTH allow yourself to be excited AND remind yourself that you are getting to know the person still.
- Check in with what you know about them, not just what your brain tells you they might be in the future. Ask questions. Breathe. Move one step at a time. Date someone for who they are right now. Not for who they might be.

Attachment Styles

When it comes to dating, your attachment style may predict how quickly you get hooked or

Is it desire or just an activated attachment system?

jump ship. It may also predict how you interact with dating apps. Research is starting to show that people with an anxious attachment style spend more time on swipe-based dating apps (such as Tinder) than people with avoidant attachment styles.

When it comes to long-term relationships, your attachment style may predict how you respond to arguments and how close or distant you need to be to your significant others.

In Chapter 1 I told you that our earliest relationships form the blueprints (read: the predictions we make about people, how anxious/or not we will feel in our relationships and how we will respond, based on all of the above) of our later relationships, and that through these experiences we develop an attachment style – a way of relating to others and to ourselves that shows up throughout our lives.

I told you that:

- **People with secure attachment styles** learned within the first few years of their lives that people want to, and will, be there for them, and that relationships can be relied upon. They therefore tend to feel safe, calm and worthy in relationships and can offer and receive care and love freely. If you have a secure attachment style you may not feel the anxieties I described above.
- **People with avoidant attachment styles** learned that people can be rejecting and distant. They adapted to this

322

by becoming extremely self-reliant (smart). They may therefore seem very independent and describe themselves in this way, wanting connection but also pushing away anyone that gets too close, as 'too close' triggers an underlying nervousness or fear (that other people cannot or will not want to be there for them), which they managed in childhood through distance and self-reliance.

- **People with anxious attachment styles** learned that people may meet their needs intermittently (read: they may be emotionally present and in tune with them one moment, but not the next). For many, this means they learned that if people pull away they must lean in, taking every opportunity to connect (also smart). They may describe themselves as clingy or needy – if this is you please don't criticise yourself with these labels; this is not a flaw; this is a survival skill that helped maximise your chances of having your needs met as a child.

The secure attachment style and dating

Assuming nothing significantly devastating has happened to the person with a secure attachment style, they will remain secure and calm in relationships. If this is you, you likely believe others can be there for you and that you deserve love and attention – this is not arrogance, this is a calm knowing and reassurance.

Making friends and dating may come easily to you. You are likely to believe that other people's behaviour is not a reflection of your worth (brilliant!). You won't tend to engage in games or hot–cold behaviours, as you aren't feeling anxious and aren't trying to calm your nervous system by whatever means necessary.

You might 'couple up' quickly when dating and may not date that many people before you decide on someone (or **someones**, if you're polyamorous).

If you (we, as I fall into this category too) have an insecure attachment style, your relationship experiences may feel quite different from those with a secure attachment style. You may feel anxious or shut down, your fight–flight–freeze–fawn system activating whenever you meet a new person or have any kind of uncertainty within your relationships.

The avoidant attachment style and dating

In the dating world, the avoidant attachment style plays out in a particularly interesting way, as your brain protects you by preventing rejection by never getting too close to anybody. One way it does this is by continuously looking for all the reasons a relationship won't work. This is why you could be on a date and be put off by someone at the drop of a hat, or, if you are me, the sight of an ugly shoe – judgemental, I know! I have work to do too!

When you start dating, you may believe you want a partner but find that things keep getting in the way of you having a relationship that works out. You may see sex as a safe way to connect with people, sacrificing intimacy.

Over time people may tell you that your walls are up, or that you are emotionally distant, cold even. They may tell you that you engage in a push–pull behaviour: one moment you initiate contact with someone, you genuinely want to engage. Then, when they come close, intimacy starts to build or they say something strong or affectionate, anxiety rises in you and you suddenly shut down. You push them away, leaving them confused and hungry for emotional nourishment. This push–pull behaviour isn't that subtle either.

> **If you're dating someone with an avoidant attachment style, the push–pull behaviour may play out in the following way:**
>
> You go to sleep, the person with the avoidant attachment style looking into your eyes, telling you how incredible you are – 'You really understand me, you're so wonderful, I think about you all the time, why don't we plan to do something incredible together soon?' You wake up to find the very same person now emotionally shut down, possibly distant for days. It's like the night-time never happened.
>
> If this behaviour is genuinely down to an avoidant attachment style (and it's not just that they are messing you around), then this person will be distant for as long as it takes for their attachment system (psychology speak for their emotional response directly related to relationships) to settle. Then they will be back, able to give you their attention, until they feel too emotionally close, and temporarily shut down again.

You (the person with an avoidant attachment style) may have a belief that others are going to take away your independence and, therefore, maybe you unconsciously seek out people who can't give you any form of long-term connection.

If you date someone who clearly wants to be with you,

you may find it is manageable if the other person allows you to keep them at a distance, or allows you to be present and then disappear. However, if the person you date makes you feel they need you, you may start to feel trapped. You may want to disappear temporarily, or want to end the relationship, feeling they have confirmed your belief that you can't date, as everyone else in the world is so needy and time consuming – not knowing that underneath what you really fear is abandonment, not being supported, and what would really happen if someone got close.

Your inner critic will support the thoughts and fears you have. It may tell you: *You don't need anyone. Others can't be trusted. Only trust yourself.* Or: *Protect yourself or you'll get hurt.* It might say: *Others won't commit to you.* Or, conversely: *They'll take away your independence.* Your inner critic isn't correct. It is, in its own bizarre way, still trying to protect you. But in doing this it is likely contributing to you feeling unable to connect with others deeply, and may leave you feeling isolated.

Also, if you have an argument with someone, you are likely to remember all the negative aspects of the other person after it's done. Yep, the brain of someone who has stayed safe through avoidance is constantly trying to minimise any chance of intimacy. If this speaks to you, try to remember this, and purposefully remind yourself of the positives of the other person so that you don't buy into your brain's tendency to push people away.

If, or when, you break up with someone, your attachment system will calm down, meaning your brain doesn't have to protect you by pointing out all the negatives anymore. This can mean that the way you think about your ex suddenly shifts, leaving you remembering all the great bits and wanting them back.

People with an avoidant attachment style can become more securely attached if they date someone with a secure attachment style, as the secure person lets the avoidant person push and pull and doesn't tend to play into it.

Knowing all of this, plus dating people with secure attachment styles, has helped me immensely. My avoidant tendencies mean that in long-term relationships I have to disconnect on occasion – I go travelling on my own and have solo hobbies. I disappear for a while, then I pop back up. The difference is that now I understand the avoidant style, I know what I'm doing. I don't pull away without explanation. I explain what I need and make plans around how to meet this need while also being present to the other person's needs; sometimes they need me to call or text them each day, sometimes they need me to not disappear in the mornings.

Push-pull, but this time with compromise

Even though only a small proportion of people fall into the avoidant attachment style, they make up the largest section of the dating pool. This is because they often cycle in and out of relationships, meaning they arrive back on the dating scene regularly. So, if you are not avoidant, and you feel someone engaging in the push–pull with you, maybe they are! It doesn't mean you need to ditch them; it means you need to get good at communicating what you need from your date. If they can meet your needs, great. If not, ditch them.

The anxious attachment style and dating

If you have an anxious attachment style you may believe that romantic relationships are rare, and you may notice that you become preoccupied with people very quickly. This is solely because your brain kept you safe as a child by centring your caregivers in your mind at all times.

You may also see the absolute best in everyone you meet – 'Wow, they're so incredible. I can't wait to tell you everything about them. I'm sooooo excited!' This is a wonderful thing. However, this can mean that almost everyone lets you down, as your hopes and bars were so high in the first place.

You may also notice that you start to predict abandonment and rejection constantly, seeing it everywhere, including *what wasn't said* in text messages. When you feel anxious, if you feel someone may be pulling away, you will want to connect, finding any way you can to do so: 'Ooh, they'll like this book/ article/picture I took that looks a lot like something we once talked about. I think I'll send it to them. I'm not trying to get their attention, it's just a nice thing to do.'

In fact, someone with an anxious attachment style may behave like an excited (possibly overzealous) gardener who, on occasion, overwaters the seeds of a new relationship. Excited about the relationship, they lean in, giving it all of their attention (water). The person seems to pull away, so they lean in further (more water) – 'More water? More sun? More light? A playlist to help you grow? What do you need? Because I'm sure I can offer it.'

If the person you date shows they care, and you (the person with the anxious attachment style) like them in return, you'll notice you start to feel calm and connected and able to slow the process down (no more overwatering). However, if they're aloof or pull away further, you may notice that not only does anxiety arise, anger does too. You may feel you need to express this emotion, so the other person can know how you feel and therefore reassure you. Or you may feel you're unable to do this, in case the other person runs a mile. The problem is the feelings can get so intense that they burst out of you, and you end up swinging between anger and requests for forgiveness and love.

Your inner critic will also support your fears and beliefs. So, watch out for it. For example, it may tell you: *You're so needy, it's no surprise they don't want you.* Or: *They're losing interest, it's so obvious. If they really loved you they would . . .* When this happens, the thought-distancing techniques in Chapter 7 and the self-compassion exercises in Chapter 15 will be your friend.

Good news: If you have an anxious attachment style and someone clearly shows you they are there for you and will stick around, these alarm bells will switch off and you will feel genuinely soothed, cared for and ready for true, deep intimacy.

Bad news: If you date someone with an avoidant attachment style, you may notice you become more anxious and they become more avoidant. You lean in, they pull away; you lean in more, they pull even further, maybe shutting down, then reappearing again. You need closeness to feel safe; they need distance. This is a painful (understatement) and powerful mix. It can only be navigated through clear communication about everyone's needs.

It is very difficult to know whether someone is pulling away because they aren't interested or whether they're avoidant. One simple way to find out is to directly ask, 'Are you interested in me?'

How to become more securely attached as an adult

Adult attachment styles are stable but can change – for the better and for the worse. If you are secure and someone breaks your heart or shatters your belief systems around relationships, you could be shoved into an insecure category, either momentarily, long term or until you get therapy.

Likewise, secure people can help heal insecurely attached people. Making them feel secure enough to be able to show up without their protection strategies.

Think about your relationships. There will be certain people and places that make you feel safe and at ease. For example, you may feel more secure in platonic friendships than in romantic ones; totally anxious with certain work colleagues but confident as hell with your boss.

During times of stress, however, which dating often is, we usually revert to our earliest attachment styles.

To adapt your attachment style, you can practise the following steps:

1. **Identify your attachment style.** Learn what you can about your specific style to normalise your

---

feelings and behaviours. There are many online quizzes that will help you assess this.

2. **Think about secure role models.** List all the secure people you know who take relationships in their stride, neither 'overwatering' nor pushing people away. This could include friends, colleagues or family. Visualise the specific things they have said and done around you that make you and others feel calm and connected. Think about how they act in relationships, how they treat you and others. Are they reliable? Sensitive to other people's needs? Communicative about their own? Are they supportive or able to compromise? What do they pay attention to in relationships and what do they ignore? Do they use effective communication? Write down the answers to all of these questions. How do you feel when you're around that person and which of their characteristics you would like to adopt? Practise acting in the ways they would.

3. **Create a list of your past romantic relationships.** Amir Levine and Rachel Heller wrote a seminal book on attachment and finding love. They recommend creating a 7-column table. In column 1, list your exes and anyone you're dating currently. In column 2, write down the main features and themes you remember from each of these relationships. In column 3, focus on specific moments in each relationship that caused you to feel threatened

and anxious, or soothed and connected. In column 4, note what you did in response to each of these moments. Did you act out? Did you punish the other, hoping this would make them lean in or distance themselves? In column 5, write down whether these behaviours link to an anxious or an avoidant attachment style. In column 6, write what you lost or gained from these behaviours. Now, look over the list. Are any patterns arising? What do you need to be aware of, moving forward? Finally, complete column 7 by visualising how your secure role models may have responded if they had been in those situations. Write these down as new potential ways of responding. Imagine that you actually did this. With practice, you will find it easier to respond in these ways more naturally.

4. **Seek out securely attached people** and look out for conflicting attachment styles in relationships. Know that insecure attachment styles often gravitate to one another, as many of us confuse an activated attachment system with passion and sometimes love. Seriously, sometimes that feeling of lust or desire is actually just a complicated and unrecognised form of anxiety. A great question to ask yourself is: *Am I in lust or am I just anxious?* Conversely, when we date people who don't trigger our attachment system and make us anxious,

we may confuse this lack of anxiety with a lack of attraction. So, give people time. If you meet someone who makes you happy in other ways and you are intrigued, give them a chance. The feelings may develop into something deep and connected.

5. **Learn to communicate your needs.** Many of us have been told that when we meet the right person they will know what we want and need. It just isn't true. While people can be in sync with us, they are not us. If you feel anxious about something, tell the person you are dating. Ask them if they can work with you to address this. For example, if you want someone to text you more, ask them to text you more! If you are someone who shuts down and needs regular space to reset, ask for this too! This way you will give the other person a shot to be there for you, and you may find out faster whether you should stick around.

Also, learn how to express when you have been hurt, otherwise you will act this out in what we call protest behaviours. A funny example: my wonderful literary agent, Abigail, has a (gorgeous) Italian greyhound called Luca. Whenever Abigail goes away, Luca is upset. Then when Abigail gets back, Luca ignores her, snuffling around whoever else is there, snuggling up close to them, nose and head turned away from Abigail. This is textbook protest behaviour and we can all do this from time to time. Punishing via behaviour rather than speaking up about what we need and want.

6. **Be really bloody kind to yourself!** Remember, your attachment style comes from somewhere – your anxiety, your avoidance. Be kind to yourself.

And to everyone: Stay away from anyone who makes you feel like you're dating a slot machine. You know the people I mean – the ones who were there at first, then disappear, then message you just as you are about to give up on them. Suddenly you feel like you've hit the metaphorical jackpot, heart-shaped dollar signs in your eyes, even though this really was the least the person could do. You respond excited then they disappear again. If this feels like more than an avoidant attachment style, as they haven't told you they like you, yet have been keeping you on hold for quite some time, ask them to stop disappearing, to be more reliable, and if it doesn't get any better ... ditch them.

We need to get better at telling people what we need in relationships. We also need to get better at leaving the people who continuously treat us badly, and who don't and won't change when we explain what we truly need from them.

Quick check-in. How's your head? How's your heart? What's happening for you right now? If you need to pause, ground, come back later, I will still be here for you when you're ready, so do what you need. If you need to message a friend to say hi, reminding yourself you are not alone, do that now too.

What even is love?

> *We learn about love in childhood. Whether our homes are happy or troubled, our families functional or dysfunctional, it's the original school of love.*
>
> —BELL HOOKS

No wonder dating and relationships can feel so flipping difficult. There are so many factors at play. Especially in modern dating. Whatever stage of dating you are in, there is a huge question I want to finish with . . .

What even is love?

Seriously, what do you think it is? Your answer to this question will affect how you behave in your relationships.

If you believe it is a physical experience, you might wait until you feel something in your body that tells you you are in love. If this physical feeling disappears, you may think your love has too, assuming this is a sign that the relationship has run its course.

If you believe love is possessive, you may interpret someone's jealousy of your connection to others, and their desire to control your social diary, as true love. True commitment.

If you believe it is wild, uncontrollable and passionate, you may interpret whirlwind emotions and arguments as a positive sign in your relationships.

If you believe that 'love is a ball and chain' or 'love hurts' or 'love will make you weak', or if you were ever punished and told, 'I'm only doing this because I love you', you may believe that love is painful.

If you believe that love is service, and that you deserve service, you may expect to sit around while your partner carries out the household chores, bringing you everything you wish for and need. It could be the other way round, of course, should you believe that, once in love, you are meant to be the one carrying out service.

If you saw Disney films, and learned that men rescued women from their poor, lowly, trapped lives and whisked them away to be princesses with a pure and enduring love, you may have ... well ... an unrealistic notion of what it's like to be in a relationship!

What we believe about love derives from what we learned about love. What did love look like in your family? Was it nurturing? Was it affectionate? Was it there for you no matter what? If so, what did you learn that love could look like for you? Did you pick up expectations from TV shows and films? Probably. We all do. How do your answers to these questions affect how you feel about love and relationships now?

I worked with someone who 'so wanted a relationship and to find love'. Yet, they were stuck in a pattern. Whenever they started something new that had a chance at success, they suddenly 'wanted out'. Or, conversely, they found that they were dating 'the eternal bachelor', the ones who made it clear they would never settle down.

When we looked into this, they realised that on the surface they had bought into the Disney version of love, and they thought this is what they had been seeking. But underneath this, their beliefs were conflicted, as the relationships they had seen at home were full of conflict. To them, 'love' was unkind and painful, and when they thought about it, it made them feel claustrophobic.

When relationships were going well, and connection was truly possible, the old fears started to emerge, they panicked and pushed people away – a confusing mix of: 'I like you and want to be with you, but please get away from me, as I can't bare the risk of repeating what I saw growing up.' It also meant they often dated people who could never commit to them – 'Phew, danger averted, they won't trap me.'

Like so many of us, my client needed to unpack their old beliefs; they needed an upgrade in their understanding of love.

My favourite description of love is written by M. Scott Peck, who said love is 'the will to extend one's self for the purpose of nurturing one's own or another's spiritual growth'.

Love is a verb

Love is something that we can choose to be doing every moment of every day; something that is there to benefit and nurture ourselves, another or many others.

If you think about love in terms of nurturing your own or another person's spirit, personhood, soul, the essence of us/them – whatever word you use to describe that very central part of what makes people *people* – does it change something for you?

It did for me. And it did for my client too. It simplified the concept, and suddenly meant we saw relationships as a place to connect and nurture. A journey, with each moment a new chance to show love.

When in relationships, it made me think, *How can I nurture that person in a way that suits who they are, and what they want in life? How can I connect with them right now and show them I'm here.* It made me realise that, rather than trying to read their minds, I could ask them what they want and need. Suddenly I had a shot at the most human experience of all – I had hope that I could find and create love.

The final new rules

People often say, why plan around dating and relationships? Shouldn't it be natural? If dating works out for you that way, brilliant! But a lot of us fall into old traps: we confuse anxiety with lust and love; we chase the people who push us away, and we push away the people who run towards us. So, we have to do the work! Here are your final new rules:

- **Immediate attraction is not a sign that they are 'the one'.** It may be a sign that your attachment system is activated.
- **There is no such thing as 'the one'.** There are many possible 'ones' for you – how fab is that!
- **When you date, watch out for time-travel!** Discovering who people are over time is actually meant to be one of the joys of dating. Don't let your past experiences and your brain's determination to time-travel ruin this moment.
- **You can 'earn' secure attachment** by making sense of your childhood experiences (which we have been working on throughout this book), understanding how they influence how you feel and behave in relationships,

and choosing to practice mindfulness to notice and let go of old patterns. To start practising mindfulness now, turn to Chapter 13. Read *Attached: Are You Anxious, Avoidant or Secure? How the Science of Adult Attachment Can Help You Find – and Keep – Love* by Amir Levine and Rachel Heller, to understand attachment in more depth.

- **Dating is two-way.** You aren't there to find out if you got the job. Or to prove they should pick you. You're there to interview them too, and find out, for real, who they are.

- **If you don't like someone after the first few dates, don't 'ghost' them.** I know it can be hard to tell people you're just not that into them, but disappearing on people is painful and unnecessary. If you don't want to see someone again, simply message them and say: 'Hi, it was great to meet you. I loved hearing about _____ [insert something you liked hearing about during your date, e.g. their band, their failed attempt at baking during the COVID-19 lockdown]. I didn't feel the spark of chemistry I'm looking for right now, which I think you didn't feel either. You seem like a brilliant person. I wish you the best in the future. xx'. You can copy this directly into your message if you want. Also, dating regularly can be exhausting, so be really kind to yourself while you do this. If you let the occasional date fizzle and don't end it perfectly – totally fine as well.

- **If while dating someone you start to feel like they don't like you, read this** from the wise and wonderful poet Vean Ima Torto: 'When you're not their cup of tea, do not reinvent yourself as their cup of coffee. Stay true. Stay you.'

- **While dating, ensure you work on all areas of your identity**, otherwise it may shift into being all about the relationship, and this will derail you. If you can focus on all parts of you, and the things that nourish you, you will be able to stay more grounded. Also, there is nothing sexier than someone who knows what they like.

- **All relationships take work.** They take time and care. And at the same time, not all relationships take a *lot* of work. This is another 'both/and'. If you don't put in any effort, your relationships will obviously flop. However, this doesn't mean all relationships are hard or should be a real challenge. So, relationships take work, but shouldn't be so hard that you are exhausted and stressed out all the time.

- **We all have different experiences that affect what we expect in relationships, what love means and what we hope for.** Ask people what they hope for, what love was like for them growing up. And some hard and fast rules: possessiveness and/or jealousy is not 'proof' that someone really, really likes you. The book *All About Love* by bell hooks is a must-read if you want to explore the meaning of love in more depth.

- **Monogamy is not the only way, you can choose what your relationships look like.** You could be monogamous, in an open relationship, a polyamorous relationship, you could swing. There are so many ways that relationships can work. What matters is that you and your partner(s) are happy and feel emotionally safe.

- **Desire can fade but that doesn't mean the relationship is over.** If this happens to you, you can work on this. Conversation is key. Talk about what you would like to be happening with your partner and make a plan. Schedule in some time for sex or gentle touch or other forms of contact, and see how it goes. See the book *Mind the Gap* by Dr Karen Gurney for specific guidance. And if your sex drives are non-negotiable, you can negotiate, should you wish to, to open the relationship up to meet sexual needs in other agreed spaces.

- **No one can read our minds, so say what you want and need in relationships.** If we do not tell our partners what we want or need, or how we wish to be cared for and supported, we cannot expect them to know. So many of us get cross that others don't know how to support us, but if they aren't us, we may need to show them!

- **A relationship that ends is not a failed relationship.** People say their marriage 'failed', or that they feel shame for the end of a relationship. But what if the relationship was good for the time it was around, and if endings happen and this is okay? Of my clients, it tends to be the ones who have been through marriage and divorce that go on to have the most nuanced and profound relationships. Maybe they realised the 'happily ever after' narrative they were sold didn't work for them, and went in search of a more authentic life – hell yeah!

- **People grow and change.** This means they can grow apart too, and this is okay!
- **Know your red flags and alarm bells in relationships** – the things that have happened in the past that made you realise the person was going to trigger old fears, old patterns, making you hungry. Share them with friends so you can support each other to notice patterns. Leave relationships when you see those patterns. Also, however, if you miss them, do not beat yourself up – this happens. It's very human.
- **Remember, your worth is not dictated by your relationship status** – being single can be utterly fantastic.

A final word: you deserve love. You always have.

Don't forget to love yourself

Thinking of love as a verb, the way M. Scott Peck does, can make all those self-love posts on the internet seem possible . . .

'Just love yourself.'

'I'm in love with . . . me!'

'Just own it, babe.'

. . . statements that can seem fake, toxically positive, 'basic' or too big a leap, but actually *do* hold a truth that love (including self-love) is a possibility and an option at any point.

The reality for many of us is that feeling love for ourselves every minute of every day feels impossible. But thinking of love as a continuous opportunity, rather than a feeling, means that we don't have to expect the warm and fuzzies about ourselves all the time.

For me, it means that the days when I feel unsettled, unsure, unhappy, angry, self-critical, I know there is always the choice to offer myself love.

Instead of asking, 'What's wrong with me? Why do I feel this?' I instead ask, 'What do I need right now? What would make me feel soothed right now – a cup of tea? A walk? A chat with a friend? A bath? Do I need to scream into my pillow, rage-journal or go boxing?

I can offer myself an act of care or a moment of stillness, whatever I need in that moment.

You can do this too.

If your answer to the question 'What do I need right now?' is 'I don't know', this is the perfect opportunity to throw your hand down into that coping-skills jar we talked about making in Chapter 8.

When we came into the world, we did not choose who supported us, or how they would support us. We did our best to lure them in – with our cheekiest grin, our cutest giggle. Yet, we could not control whether they would meet our needs in the way we needed them to.

Contrary to popular belief. You do not need to love yourself before you let someone else love you. You are deserving of love however you feel right now.

As adults, we may feel the remnants of those early days, and we still cannot control how other people will feel about us, or how they will treat us.

But . . .

- We can decide to give ourselves the love we deserve. And oh, you do deserve it!
- We can decide to surround ourselves with the people we choose, who we know care about us.
- We can decide to ask how others wish to be loved, and we can be there in the ways they wish us to be there for them.
- We can decide to communicate what we wish for and need to the people we care about too, and we can choose to stay around those who are able to meet us where we are at.

When we feel anxious, overwhelmed, sad, or another feeling, we can **both** co-regulate as we did as a child, surrounding ourselves with friends, having a cuddle and a potential cry over a cup of tea (the main British coping skill) **and** we can be the person that we needed all along.

We can offer ourselves the soothing and love we so needed from the moment we took our first breath.

A Note to You

Hello!

You finished Part One and Part Two! You now have more information about yourself and what it is to be human than most people gather in their lifetimes. Wow!

Were there pages where you saw yourself in every word, and other moments where you caught yourself thinking, *Huh? People do that?!* or even *What's she on about? That's not a thing!*

I imagine it was a little of all three. A little secret: until very recently, I didn't believe any of the stuff about our childhood affecting our here and now. I also didn't see the point in talking about it. *What's done is done . . . Why are some therapists so obsessed with the past?*

It took me many years of studying and reading the research papers and books to learn what I've shared with you in this book. And it took seeing the benefit that I and others gained from understanding ourselves through the lens of the past – recognising that we are normal, that there are good reasons we feel the way we do – for me to realise that revisiting the past and the pains isn't 'depressing', and doesn't 'keep you stuck there', as I'd previously thought. Instead it can liberate you.

So . . . if some stuff in here is a leap for you, it was a leap for me once too. And that's okay!

Maybe one day you'll suddenly think, *Eek! That thing I read does match what I'm doing*, and maybe you won't continue to do it. This book is here for you to take what you need to make your life make more sense. And it's here for you to return to whenever you need.

Before we move forward, I want to summarise the entire book to this point in a few sentences.

There are things in life that shape us: our childhood home, our school and the people who influence our identity development during our teens, the media we consume on a daily basis, the structures, prejudices and beliefs in our society that affect us every day, and the life events that come out of the blue. And each of these things can affect our internal experiences, our emotions, our thoughts, our coping skills, the way we talk to ourselves, what we expect of ourselves, and the way we date and relate. Which then affect how we interpret the behaviours of others, and how we treat them, creating a knock-on effect in the world around us.

As our brain likes to keep us on autopilot, the majority of us walk around unaware of these interactions. Sometimes we sleepwalk through our own lives. And as psychology has been kept behind closed doors for so long, few people have the tools to change, even when they become aware and would like to know how to act in a way that is aligned with what they want, rather than what they have been told to want and believe.

But you don't have to sleepwalk through your life. You can choose. And you have the tools right in the palm of your hand.

So, now you have all this information at your fingertips, what are you going to do? Are you going to put the book down and venture out into the world for a bit? Are you going to journey straight forward into Part Three, to equip yourself with the coping skills I wish we were given in school? Whatever works for you, works for me too.

Much love, Dr Soph xx

Part Three

How You Can Move Forward:

Your New Toolbox with Go-To Techniques

> *Real change, enduring change, happens one*
> *step at a time.*
> —RUTH BADER GINSBURG

Understanding ourselves and why we think, feel and act in specific ways has a profound impact on our lives. However, no real, life-changing experience can occur without adding action into the mix.

Reading psychology or self-help books without taking action is like learning all about a country without ever really going there. This means you can never know if what you have learned is really the truth or really worth bringing into your life.

I have been guilty of this too. I realised, not so long ago, that reading these kinds of books can be another form of avoidance, because we can use them to intellectualise our experience without doing any of the actions needed to move through our actual pain or change things.

Sometimes the act of buying a new self-help book or lining up a podcast is enough to make us feel a bit better. This means we don't address what we need to address and, when the discomfort arises again, we just go online and cue up the next book or podcast.

You're past that point now – well done! This is where real change happens.

The chapters in this section are organised in the way I think is most useful for learning the techniques within them. They start by showing you how to ground yourself when your emotions threaten to overwhelm you. While some of the skills, such as dunking your face in iced water (yes, I suggest this) will ground you in an instant, others will take time and practice.

You can move through this part of the book chapter by chapter, for a comprehensive skill set. Or you can dip in and out, taking what you need in the moment.

If you are working to stop avoiding the places you associate with panic, or another scary emotion, remember there is a step-by-step guide for you in the Appendix, which includes how to use your imagination to kick-start the process.

Why we have to practise, practise, practise

Almost every time someone departs my clinic for the first time equipped with what they need, they leave excited . . . and then they return, saying, 'It didn't work.'

Your brain will resist some of your new strategies at first.

Why? Because it has been using the fight-flight-freeze-fawn response as a coping and survival skill for millennia.

It may therefore look at your new strategy and say: 'Hang on, there's a tiger at our door and you want to mindfully breathe your way out of this life-or-death situation? Yeah right! I've been doing this my way for thousands of years and you've done that breathing exercise, what, twice? As if I'm going to let you do that!'

It may then double down momentarily on its grip over you, upping the fear feelings in your body or the stream of negative thoughts – *THIS ISN'T WORKING. IT NEVER WILL!* – as it tries to take back control. This is normal and nothing to worry about.

I remember the first few times I tried to use breathing exercises to manage my panic attacks. I remember them because two breaths in I would stop, as the panic felt like it was getting worse. It made sense that it seemed worse. It was the first time I had made myself focus on my chest (where the panic sat, a place I tried to avoid paying attention to at all costs) and this attention made my fear much worse – *Oh God, it's so tight, my heart is racing, this is so bad.*

I had been told that panic will always pass if you let it, so I decided to imagine my panic (and other emotions) as a wave in the ocean. As I did my breathing exercises, and the intensity of my feelings grew, I imagined the wave getting bigger, knowing that if I kept breathing the wave would eventually crest, and the panic would start to fade. The first time this worked I could not believe what had happened. My therapist had been right! The breathing exercises had seemed to make it worse at first, but when I stuck with them, I learned they could and would work for me. From then on I did them as if my life depended on them, which isn't an understatement, by the way – it very much felt like my life did depend on it.

Whenever you try a new coping strategy, know that the feelings may intensify at first, but that this will pass. Know that you are going to need to practise, practise and practise some more. You will get there.

Practise your new strategies when you feel calm. Especially the strategies linked to grounding, triggering the relaxation response and mindfulness. Practising them over and over at this time will make them easier to use, and more effective when you need them during times of distress. Don't wait until you need them.

Please, **avoid the urge to practise only when you are feeling emotional or anxious.** You might think, *But I feel good right now. I don't want to do something that will remind me of the times I feel bad.* This is a fair point, but it's a common thought that gets in the way of people putting in the practice they need, which will help them cope and stop them feeling so bad in the long term.

If you leave practice until you're struggling, it'll be much more difficult, as you'll be in autopilot, with the fight-flight-freeze-fawn response running the show. This makes it feel nigh-on impossible. If you're having panic attacks, or are generally really stressed out, and it feels like there's no time when you feel calm, that's okay – you can start right away anyway. Once these skills become second nature to you, they will be easy to use.

Maximising your chances

Motivation and commitment are required whenever we start a new skill and try to make a new habit.

So is forgiveness.

Yep, I want you to **forgive yourself** before you start any new habit in life because **you are going to slip up** and fall back into your old ways sometimes, especially if you are stressed out. And that is okay!

Say you're hoping to cultivate a new skill in mindfulness and breathing exercises. One moment you'll be breathing your way through an emotion or a stressful period in your life, and the next you may find yourself taking out the stress you feel on the person closest to you, or even compulsively scrolling on Instagram, maybe even checking your ex's Instagram account – never a good idea!

Don't beat yourself up when you do this. Simply notice that you are not practising your new skill, and then start practising!

New habits are most likely to be made when:

- **You feel energised.** Try to be well-slept and well-nourished. Try to start new habits when you don't have too many tasks competing for your attention and energy at the same time.
- **You are held accountable.** Find others who can start your new habits with you, hold each other accountable and support each other through the low-energy days.
- **You are prepared for barriers.** Look at what's in your diary that may disrupt your new daily practice. For example, if you want to start practising mindfulness

every day but have family coming to stay – and know you won't have a moment to yourself – plan ahead, decide how you'll manage this.

- **You note down every small success.** Your brain may not focus on small successes by itself (as it is so often predicting and remembering the negative). Each time something goes well (e.g. you did your breathing practice, or had a cold shower, and it slowed your panic response) spend 10 seconds focusing on it, really thinking about the success and the feeling.

- **You reward yourself.** When a new activity isn't fun or rewarding in itself we don't look forward to it, and it's easy to let our practice slide. Choose something you can do immediately after each mindfulness, breathing or other practice that feels good. The rewards don't have to be big. Mine are usually calling a friend, dancing around my room to loud music and going to the dog park to look at all the furry friends. I will never be the woman who does 50 crunches after breakfast but, with the right incentive (money, bribes, puppies), I just might. Your rewards have to work for you, and not everyone has to agree on whether they are 'good' or not. For example, you may worry that your rewards are counterproductive, such as having a whipped-cream latte or fries and a burger after going for a run. However, if you are running because you value moving your body and committing to a hobby, then having a whipped-cream latte that makes you feel happy and rewarded is a brilliant choice. The most important thing is that the reward occurs immediately after the new behaviour, so your brain learns to associate the two things. In the future the reward will hopefully motivate you to practice.

- **You start with a very small step** and then build from there.

To make a habit-like practice stick you must make it small enough for it to be unfailingly consistent from the very beginning. Floss just one tooth, do just two push-ups, walk for three minutes, drink just one glass of water each day, write a single paragraph, or perhaps, practice just one measure of music for 5 or 10 minutes.

—DR B. J. FOGG

Floss one tooth! Why? Because consistency is the most important thing here, and we often start off too big. This is what I see every day. People start off committed – day one, they journal for 45 minutes. Day two and three, they do the same. Day four, they genuinely don't have 45 minutes, so they skip it altogether. On day five, writing for 45 minutes suddenly seems like a big task. The practice is dropped.

It's better to do something for 5–10 minutes, 5 days a week than 45 minutes once or thrice.

Whatever you choose to do, breakdown the change you want to see in your life into manageable and realistic steps. Focus on the frequency of your practice rather than the duration. Gradually increase the task when you can unfailingly repeat the first step.

Start so small that the first step barely disrupts your usual life at all. Build from there. Start now!

11. Grounding Exercises

These exercises:

- **Create an immediate sense of grounding and safety.** If you feel like you are in an emotional emergency, these skills are for you.
- **Are helpful for all forms of feeling emotionally overwhelmed,** including panic attacks, feelings of rage, dissociation, flashbacks, other trauma responses, and managing urges linked to substance use and self-harm.

When we start to feel overwhelmed by our emotions or thoughts, we can feel as if we're on a runaway train, hurtling down the tracks, getting faster and faster, with no way of slowing down.

When this happens, it's as though we've lost connection with the present – as though everything around us has temporarily stopped making sense. Words are suddenly hard to process, sentences hard to construct, as the only thing in our mind is the emotion we feel in the moment we are in. No amount of 'thinking our way out of the situation' is going to work when we are in this state, as our brain isn't thinking any more – it's in survival mode. Fight. Flight. Freeze. Fawn.

Whatever emotion is consuming us in those moments of overwhelm – whether it's anxiety, anger, jealousy, despair, or whether you are dissociating or having flashbacks – we are going to need something that will bring us back to the present, and back to safety, fast. Something that will help us apply the brakes, stopping our metaphorical runaway train in its tracks.

This section will give you the grounding techniques you need to do exactly that.

Each of these strategies asks you to look outside yourself and away from the emotional experience. They are the opposite of breathing exercises and mindfulness, which require you to focus inwards by asking you to concentrate on the breath and the sensations in your body.

Sometimes focusing inwards only increases distress. This is particularly common for people who have experienced trauma, where focusing on their breath and body may trigger trauma memories leading to more panic and overwhelm, not less. Therefore, the techniques in this chapter use external features, such as what you can see and touch, to avoid that kind of retriggering, safely bringing you back into the present moment.

We are starting with grounding exercises and other techniques to help you apply the breaks for two reasons:

1. We all need to be able to know we have access to safety even in our darkest moments, hopefully in advance of that need.
2. Without feeling like we have a firm foot on the ground,

we will never feel safe enough to work on the other coping strategies detailed in Part Three that will help us long-term.

Here's how you apply the brakes to the runaway train.

54321 Technique

My favourite coping technique is the 54321 technique, as you do not need to use anything other than what is around you at the time. As with all coping strategies, this will work best if you practise it in advance – in other words, before you actually need it.

How to do it

Look around you. And without rushing:

Name 5 things you can see. Either say them out loud or to yourself. Really look, take your time. They can be anything in your visual field. There is no right or wrong answer. For example: *I can see a bus. I can see a table. I can see a . . .*

Name 4 things you can touch. Choose different items. Touch them. Feel them under your fingers. Notice the sensation. Name the items you're touching and describe what they feel like. For example: *I can feel the wood of the table – it feels smooth. I can feel the fabric of my top – it's soft and fleecy. I can feel . . .*

Name 3 things you can hear. You may have to listen really hard for sounds, depending on your location. You can include your breath, your heartbeat. Notice the sounds. Say them to yourself. If a judgement comes up, notice it and move onto the next item. For example: *I can hear a bird singing in a tree. I can hear an aeroplane flying overhead. I can hear . . .*

Name 2 things you can smell. Purposefully smell something near you. You can smell your hand or top if there isn't anything around you that is easy to grab and/or sniff. You can also carry something strong-smelling with you if you need to do this often. Name the things you can smell. For example: *I can smell garlic cooking. I can smell the roses in the garden . . .*

Name 1 thing you can taste. Purposefully taste something. If you don't have a drink or other thing to taste, notice if your mouth has a flavour (like toothpaste). Otherwise, say your favourite thing to taste. For example: *I can taste my tea – it is milky but strong. I like to taste Grandma's roast potatoes.*

If you need to, repeat this. You can do this as many times as you need. You're okay; you just need to reconnect with the now and this technique will help you do that.

Adaptations: if you cannot use one of your senses, don't worry, simply skip that step and move onto the next.

Why does this work?

When you are flooded with emotion, your brain is solely focused on surviving the threat it thinks you're in. By turning your attention to items in your environment that are safe, you start sending signals to the brain that you too are safe. But more than that, you use every sense to do this and to come back into the present moment, out of your emotional response and into the world again.

Personalising the 54321 technique

If you know you're going to need to ground yourself in advance – for example, during a stressful week at work, or before, during or after a presentation you've been feeling anxious about, or if you have decided today is the day you will do that thing you've been avoiding for forever (the London Underground was my nemesis but you will have your own), or simply because you know your anxiety or scary thoughts have been bad recently – it's always good to be prepared with solid coping skills that you know can help you.

I recommend you write down the 54321 steps on a piece of paper, take a screenshot and have it as a background on your phone. This way you won't need to remember it when your fight-flight-freeze-fawn is screaming.

You can also carry around items that will help ground you, personalising your 54321 grounding experience so you'll always have the things you find grounding on hand.

Some people carry smooth stones or soft items in their pockets that make them feel soothed when they stroke them. Others wear elastic bands around their wrists that they can snap when they have a sudden burst of feeling, to draw them away from an urge (such as the urge to drink when they're working to become sober, or the urge to self-harm, if this has been their emotional release-valve in the past) that is threatening to overwhelm them.

Some people carry lavender oil, others perfume, or any

scent that soothes their soul. If you do this, make sure to switch the smells every so often. For example, you could use lavender one week, lemon another week, and bergamot another. Sticking with the same fragrance may mean you begin to associate stress with that specific smell, rendering it unhelpful to you in the future. Avoid this by having a few different scents to hand.

You can do this exercise alone or with someone you trust.

In fact, if you're reading this and thinking of someone you know who sometimes needs to apply the brakes to their emotional state, practise this exercise with them. Kids really love the 54321, so this isn't just reserved for adults and their emotions.

Submerge Your Face in Iced Water

This will ground you fast, possibly faster than the 54321, as yes, you guessed it, it involves dunking your face and/or body in ice-cold water.

It helps if you feel a panic attack building, or anger coursing through your veins, or the urge for another drink, hit or other form of fast relief.

How to do it

Fill a sink or bowl with cold water. Add ice. You do not want the water to be freezing (keep it above 10 degrees Celsius or 50 degrees Fahrenheit).

Hold your breath, lean forwards and submerge your face under water for around 20–60 seconds, depending on what's possible for you. Lift, breathe, repeat if necessary.

If you can't set this up, or know that submerging your face will trigger more distress, you can still lean forwards and hold your breath (if this feels safe, otherwise don't) but this time place an ice pack over your eyes – or anything else from the freezer. Bag of peas, anyone?

You can hold an ice cube and see how it feels in your hands, how it melts. If you don't have access to those, a blast of an icy shower will do.

I realise none of this sounds fun, but they work and that's what matters!

Why does this work?

For those of you who can swim, have you noticed that diving into a pool, a lake or the sea rapidly soothes your internal state? Think about the last time you plunged with intention into the water, fingers hitting the water first, then your face ... how did you feel?

I am in no way graceful, so I don't really dive, but even my belly flops can shift how I feel. This is because the sudden change in temperature and the contact with the water activates the mammalian dive reflex.

The mammalian dive reflex is incredible and is in all air-breathing vertebrates, such as seals, otters, dolphins, ducks and ... you!

It developed as a survival strategy. When it is triggered, our breathing slows, our heart rate too, and oxygen is sent towards the brain and the heart, meaning, should you need to, you can survive without breathing much longer than you would above water.

It is triggered whenever our breath is held and water touches our nostrils and face.

And here's the important part, the reason we choose to subject ourselves to an icy shock at a time where it feels like the last thing we'd wish to do: it can drop our heart rate by 10–25 per cent, a huge and deeply relaxing shift, and it sends the blood from the limbs back to the heart, which, if you remember what I said in Chapter 7, is the opposite of what happens during the fight-flight part of the threat response. That muscle tension, that shakiness and achiness that can accompany overwhelm, suddenly drops. Sudden calm left in its wake.

Some people swear by ice-cold showers each day, and this may be one of the reasons why.

A Safe-Place Meditation

This guided meditation involves visualising a place where you feel safe, grounded and calm, a place you can go to (in your mind) any time you feel frightened or emotionally unsafe in any way.

This is a particularly useful exercise for anyone who struggles with other forms of meditation that focus on the breath, the body or something else internal.

As with all the skills in this book, the more you practise this exercise the more quickly you will be able to access a place in your mind that creates a tether to calm you in your time of need.

I recommend reading the script and adapting it to suit your needs before you do anything else. Read it, see how it sounds to you, notice and remove (cross out) anything that makes you feel scared or doesn't feel like it applies to you.

Then think about the place you are going to choose as your safe-place. I don't recommend that this is your home or your bed, for two reasons.

Firstly, your safe-place needs to be as pure and as calming as it can possibly be. Homes and bedrooms sometimes aren't purely calming. We may argue there, feel anxious there, lie awake fretting through the night there, making our safe-place suddenly not so safe.

Secondly, even if home and bed are pure magic for you, with zero negative associations, we don't want to start associating your bed and home with the stress you may feel in the moments you practise this exercise.

It can be anywhere else. If you can think of somewhere outdoors that makes you feel safe (nature is proven to naturally soothe us), this is a great place to start. Maybe a beach, a forest, a patch of grass near a lake, a garden or a park. Or maybe this place is indoors, somewhere you have been in the past that reminds you of a special time. You don't need to have been to this place before, by the way; it's somewhere for you to create, and what you create is up to you.

Each time you use this meditation you can add more details. You can build on it, plant flowers or trees, or add rooms – whatever feels good. You can also invite someone, or a pet, into the imagery whenever you wish; someone that makes you feel safe and calm.

If this place ever starts to feel like it needs an update, e.g. if it starts to remind you of feeling anxious, you can create a new place at any time.

Once you have decided on your place, cross out the parts of the script that you don't feel suit you.

If you're able to, grab your phone or laptop and record yourself reading the script out loud so you can listen to it and be guided through it each day – because remembering scripts when in the depths of emotion can feel impossible.

Or, get someone who makes you feel soothed to read it for you. I always record these for my clients, as it means they can take the soothing quality of our sessions out into the world with them. So, if you have someone who can do this for you, please ask. I know I would be deeply honoured if a friend of mine asked me to do this for them.

Listen to the safe-place imagery every day, or as many times a day as you need to, if things are really difficult.

Are you ready? Here's the exercise.

How to do it

Sit or lie down somewhere that feels comfortable. Make sure you feel supported if you are sitting up.

Either close your eyes or lower your gaze so that your eyes are still open – if you feel scared at any point, or feel over-whelmed, simply open your eyes and look at a patch of ground in front of you, or wherever feels good.

Breathe, remind yourself that you are safe and in control of this exercise. You can stop at any time.

If it feels safe to, take 3 slow deep breaths, inhaling slowly, exhaling fully.

Imagine a place where you feel calm, where you feel peaceful and safe. What's the first place that comes to mind? It's okay if it's somewhere you haven't been before, or if it's somewhere you've created purely for yourself. Wherever you choose, know that no one else can enter this safe-place without your permission, and that this place will always be there for you, and will always offer you peace.

Maybe you've chosen somewhere outside – a garden, a park, a beach, a field or somewhere in the mountains. Whatever it is, allow yourself to start noticing what's there. The more times you come to this place, the more detail you can add to the picture.

What can you see? What colours and shapes can you see?

If there are leaves, flowers, plants, trees or sand, pay attention to them. How do they look?

Are there any people nearby? Is a friend with you? A beloved pet? Or are you alone? If someone is with you, notice them, feel the warmth of their presence. If you are alone, notice how safe you feel in your own presence.

What time of year is it? Is it summer? Is it autumn? Or is it another time?

What can you hear? What sounds are around you? Are there birds chirping nearby? Can you hear the breeze or running water? What sounds are furthest away, and which are closer? Is it silent?

What can you smell? If there are flowers nearby, can you smell them? How does the air smell? Is it fresh? Floral? Salty?

What can you feel? Can you feel a warm or cool breeze on your skin?

What does the ground feel like beneath you? Are you standing on soil? On sand? On grass? Something else? Do you have shoes on or are you barefoot? If there is water nearby, what does it feel like on your skin?

Notice all of your senses and how this place makes you feel calm and grounded.

If you wish to, imagine sitting or lying down on the ground in your safe-place. Notice how sitting or lying on the ground makes you feel. Notice the warmth of the ground and how it warms you too. Notice how it holds you, making you feel even more safe and relaxed than you did before. Notice how the tension leaves your body as it is released into the ground.

Can you still hear the sounds around you?

Can you still smell the smells?

Can you now see the sky too, as you lie there? What colour is the sky? Is the sun out? Can you feel its warmth on your skin? Are there any trees above you? Or anything else in the sky? Notice whatever is there.

If you want to, name this place. Give it a name that you can use to remind yourself of this place and help you return to it when you need to in the future.

Stay here for as long as you wish, enjoying the safety and peace you feel in this place.

When you're ready to leave, simply open your eyes fully and bring your attention to the room or wherever you are.

Know you can return at any time. This is your safe-place.

Why does this work?

In the safe-place meditation, we harness the power of the imagination and we visualise lots of the things we find make us feel safe in our lives.

We also use all of our senses to ground ourselves in the moment we are visualising, making it feel like we're actually there. Giving our brain a chance to say, *Safety, finally.* A deep and deserved exhale.

Did you know that simply thinking about beloved

memories from the past can bring up positive emotions, as we relive those moments and the nostalgia floods in? Using our imagination and memories helps change our mood, and, when we visualise safety, we increase our feelings of safety.

This exercise has been reported to decrease distress and increase people's sense of control, which is deeply important for anyone who has experienced trauma – which almost always involves a profound loss of control. They learn they have a place to escape to where they feel calm and safe, even when our world is totally unstable.

12. Breathing Exercises and Relaxation Skills

These exercises:

- **Help trigger relaxation** in the body and the breath, and **switch off the fight-flight-freeze-fawn response.**
- **Are particularly helpful for managing stress, anxiety, anger, panic attacks, poor sleep** and other experiences that cause extreme distress, such as intrusive thoughts and health conditions.

Caution: for those of you who do not feel emotionally or physically safe focusing on your body or breath, do not start here. Start with the grounding exercises.

When our fight-flight-freeze-fawn response is activated, our whole body-state changes. We shift from feeling relaxed, calm and open into preparing to fight, run, freeze or please.

Our breathing changes – we take in short, shallow breaths, gathering the oxygen we would need to fight or run for our lives.

Our heart races, pumping oxygen to our muscles, leaving us tight in the chest and potentially shaking, as tension builds inside our body.

To stop the threat response, we either need to burst into action, exercising hard and fast – as this will signal to the brain that you have fought and/or run, and survived, meaning the threat response can be switched off – or we need to trigger the relaxation response.

The exercises in this chapter are not solely for people who feel acutely anxious or distressed. The pressures of modern living mean that many of us, who wouldn't call ourselves anxious or distressed, are stress-breathing without realising.

Are you stress-breathing?

Let's find out . . .

Pay attention to your body.

Now take a deep breath in and a deep breath out. Fill your lungs all the way to the top and then let it all go. Do it again, breathing in and breathing out.

Did anything move? Did your shoulders move up and then drop down? If so, take the next inhale and exhale and try to keep your shoulders still.

Now, place your right hand on your upper chest and your left on your lower ribs. This time pay attention to your hands as you breathe.

Breathe in fully, exhale fully.

Which hand moved the most? Was it the upper hand or the lower?

Most people who live busy or tense lives breathe into their

shoulders and the top of their chest (their upper hand), which is a sign that our muscles are tense, and that we are breathing as though stressed.

If you did that, don't worry, it's common.

Take a moment now to bring some relaxation into your muscles. Purposefully circle your shoulders forwards, then up to your ears, letting them drop backwards and down on your exhale. Do this one more time, circling them forwards, up and back. Now, gently look to the left, to the centre, then to the right, and back again. Circle your shoulders again, and finally check your jaw; unclench it and unstick your tongue from the roof of your mouth (maybe even stick your tongue out and waggle it around). We carry a lot of tension in our shoulders, neck and face, so add these little movements into your day if you can.

The tendency to shallow-breathe, and the stressful nature of so many of our lives, means we need to actively learn how to breathe into our full lung capacity in a way that sends a signal to our brain that we are safe. We probably also need to include more rest in our days, but that's a different topic altogether.

For those of us who feel very anxious or stressed, the need to learn how to trigger the relaxation response is even more important. Below are two easy ways to do just that.

Remember, if you have been avoiding your physical feelings of anxiety, then the first time you try this you may feel a spike in anxiety because you are not used to focusing on your body. You may become doubly aware of your heartbeat or the tension in your chest. This is normal and doesn't mean anything dangerous.

Practise these exercises in the same way that you practise

brushing your teeth, safe in the knowledge that you are not in danger and that these exercises will slow your heartbeat and relax your muscles. It may just take time and practice. These skills have superpowers, but you have to nurture them in order to benefit from them.

Breathing Exercises

You already know that changing your breath changes the way you feel. Think about the sigh you let out when you feel overwhelmed, tired and frustrated – the deep inhale that precedes, the whooshing sigh that follows – leaving you feeling a little more balanced than the moment before. A yawn is your body's attempt to get more oxygen into the body to perk you up.

There are ways you can proactively breathe better, which will help your mood.

The first part shows you how to breathe into your diaphragm – the area linked to the lowest part of your lungs.

The second part shows you how to breathe in through the nose and out through the mouth (to steady the amount of oxygen you can take in).

The third part puts it all together and shows you how to ensure you breathe at the right speed.

I find doing this with an audio recording of the exercise works best for me. If you're the same, read the exercise through a few times, then record it onto your phone or computer. Again, you can ask someone who has a voice you find soothing to do this for you.

Part 1: Breathing into the correct place

- Get comfortable – you can sit or lie down for this.
- Place one hand on the centre of your chest.
- Place the other over your lower ribs – if half your hand is on your ribs and the other half on your stomach, you've got it. ·
- Close your mouth and breathe slowly through your nose.
- Turn your attention to your hands. Notice which hand is moving the most as you inhale. Are you breathing mainly into your upper hand – your chest? Or mainly into your lower hand – your diaphragm?
- Send your next breath down into your bottom hand. Purposefully breathe into the lower part of your lungs first, making the bottom hand move. If you can't make this happen at first, don't worry – you can just imagine sending your breath there.
- Keep breathing.

Part 2: Breathing in the correct way

- Keep breathing into your bottom hand.
- Inhale in through your nose
- Purse your lips. Imagine you are about to whistle a tune, or that you have a candle in front of you and you want to blow gently enough to make the flame flicker. Exhale gently.
- Repeat, inhaling through your nose, exhaling through your mouth.

- Notice the place where your breath feels most vivid. Can you feel it most strongly at the tip of your nose? Or in the back of the throat? Simply notice the breath.

Part 3: Putting it all together, with extended exhale – the 4-1-6-1 breath

- Check you are still breathing into your bottom hand.
- Inhale through your nose for a slow count of 4.
- Hold your breath for a count of 1.
- Exhale through your mouth for a count of 6.
- Hold for a count of 1.
- Repeat for as long as you need. Do a minimum of 10 of these each time you practise.

Repeat this breathing exercise at least twice daily, ideally for 5–10 minutes at a time. However, 8 repetitions will be fine if you're in a rush. Remember: to create a habit, it's better to floss one metaphorical tooth every day than a whole mouth of teeth only once.

When my panic attacks were bad, I did this breathing exercise near-constantly. This meant it became second nature. I was then able to do it even when the fight–flight response had hijacked my brain. It was in my unconscious mind; I didn't need my conscious control to do it!

If turning your attention to your breath in this way feels strange, or in any way alarming, I strongly recommend you do it with someone you trust. Especially if that person makes you feel calm. Ask them to read the script above out loud, and simply breathe as they breathe.

Caregivers, you can teach this to your kids too; you may just need to adjust the length of the inhales and exhales to match the length of their breath. You could try to breathe in for a count of 2 and out for a count of 4 – or any iteration where the exhale is longer than the inhale.

Again, this is not about doing the exercise perfectly. It is about practice.

There are alternatives to 4-1-6-1 breathing. People always have a breathing exercise they prefer, so here are a couple more variations:

- 4-7-8 breathing – inhale for 4, hold for 7, exhale for 8.
- Box breathing – inhale for 4, hold for 4, exhale for 4, hold for 4.

Box breathing doesn't have a longer exhale; however, it still slows the breath and stops over-breathing. It can also be the easiest to remember, as all the numbers are the same.

Why it works

These breathing exercises work because they are the opposite of the fight-flight breath. Instead of slow and shallow, they are long and deep. Instead of pulling in oxygen, they limit the amount of oxygen we take in and maximise the amount of CO_2 we exhale.

If you're reading this, thinking, *But when I panic, I feel like I'm not getting enough oxygen. Why would I want to limit my intake?*, the answer is that panic can make us feel like we cannot breathe. Like we need more air. This is because we aren't breathing into our lungs fully, and our muscles are tense around our chest, making it feel like we're struggling to breathe when we aren't. So, slow, steady, deep inhales and slow, steady, longer exhales.

Diaphragmatic breathing also works because it stimulates the vagus nerve (the nerve that runs through the body and is responsible for the fight–flight–freeze response) and triggers the rest-and-digest response (the state we need to be in to sleep – so, remember this exercise if you are struggling to sleep).

Progressive Muscle Relaxation

This exercise targets the tension that the fight–flight–freeze–fawn response creates in the body.

When tension is in your body, it can start a cycle:

Brain creates tension in the body to prepare
you to respond to a perceived threat

Brain interprets tension in the body as a
threat, creating more muscle tension

To stop this cycle, progressive muscle relaxation involves tensing and then relaxing different muscle groups, moving from the soles of your feet all the way to the top of your head. Every time you relax a muscle, the tension in your body decreases and a message is sent to your brain that it's time to relax.

This is why I like to do this one just before I go to sleep.

This exercise will not only help you feel more relaxed in the moment, it will also help you become more aware of what tension feels like in the body. This is important, as many of us miss the first signs of tension, only noticing we're stressed or anxious when our shoulders are up by our ears and our head and neck are hurting.

With this newfound body awareness, you'll be able to employ stress-relieving exercises (by practising the breathing exercise above, physically exercising or going for a walk) the moment you notice tension arise. Nipping it in the bud.

Caution: do not tense any areas of the body to the point of pain. Likewise, do not tense areas where you have a physical injury. If you are injured, please consult your doctor before trying this exercise.

How to do it

Either sit or lie down somewhere you know you will not be distracted. Let your arms fall by your sides. Either close your eyes or look down towards the tip of your nose.

Close your mouth and breathe slowly through your nose. Purposefully practise breathing slowly and deeply into your diaphragm.

Turn your attention to your breath. Notice the sensation of the breath as it enters your nose, goes down your throat and into your lungs. Then notice the sensation as it comes back up and out through your nose. Notice that the air is slightly cooler on the inhale and slightly warmer on the exhale.

Turn your attention to your feet.

On an inhale, scrunch your toes and tense all the muscles in your feet.

Hold the tension and breathe, noticing the sensations there for a count of 5.

On an exhale, release the tension. Visualise the tension

leaving your feet and disappearing into the floor or mattress below. Notice how your feet feel now; notice the relaxation.

Repeat this one more time, tensing on an inhale, holding for 5, then releasing, visualising the tension draining away.

Turn your attention back to the breath.

Take 3 diaphragmatic breaths. Notice the sensations of the inhale and the exhale.

Turn your attention to the lower part of your legs. Repeat the process above. Tense on an inhale. Hold. Release on an exhale. Visualise. Repeat.

Come back to the breath.

Continue this process, moving up the body one section at a time. Follow this order:

- Feet.
- Lower legs.
- Upper legs (from your knees to your hips including your bum muscles).
- Both legs and feet together.
- Chest and stomach.
- Shoulder blades and back (pull your shoulder blades together as you push out your chest).
- Shoulders (bring your shoulders up towards your ears).
- Hands (make your hands into fists).
- Wrists and lower arms.
- Upper arms (squeeze them against your sides).
- Both arms and hands together (bring your arms directly out in front of you and squeeze).
- Face (scrunch it all up!).
- Whole body (yep, everything).

After moving through the body, finish by noticing how you feel. Is your body more relaxed? Take 5 final slow deep diaphragmatic breaths (which you now know how to do) and slowly bring your attention back to the room.

Learning how to switch off your threat response is one of the most empowering things you will ever do. This is another activity that gets easier with practice. Practise each day and see what a difference this makes.

13. Mindfulness

Between stimulus and response there's a space. In
that space lies our power to choose our response.
In our response lies our growth and our freedom.
—VICTOR FRANKL

These exercises:

- **Give you the power to pay attention to, and stop, your usually unconscious patterns.**
- **Help cultivate acceptance**, getting you comfortable with even the most painful emotional and life experiences.
- **Are helpful for everyone** and are particularly helpful for managing rumination (repetitive worry thoughts), all forms of emotional stress and distress, sleep problems, high blood pressure, chronic pain and other health conditions.

Mindfulness is a form of meditation that is rooted in ancient religious practice, and has become highly fashionable in the twenty-first century.

The first texts on meditation were found in the Vedas, the sacred texts of Hinduism, from around 1500 BCE. In the sixth to fifth centuries BCE meditation was also developing in Taoist China and Buddhist India. The mindfulness practised in this chapter is a secularised iteration of the Buddhist Insight Meditation and one of the oldest Buddhist meditation practices – Vipassana.

Mindfulness in the current context means: 'Paying attention to the present moment, on purpose, and without judgement' – John Kabat-Zinn (who brought mindfulness into Western medicine in the 1960s).

Have you ever been in conversation with someone, assumed you knew what they were about to say to you (assuming it was an insult) and then verbally jumped on the person, only to find out they weren't going to insult you at all? Have you ever been to an event and assumed it would be awful, only to find that when you got there it was fine, and there was no need to fret?

Mindfulness gives us a chance to create a pause between our automatic predictions (thoughts and feelings) and the knee-jerk reactions we so often engage in. Allowing our habitual thoughts and feelings to come and go, without affecting our lives so intensely.

Mindfulness means we can choose how we want to respond in any given moment. It helps us to see the world exactly as it is, rather than as we assume it is. It also helps us know that all experiences are temporary, even the ones that feel the most distressing.

A helpful metaphor

Think of your thoughts, judgements, feelings and urges as trains pulling into a station. More often than not we get on the first train that pulls in without realising, then, suddenly, we're miles away and we don't know how we got there.

With mindfulness, we observe the trains (our metaphorical thoughts, feelings and urges) coming into the station but we choose to remain on the platform (our metaphorical present moment). We acknowledge the trains but don't engage with them, allowing the trains to come and go.

Or, and this may feel more likely, we may still get on the train (get caught up in the thought, feeling or urge), but through mindful observation we suddenly realise we are on it, and decide to get off quickly.

Three Mindfulness Exercises

Here are 3 mindfulness exercises you can try right away and take into your daily life. As with the safe-place meditation, please read and see what works for you, then record yourself (or someone you care about) on your phone or computer, so you can listen back. If you're starting a mindfulness practice, choose one of the formal meditations and one of the informal practices and use them daily. Some formal mindfulness courses (e.g. the mindfulness stress reduction course) require you to practise a formal mindfulness exercise (usually a body scan) for 45 minutes a day, 6 days a week. If you want to see results fast, this is the way to go.

However, if you are not dealing with acute stress right now, and this length of commitment is going to stop you from practising (which it does for many of us), 10 minutes each day is fine. When it's part of your routine, you can build from there.

It is important to know that mindfulness is not easy.

It is the opposite of what most of us have been trained to do in our lives – the great 'what next'. Therefore, at first it can feel like you're going against your nature. Asking your mind to stay here, curious, accepting and present, when it wants to rush, produce, avoid and judge.

Having a wandering mind doesn't mean you're 'bad at mindfulness'; it's the moment we catch our mind wandering yet choose to bring our attention back to the present moment that IS mindfulness.

Think about being in the gym. We don't get strong by merely holding weights. We get strong by flexing our muscles while holding the weights; getting stronger every time we flex our arms. In mindfulness, your ability to be in the present gets stronger every time you catch yourself floating away but choose to bring your attention back to the body. It's the same principle.

Don't expect have a totally empty mind – that's impossible. And don't judge yourself for being distracted. Simply pause and return to the breath as often as necessary.

1. Focusing on your breath and sounds (5–15 minutes or as long as you wish)

Find a comfortable place to sit or lie down. Close your eyes if it feels safe to, or simply lower them.

When you are comfortable, take three slow deep inhales and three slow deep exhales through your nose.

Now, turn your attention to the sounds furthest away from you – what can you hear?

Next, turn your attention to the sounds closest to you – what can you hear?

Turn your attention now to the sound of your own breath – listen to the inhale and to the exhale.

Now, turn your attention to the sensation of your breath. Follow the breath flowing into your body. Start at the tip of your nose, feel it passing into your throat, down into your chest and your belly. Then follow it all the way back out, noticing the sensations – belly, chest, nose, throat. Notice how the air is slightly cooler on the inhale and slightly warmer on the exhale. Now, notice: where does the breath feel most vivid? The tip of the nose? The back of the throat? Somewhere else?

Keep noticing the breath – following it in and out or staying with the area where you can feel it the most.

If your mind has wandered off, don't worry, simply say 'Hi' and nod your head towards the thought or feeling the way you would to a passerby in the street, and come back to your breath. Breathing in. Breathing out.

Again, notice where your mind is – is it here with the breath? If not, again nod towards the feeling and return, or simply label what is happening. If it is a thought, say 'thinking'; if it is a judgement, say 'judgement'; if it is a feeling, say 'feeling'. Then, knowing it will pass, choose to come back to the breath.

Focus on the area where the breath feels most vivid.

When you're ready, turn your attention to the last few inhales and exhales. Follow the inhale all the way from your nose into your belly and back out.

Next, turn your attention to the sound of the inhale and then the exhale.

Next, turn your attention to the sounds closest to you – what can you hear?

Next, turn your attention to the sounds further away – what is the furthest thing you can hear?

Finally, knowing you can come back to this any time you like, bring some movement into your fingers and toes, and feel yourself fully back in the room, or wherever you are.

2. Thoughts-as-the-sky metaphor (10 minutes or as long as you like)

This meditation is adapted from a rather lovely metaphor put forward by Russ Harris in his book *The Happiness Trap*.

Find a comfortable place to sit or lie down. Close your eyes if it feels safe to, or simply lower them. When you're comfortable take three slow deep inhales and three slow deep exhales.

Notice your body against the chair or the bed, whatever you're resting on.

Keep noticing the breath as I talk to you. Maybe following the breath as it comes into your body, starting at the tip of your nose, moving down into your lungs. Follow the breath as it leaves your body, flowing from the bottom of your lungs up and out of your nose. Focus on this, or the sound of my voice, as I talk you through this exercise.

If at any point you notice your mind has wandered off, don't worry – simply notice this has happened and, without judgement, come back to the breath or the sound of my voice. It doesn't matter how many times you need to do this.

Our thoughts come and go, affecting how we feel and what

we do. Sometimes thoughts affect how we feel so powerfully that we get stuck on them, following them down a rabbit hole.

If we bring our awareness to our thoughts, observing them and the feelings and urges that arise with them, allowing them to be present and then letting them go as we come back to our breath and the present moment, over and over, we can start to see our thoughts are temporary events. We can start to see that they are not facts and they are not *us*. We can start to gain distance from our thoughts and feelings.

I want you to imagine that your thoughts, feelings and all the sensations in your body are like the weather.

You know that the weather changes, throughout the day and throughout the year. Think about the weather now; think about all the kinds of weather you have seen and lived through.

You know that the sunshine comes and goes, as do all other types of weather. Clouds, rain, storms, they come and go. No matter how dark the clouds, how bad the rain, the thunder and lightning – they all pass. The biggest storms and even tsunamis pass.

This is just like us and our emotions. Sometimes emotions roll in, turbulent and overwhelming, like clouds or thunder rolling across the sky. Sometimes emotions build, and when they burst they feel like rain falling from the sky. Sometimes we get caught up in the emotion, responding as if we ourselves are the weather, thundering, raging, cloudy or stormy. Sometimes we feel we cannot contain it all.

I now want you to imagine that you, your mind and your body are the sky.

You know that the weather is always contained by the sky.

No matter how extreme the weather is, the sky always makes room to hold it. The sky can never be harmed by it.

After the biggest storm, the hottest sun, the strongest blizzard, the sky always returns to its clear blue. In fact, that sky was clear and blue and stable the whole time the extreme weather raged on. It was just temporarily obscured by clouds.

What happens when you think of yourself as the sky, and your thoughts and feelings as the weather?

When you observe every sensation here as part of the weather, knowing that it will pass and change again and again, and when you know that you cannot be harmed by it, as you can contain everything that passes through you, what happens then?

Remember, the sky is not a part of the weather, but it *contains* it. Whatever the weather is like, the sky always has room for it. No matter how bad the weather, no matter how violent the thunderstorm, no matter how severe the sun, the sky cannot be damaged in any way. And of course, as time passes, the weather will change again and again. Meanwhile, the sky remains as pure and clear as ever.

Take a moment to reflect upon this metaphor. If you can, bring your awareness to the thoughts and sensations in your body.

Imagine you are the sky, and your thoughts are the weather passing through. Don't judge the thoughts or sensations. Don't label them good or bad. Simply notice that they are there. Whatever you find there is okay. They will pass through. Watch them pass.

If it feels hard to separate from a thought, say to yourself: 'I'm having the thought that . . .', adding the thought to the end of the phrase. This can help create distance between you and your thoughts, allowing you to imagine them as the weather, allowing you to watch them pass, as you come back to the breath or the sound of my voice.

Now turn your attention back to your breath. Take 3 slow deep inhales and exhales.

Finally, knowing you can come back to this any time you like, bring some movement into your fingers and toes, and feel yourself fully back in the room, or wherever you are.

3. A body scan (10 minutes or as long as you want)

A body scan is similar to the Progressive Muscle Relaxation exercise in Chapter 12, but without tensing or relaxing muscles. You simply turn your attention to each area of the body, one section at a time, and see what's there. Turning our attention to our body not only gets us out of our head and into our body, it lets us know what we are feeling, and importantly, when we pay attention to areas of tension, those areas start to relax. It sounds counterintuitive to anyone who has been avoiding their physical sensations for fear of making them worse, but it's true – when we learn it's safe to pay attention to the sensations it can feel like shining a light into the darkest corners of a room, transforming it.

Find a comfortable place to sit or lie down. Close your eyes if it feels safe to, or simply lower them. When you're comfortable, take three slow deep inhales and three slow deep exhales through your nose.

Notice your body against the chair or the bed, whatever you are resting on.

Turn your attention to your feet. Notice any sensations in

the soles of your feet, your toes, the tops of your feet and your ankles. Acknowledge any sensations you find, any thoughts that arise, and keep breathing.

If you notice any tension or pain, and it feels okay to do so, turn your attention to that area and imagine sending your breath to that area. Visualise the tension leaving your body as you breathe.

Now repeat the exercise, moving up through your body.

Start with your feet. Move up to your lower legs. Then to your upper legs (thighs and bum). Then your lower body (stomach). Then your upper body (chest and shoulders). Then down your arms to your hands. Then turn your attention to your neck. Then your face (chin, mouth, forehead). Then notice the sensations in your whole body.

After moving through the body, finish by noticing how you feel. Is your body more relaxed? Take 5 final slow deep diaphragmatic breaths (which you now know how to do) and slowly bring your attention back to the room.

Mindfulness in everyday life

The guided exercises above are just that, practice. Mindfulness is most effective when brought into your everyday life.

You can be mindful in any moment.

You might be washing up and notice that you are bored of the task, or stuck in your head, worrying about the date who hasn't texted you back yet, or your most recent intrusive thought, and choose to practise mindfulness. In this instance all you would need to do is notice your hands in the water – what does the water feel like on your skin? What do the bubbles in the water feel like? What does the cutlery or the plate you're currently washing feel like in your hands? Is it smooth? Does it have a pattern? Any time you notice your mind drifting, come back to the washing up!

The STOP Technique

This is a quick trick that takes a matter of moments and can, with practice, help bring mindfulness into your day, making it come to you naturally in the long run. It can also help you whenever you notice you're suddenly stressed, angry and about to respond in such a way.

For example, if someone sends you an email at work that makes you flare up in frustration or rage, before you respond from a place of annoyance (which you may later regret), use the STOP technique to slow down your emotional response, ground you back into the present moment and give you a chance to respond in a way that feels more helpful. You could also try this if you're about to flare up at your friend or partner, creating just enough of a pause to stop you from putting your foot in your mouth!

I use the STOP technique multiple times throughout the day. I have a reminder set on my phone that goes off 5 times during the day. The reminder simply says: STOP.

Here is what it means:

- S – stop what you're doing.
- T – take 3 deep and slow breaths (remember your dia-phragmatic breathing).
- O – observe what is present in your body with a short body scan, starting at your toes, working up to your

head – what urges are here, what sensations? – and then move to what is around you, simply noticing what's there.

- **P** – proceed. Choose what you want to do in the next moment. Choose how you will proceed, rather than what your knee-jerk response tells you to do. Will you still send the 'screw you' email? Will you still shout at your friend? Or will you choose to do something else?

Mindfulness is about observing, accepting and letting go, but it doesn't mean always accepting the status quo or turning the other cheek and welcoming harm. Sometimes you'll still want to send that email. And stand up to your friend. Mindfulness *does* mean, however, that you will make your decision from a position of calm and consideration – making it more likely you'll say what you need to say, rather than lashing out.

Why does mindfulness work?

Mindfulness doesn't just help us be 'more present' and in the driver's seat of our life, it changes the structure of our brain. Dr Yewande Pearse, neuroscientist and expert for the meditation app 'Headspace', taught me that practicing mindfulness can change the structure of:

- The prefrontal cortex – the part of your brain responsible for complex tasks and being in the present moment. This means mindfulness can improve our attention span, help us filter out thoughts and other distractions we don't wish to attend to, improve our ability to learn new information, make complex decisions, and also, have more control over our stress responses.

- The pons – the part of your brain responsible for regulatory neurotransmitters, the chemicals that regulate our mood and our sleep (among other things). Improved mood and improved sleep? Yes please.
- The temporoparietal junction – the area associated with perspective-taking, empathy and compassion. Again, we all need to be better at these things, so again, yes.

Mindfulness has also been linked to a smaller amygdala – the amygdala is one of your fear centres and is central to the fight-flight response. If it's smaller, it can't be as active – another good thing. And mindfulness has been linked to preserved brain structure and cells as we age.

No wonder mindfulness is so fashionable. It doesn't just give us a psychological tool; it doesn't just give us a new framework through which to see the world and each other; it gives us a life-changing, brain-changing way of being.

If you like these exercises, moving forwards you can choose whether you wish to engage in a full spiritual immersion with mindfulness, or whether you would prefer a packaged approach, using an app like Calm or Headspace.

14. Journalling

These exercises:

- Offer a place to **express your emotions**.
- Help you **find out more about yourself**.
- Are **helpful at any time, and also after a significantly distressing life event**, such as unemployment, a break-up with a life partner, the death of a loved one, a natural disaster.

One antidote to the bottled-up emotional experiences most of us carry around is emotional expression. Journalling is a safe way to express how we feel without having to worry what other people think or whether there is anyone we can trust to listen. It's also free!

People often resist doing it, as it makes them feel like they're back in school, or because they can't quite believe that it can actually be useful. However, writing has powerful and almost inexplicable effects.

Dr James Pennebaker showed that writing for 15 minutes each day about a difficult experience leads to improved feelings of wellbeing, better sleep, decreased blood pressure, decreased pain, improved immune functions, general health and fewer trips to the doctor. And other researchers have since shown writing 20 minutes per day, 3 days in a row, can help wounds to heal faster (what?!), improve 'moderate asthma' (again, huh?!) and improve mobility in people with rheumatoid arthritis (wow!). It sounds improbable and impossible, doesn't it? But I've read the studies, and the findings are consistent time and time again.

Writing changes your physical health and biology. Wow, wow, wow.

Ready to give it a go?

How to do it

Any time you feel emotional and need a place to dump your emotions, try expressive writing. It could be when your thoughts and feelings seem jumbled and you don't know why; or any time you are going through something devastating, e.g. a break-up or a loss. You can also write about past experiences that you want to make sense of. Or, it can simply be a healthy habit.

- **Choose a topic to write about.** You can focus on one event, or concentrate on a few different topics – one each day. Write about something extremely personal and important to you (a break-up, a row at work, the day your pet died), but if something feels too overwhelming to think about, choose another subject. If you can't think of anything, have a look at the prompts below. You could also simply start writing and see what flows!

- **Write for 15–20 minutes each day for four consecutive days.** This will be more effective than writing four times over an extended period.

- **Write continuously without stopping.** Don't worry about your spelling or grammar, or about writing beautiful sentences, or even ones that make sense. If you run out of things to say, don't worry, you can repeat what you've already written. Also, don't worry if you suddenly change topics; just keep writing until the time is up. No one is going to see what you've written, so write freely knowing this.

- **Explore how you feel.** While you write, explore the emotions (physical sensations) and thoughts that arise for you. Think about why you may feel that way and whether they remind you of another time in your life, another relationship. Think about how they connect to who you were in the past, how you feel you are now, and who you would like to be in the future.

- **Stop writing if you become overwhelmed.** Step away, breathe, ground yourself, cuddle, exercise, and maybe consider a different topic, one that feels safer.

- **After you have written for 15–20 minutes, do something that makes you feel good.** You may notice that, after writing, especially on day one or two, you suddenly feel more emotional. This is normal and to be expected, as you are allowing your brain to process and make sense of your experiences. Plan time after each writing session to do something that feels good for you. Maybe pull something from your coping-skills jar. Whatever helps you feel good.

Quick tip: don't write about the same topic for more than a couple of weeks, otherwise you risk ingraining your distress rather than releasing it.

Journalling with prompts

Using prompts can be helpful if you journal regularly and need to find new topics. Choose any of the prompts that you like and feel good for you.

- The emotions I have been feeling most recently are _____.

- Whenever there is a major life stress, I notice that my thoughts become _____. My feelings switch into _____ and the way I cope usually involves _____. Would I call this a pattern? When and where did it start in my life?

- When I recently felt annoyed/frustrated/emotional, what did it remind me of? Was there another time in my life when I felt similar to this moment? What would it be like to remember that original moment and imagine looking after that version of me at that age?

- When did I last respond to someone without thinking? When was I defensive recently or last? What happened? What was that defence trying to protect me from?

- I need to forgive myself for_____.

- If I woke up tomorrow and everything was okay, what would be different? What would be the first thing I would do if that was the case? What would I do next? Is there a way I can do those things right now?

- What one thing do I constantly try to push away or pretend is not here or happening? Why do I do this? What would it be like to simply allow that experience or thing to be here? Just for a moment? What grounding exercise would I need to make this possible?

- How would life be if I imagined I could be content with who I am? What do I need to do to start giving myself permission to be that right now? Who would I need to connect to who could support me with this?

- What beliefs might be shaping how I feel about myself? Is there a way I could think about this thing differently?

- When I think about who I want to be in the future, what do I see? How does 'future me' spend their days? What do they think about and care about? Who do they have in their life? What skills and hobbies do they have? And, if this is hard for me, what do I need to do to give myself permission to think about 'future me'? What do I need to do to support myself to look to the future and the opportunities it may bring?

Rage journalling

I **love** rage journalling.

If you have had an argument with someone, or feel frustrated/hurt/furious about something from your past, you may like to 'rage journal'.

To do this I start the page with: *Today (or whatever time of my life it was) X happened and it made me feel ...* I write for 15–20 minutes. I then write three things that are going well (or that I learned from writing this down). I re-read it once. Then I tear the pages into a million pieces.

If you do this, don't hope to write something pretty. You may find yourself scratching letters into the page as your rage pours out, releasing you from its grip. When you re-read it, you may feel like you have some distance from the thoughts; you may find yourself laughing or experiencing another emotion.

Ripping it up gives us a visual metaphor for release, and also ensures we know that no one will ever read what we wrote. Phew!

This is good for people who feel angry often, but even more so for those who think they 'do not experience anger' and/or who have been trained to be 'good', pushing anger away from a young age.

It took me a long time to feel comfortable with the idea of being angry. I was often in denial. And at first, letting out anger was scary. Now I can admit, *I have a dark side and I'm not afraid to go there in a safe and contained environment, like a journal.*

Connecting with my anger helped my mood (unexpressed anger has been linked to depression) and stopped me from festering after an argument (passive aggression is simply anger released very slowly over a long period of time, like a slow puncture). Allowing the anger to burst onto the page also allowed me to return to calm much more quickly, and helped me connect with who I truly am – someone who experiences all emotions.

Why does writing work?

When we are stressed, or have unexpressed emotional pain, our cortisol levels and muscle tension can soar, as can other stress-related hormones. When we write we can release our stresses and tensions, causing all of these biological markers to decrease too.

When we write we also start to make sense of our experiences. Have you ever felt overwhelmed but unsure why? Or as if your thoughts are like a jumbled ball of wool, with no clear beginning, structure or end. When we write we start to make sense of that jumble. We can see our life events more clearly, and we can step outside the brain's often automatic negative spin and tendency to jump to conclusions.

Research shows that when we create a coherent narrative about a stressful event, incorporating it into our life story, we are less likely to struggle with it in the future. For example, people who have experienced their first episode of psychosis are less likely to relapse if they manage to make sense of their experience, and see it as part of their life experience, than if they 'seal over' the event, avoiding thinking about it as a way to cope (which is associated with depression and poorer quality of life).

The combination of these two factors – decreased stress responses in the body plus emotional processing – is thought to combine to produce incredible outcomes.

At first, journalling can feel uncomfortable or overwhelming, but when we stick with it, we learn to feel curious, safe and open to who we are.

15. Self-Compassion

Love and compassion are necessities, not luxuries. Without them humanity cannot survive.

—DALAI LAMA

These exercises:

- **Are your antidote to shame and the inner critic**.
- **Help you learn how to forgive yourself** so you can move forward from anything you have been feeling guilty about or holding onto.
- Are helpful for everyone wanting to become more present in their lives, and are **particularly helpful for managing rumination (repetitive worry thoughts), all forms of emotional stress and distress, sleep problems, high blood pressure, chronic pain and other health conditions.**

Caution: if you have never been offered compassion before, you may feel more anxious at first. But that's okay. You can take it slowly.

The biggest antidote to shame and the inner critic is self-compassion: the ability to stay present with, and aware of, our suffering, offering ourselves kindness. Compassion is something we often offer freely to others but rarely to ourselves.

A friend or family member comes to us, sharing a struggle, a mistake they believe they've made, or simply looking tired and run-down. What do we do? We reach to hug them, or we flip the kettle on to make them a cup of tea. You sit, you listen, you build them up, telling them how wonderful they are and how well they're doing. If you do offer advice, you do it with compassion and kindness.

When it comes to speaking to ourselves, we are often more like a bully than a friend.

If we make a mistake, even something we could never have foreseen or that was outside of our control, we minimise and undermine our sadness; we overemphasise and punish ourselves. Why do we do this?

- We believe offering ourselves compassion is weak, indulgent or selfish. That it may make us lazy.
- We were not shown compassion when we were struggling as a kid, so we don't know what it looks like, and feel we don't deserve it as adults.
- We were ignored, rejected or minimised when we felt emotional, so now when emotions arise, we respond to them by ignoring, rejecting or minimising them.
- We believe change comes from criticism, even though all of us know how anxious and stressed-out criticism makes us, how it stops us from learning from our mistakes and gets in the way of relationships.

- Thinking about being kind to ourselves means acknowledging we are not perfect, and that, for many of us, is terrifying.

But research shows that formal practice of self-compassion is linked to:

- Decreased anxiety and depression, rumination and thought-suppression (pushing away thoughts).
- Increased emotional intelligence – which is the ability to recognise and manage our own and other people's emotions, making us feel both connected to others and also confident in ourselves, as we know we can cope with whatever life throws at us.
- Increased motivation to make the most of what life has to offer.

When we practise self-compassion, we don't collapse into a fluffy pool of sugary sweet overindulgence. No, instead we become motivated to work towards what we want and need. We allow ourselves to learn from our mistakes. We support ourselves in our time of need, we take breaks and look after ourselves in the ways that our body and mind needs, and we increase our ability to feel connected to others. Sounds damned good to me.

What is self-compassion?

Like mindfulness, self-compassion has its roots in ancient Buddhist teachings.

The iteration we talk about in this chapter is described

by Dr Kristin Neff, one of the foremost writers on self-compassion. It has three components:

1) **Self-kindness.** This involves recognising that life involves struggles and suffering; not denying this experience but instead allowing it in, offering the self what is needed in that moment for us to feel soothed and safe.
2) **A sense of common humanity.** This involves recognising that all humans are fallible, that we are all works in progress who make mistakes, struggle and get it wrong from time to time (instead of listening to that self-isolating voice that makes us feel like we alone are failures, faulty or that there is something wrong with us).
3) **Mindfulness.** As you already know, this involves observing our thoughts, feelings, urges; slowing everything down and choosing to remain present and in the moment.

Self-compassion is a way of relating to ourselves. It is the foundation for feeling safe, and for feeling empowered to try, time and time again, even when we make mistakes.

I have had to work hard at learning to forgive myself after mistakes, but I have a go-to phrase that I repeat during those times: 'I am not proud of what happened but I know that I was doing my best. I was acting in the only way I knew how at the time, and I'm learning to forgive myself.'

If you are still struggling with the idea of self-compassion, remember you can call it whatever feels good to you. As I told you in Chapter 9, I personally call it 'how to not be a total dick to yourself', but use whatever works for you. For people who are highly self-critical, or do not have trust for kindness and care in their life, practising self-compassion can be extremely anxiety-provoking. If you think you'll struggle with this exercise, take each of these practices slowly.

If you notice self-kindness makes you panic, ground yourself and practise saying this phrase to yourself multiple times a day (maybe put it on a Post-it note and stick it on your bathroom mirror, or have it as a screensaver on your phone): *I am learning that I can be kind to myself and that I am deserving of care.*

Now you know why it works, what it can do for you and how to overcome any personal obstacles, here are the exercises:

Self-Compassion Exercises

These two exercises will help you cultivate self-compassion. You can use these in addition to the 'Would you speak to your friends the way you speak to yourself?' exercise from Chapter 9.

Take a self-compassion break

This exercise only takes a few moments.

Practise this any time you notice your inner critic, or when any other feelings of distress arise. As with all the exercises I discuss in my work, the more you practise, the more successful they will be. It can be worth practising this multiple times during the day if you're working to increase this skill. You can practise it in times of calm too. Just bring a moment of recent (mid-level) distress to mind and repeat the compassion break in the same way.

This exercise involves saying three sentences to yourself. The first sentence recognises that this is a time of suffering

for you. The second connects you to others in the world, recognising you are not alone in your feelings. The third offers
kindness to yourself in that moment. Did you notice that
these sentences map directly onto the three parts I said make
up self-compassion?

Some of the statements traditionally used in this exercise
make people feel uncomfortable. You can adapt them to make
them more comfortable for you. I have included alternative
suggestions in brackets.

The exercise

Take a moment, close your eyes or lower them and look at a
patch on the ground in front of you.

If practising while calm, bring a situation to mind that is
causing you distress. Choose something upsetting but not
overwhelming. If doing this causes overwhelm, do the 54321
technique to soothe you. If practising in the moment, just
notice the following instead.

Notice the feelings arising in your body. Stay with them
for a moment.

Say to yourself: 'This is a moment of suffering.' (You can
change the words to suit what feels right to you, such as 'This
is stress' or 'This hurts' or 'This is uncomfortable'.)

Say to yourself: 'Suffering is a part of life'. (Or, 'Other
people feel like this', 'I am not alone', 'Everyone struggles at
some point').

Say to yourself: 'May I be kind to myself'. (Or, 'May I give
myself the compassion that I need' or 'May I learn to accept
myself as I am', or 'May I show myself love and care in the same
way that my mum/best friend/pet dog shows me love and care.')

You can also add any additional sentences you feel work for you. For example, you could add 'May I be strong' or 'May I be calm' as a finishing touch. This is your practice, so make it your own.

Giving yourself a hug or stroking yourself causes the same neurochemical response in the brain as actual soothing from others. Specifically, self-touch causes release of the feel-good hormone oxytocin and decreases release of the stress hormone cortisol. Therefore, if it feels right for you, try placing your hand over your heart, giving yourself a gentle hug, or stroke your own hand while you take your compassion break.

Loving/kindness meditation

The positive effects of this exercise on minimising the inner critic and reducing stress have been seen after a single 10-minute session, making it truly worth giving a shot.

Some traditional versions of this meditation start by asking us to imagine someone who makes us feel unconditionally loved, asking us to feel their warmth. Others ask us to start the meditation by sharing caring statements with ourselves. As this can be difficult for people new to this, the meditation I am offering you is a little different.

This exercise starts by asking you to visualise someone or something that you care about. It then asks you to visualise sharing your care and warm thoughts with that person before asking you to share these same thoughts and warmth with yourself.

As with all the longer exercises, read the script and decide if there's anything you need to change. Record yourself reading it out loud on your phone and listen each day. Read slowly so the experience of listening is soothing and doesn't feel like a race.

Before you record it, consider who you will call to mind in the exercise. Choose someone that brings you a sense of grounding and calm, someone who doesn't bring to mind complicated or overwhelming feelings. This can even be a pet.

The exercise

Find a comfortable place to sit or lie down.

Gently close your eyes if it feels safe to do so, or lower your eyes to a place that feels comfortable.

Turn your attention to the sounds outside the room. Now to the sounds inside the room. Close your mouth and breathe in and out through your nose. Notice the sound of your own breath. Now turn your attention to the feeling of your breath, the sensations of the air entering your body and leaving your body. Keep breathing just like this, slowly and deeply.

If your mind wanders off at any point, do not worry; simply bring your attention back to the breath or to the sound of my voice.

Picture someone close to you. Someone who makes you smile; someone who you feel a great amount of warmth for. They don't have to be human. Imagine you are there with them. Maybe you are sitting next to them or walking alongside them.

Notice how thinking about them makes you feel. Notice how this care and this feeling shows up in your body and in your heart. Notice the sensations around your heart and in your body in general when you think about them.

What do you notice? Maybe you notice warmth, tenderness,

openness, connection? Continue breathing and focus on the feelings as you think about and visualise the person or being that you care about.

Imagine that with each breath you are extending the feelings you have for this being out towards them. If you like, you could imagine a golden light that holds all of your feelings and warmth extending out from your heart towards your loved one.

Imagine that this light envelops your loved one, sharing with them the feelings that you have for them in your heart, bringing them peace and happiness. Or you could imagine placing a hand on their arm or shoulder and your feelings connecting to them this way instead.

At the same time, silently repeat these phrases:

- May you be safe.
- May you be kind to yourself.
- May you experience peace.
- May you be healthy.
- May you experience joy and ease.

Now, add yourself to this image. See yourself there. And say to yourself and to your chosen being:

- May you and I be safe.
- May you and I be kind to ourselves.
- May you and I experience peace.
- May you and I be healthy.
- May you and I experience joy and ease.

Notice how this feels. Keep yourself and your chosen being in your mind as you notice how this feels in your heart and in your body. Have the sensations changed? Do you still feel warmth, openness and tenderness? What else is here? Notice if any tension is arising. If this has happened, don't worry – so many of us struggle to offer kindness towards ourselves even though we deserve these words. So many of us are learning that we are deserving of kindness and compassion, and that it's safe to experience both.

If it feels safe to do so, now offer yourself the feelings and warmth you shared with your chosen being. Imagine extending that feeling back towards yourself. Say to yourself:

- May I be safe.
- May I be kind to myself.
- May I experience peace.
- May I be healthy.
- May I experience joy and ease.

Notice how this feels in your heart and in your body. Did the sensations change? Do you still feel warmth, openness and tenderness? What other sensations are here?

Now turn your attention to the sound of your own breath – the inhale and the exhale. Notice the sensation of the breath – the inhale and the exhale. Notice the sounds inside the room and now outside of the room. Wiggle your fingers and toes and slowly open your eyes.

Notice how this feels. Did the sensations change at all, in your body or your heart? Do you still feel warmth, openness and tenderness? What other sensations are here?

Why self-compassion works

In Chapter 1 we learned that babies need their caregivers to soothe them so their brain can develop in a stable and grounded way, meaning they can feel stable and grounded too. When we practise self-compassion, it's a little like we are the soothing parent. And over time, this practice strengthens our own ability to self-soothe and to create calm whenever we need it.

The loving/kindness meditation, when practised formally, changes the prefrontal cortex, as mentioned in Chapter 13. In addition, this type of meditation alters activity in the areas of the brain linked to 'salience processing' (meaning we find emotional and painful experiences less overwhelming and take up less of our attention) and self-reference (meaning we may be less focused on ourselves and our distress, and therefore less likely to ruminate on what could go wrong).

If you enjoyed these exercises and you want to take this practice further, I recommend reading *The Compassionate Mind* by Paul Gilbert and listening to the many audios Kristin Neff has available for free on the website selfcompassion.org.

Being kind towards yourself may sound sappy but it has the potential to change how your brain works – and there's nothing sappy about that!

16. Live By Your Values

This chapter will teach you:

- How to **identify the things you value in your life.**
- Help you **prioritise what is important to you.**

It will be helpful for everyone. I seriously wish everyone did this!

Many of us live our lives driving ourselves towards success, working harder and harder to achieve the great job, the big house, the even bigger salary, the perfect body, the 2.4 children family and other socially approved measures of success.

There's nothing wrong with having goals, as we discussed in Chapter 9 however, many of us:

- Confuse our self-worth with what we have achieved.
- Have been sold an ideal by companies who want to make us constantly buy more of whatever they are selling.
- Are trying to be who we were told we are meant to be, rather than who we truly want to be.

In her book *The Top Five Regrets of the Dying*, palliative nurse Bronnie Ware says that the top five regrets people have on their deathbed are:

1. 'I wish I'd had the courage to live a life true to myself, not the life others expected of me.'
2. 'I wish I hadn't worked so hard.'
3. 'I wish I'd had the courage to express my feelings.'
4. 'I wish I had stayed in touch with my friends.'
5. 'I wish I'd let myself be happier.'

These findings are consistent across the research in this area and they are important. They show that people often realise the quality of their lives is more important than what they achieve. They also realise what they truly value when there's little time to do something about it.

This doesn't need to be the case. We can figure out what's important for us right now, and start incorporating it into our lives today.

Goals vs. values

- **Goals are items you can write down on a list and tick off,** such as a job promotion, partner, house in the country, threesome, holiday in France, lots of money in the bank (these are not necessarily my goals, by the way, so no need to make assumptions!).
- **Values are the qualities of the experiences you want to have, and they cannot be ticked off a list,** such as commitment, compassion, knowledge, safety,

intimacy, pushing boundaries, learning about other cultures, expanding horizons, freedom.

You can tick France off the list once you've been there, but showing compassion to someone once doesn't mean you can describe yourself as compassionate. Once you stop showing compassion you are no longer being compassionate.

You can have a partner. Tick. But this goal tells us nothing of the quality of the relationship you hope for. You could be in a relationship but it could be unhappy.

When you ask yourself what you *value* about relationships, you might say reliability, honesty and compassion, and/or having a teammate to share life with. You can't tick these off, but you can sure as hell work on them every day, in any relationship you have – with friends, family, lovers, long-term partners, whoever.

Going back to the topic of death, what is really interesting about goals is that we spend our life working towards them and then, the moment we die, they are no longer relevant. They are forgotten, whereas our values are not. Rarely does someone say in a eulogy, 'They had such a big car, so many awards and a jacuzzi in the bathroom. Wow!'

Rather, what you normally celebrate at a funeral are the values by which that person lived: 'They were so loving, always there when I needed them. I always felt understood by them.' Stories are shared about the most memorable and positive qualities of that person.

Goals may be mentioned but only because of the values they demonstrated. I'm not saying that we shouldn't work towards our goals. I'm saying that we can drop the idea that we will only be deemed worthy through our external successes.

If we think about the qualities we value in ourselves, others, and all areas of our lives, we can commit to stepping up in ways that matter to us each day, growing in ways that are important to us, whether our goals are achieved or not.

You can still want the same goals when you consider your values. The important part is to understand why. For example, if you want money and success, why? What qualities of your life do you want it for? Do you want it because it'll help you be financially free? Able to take time off work? Able to spend more time with your family? If so, wonderful! Your values are freedom, flexibility, connection and being with the people you love, valuing quality time. Every day, while working towards your goal, you can look for your values in each moment.

The journey can now be as important as the goal or the grade.

Finding your values

Values are things we can be aware of and reflect in our actions every single day, and yet few of us have ever sat down and truly thought what our values might be. I would go as far as to say that when we ask what our values are, we ask one of the deepest questions we can about ourselves. We ask ourselves:

- Who am I?
- Who do I want to be?
- What do I believe in to the very core of me?
- Who do I want to work towards being in every moment?
- Where are the places I want to put my energy?
- What do I value in others?
- How do I want to be remembered?

Wouldn't it be great if we could look back on our lives at an old age and say, 'I lived a life filled with value'?

Here are the three steps you need to take to identify your personal values and start living your hoped-for future.

Step 1. Number these areas of life in order of importance

Don't number them based on how they fit into your life right now. Think which areas you value most. Put 1 by the most valued area, and continue from there (I've left a space at the left of each word for you to add your number). You can choose areas in joint positions. You can also cross out any that do not apply (e.g. if you do not have children, you can skip 'Parenting').

_____ Health and physical wellbeing

_____ Education and personal growth or development

_____ Career

_____ Recreation, leisure and fun times

_____ Community involvement

_____ Spirituality

_____ Friendships and social life

_____ Intimate relationships

_____ Parenting

_____ Wider family relationships

If recreation and leisure are at the bottom of your list, ask yourself why. Was this trained out of you at a young age? Do you feel that resting or having fun is a bad idea in some way? I say this because people do not often prioritise this incredibly important area of life, not realising that rest and play helps brain development, identity and our overall wellbeing.

Step 2. List your values

Work through the list on p.417 and, starting with the area of life that you chose as your highest priority, ask yourself what values you would like to embody in each area and how you would like to present yourself if you were able to be your most ideal version of yourself? I have given you prompts that will help you identify your values in each area, and space for you to document your thoughts.

If you struggle with this, go back to the list you made of life goals and milestones in the section between Part One and Part Two of this book. Choose the goals that you feel are most important to you. Ask yourself, *Why? What are the qualities of that experience that I would like in my life?*

Maybe you have a goal of running a 10k (or further) race. The goal would be passing the finish line or beating your best time. The values you link to this activity will be personal. Maybe you value commitment (to your training programme), moving your body, being part of something and challenging yourself, making your body feel as fit as you possibly can.

Maybe the values are something quite different. Maybe you feel you are in a state of flow while you run and you value feeling totally connected, mind and body – nothing but you, the present moment and the road in front of you. Maybe rather than valuing running because it gives you access to a running community, you might value it as something you do solely for you, giving you respite and a break from your otherwise busy life.

If you are solely focused on the goal, the many months

of training for a race may be pretty dull, even miserable. However, when you think about training as an opportunity to experience the qualities you listed above (which fall into multiple different value categories, e.g. physical health, personal growth, community), it can feel quite different.

While working on this book, there were times when I was focused solely on the goal and, because of this, I wanted to give up. I felt overwhelmed by the sheer size of the task. However, I knew my values were:

- Making psychological information understandable and available to people outside of the therapy room.
- Showing people they are human and normal and not weird or crazy.
- Consistently applying myself.
- Continuously learning.
- Self-compassion.

This meant that each day, instead of thinking about the goal, I was able to approach the task thinking about meeting these values. This gave me a focus any time my mind tried to drag me into its fears about the future. I scheduled rest periods into my diary in the same way as I scheduled meetings. I knew this is often the first thing I drop when I'm anxious or busy – the thing I need most is always the first thing to go – and by and by, with a ton of self-compassion, the book got written.

Take your time completing this. Work all the way through to the end. Remember, values are qualities that you can put into action every day, like moving your body and treating yourself well. Remember that your values will change over your lifetime, and that's okay too. This isn't a 'one and done' exercise. This is the compass by which you can live your life, and sometimes you will need to change course. Great!

Health and physical wellbeing. How would you like to look after yourself and your health? What do you value about feeling good? What actions make you feel like you are in your body? What actions make you feel emotionally well? What do you value about each of these actions?

_____

_____

_____

_____

_____

_____

_____

_____

Education and personal growth or development. What do you value about this part of life? What would you like to learn in the future? Would you like to study more? A specific topic? Why is that? What do you value about these things?

_____

_____

_____

_____

_____

_____

_____

_____

_____

Career. What qualities do you want to embody when you are
at work? What qualities would you like to find in your work?
How would you like your work relationships to look and feel?
What type of environment do you like? What do you value
about working?

_____

_____

_____

_____

_____

_____

_____

_____

Recreation, leisure and fun times. What would you like to
do more of? What areas of your life make you feel playful?
Light-hearted? In flow? What is it you value about that?

_____

_____

_____

_____

_____

_____

_____

_____

Community involvement. What kind of community would you like to be part of? In what ways can you connect to the community?

_____

_____

_____

_____

_____

_____

_____

_____

Spirituality. What do you value in terms of spirituality and faith? What do you want to believe in? What do you believe in? How do you want to connect with this part of yourself?

_____

_____

_____

_____

_____

_____

_____

_____

Friendships and social life. How would you like your friends to feel when they are around you? What qualities would cause those feelings? What kinds of relationships do you value?

_____

_____

_____

_____

_____

_____

_____

_____

Intimate relationships. What qualities do you want to show in your relationships? What would you like other people to feel when they are with you? What kind of relationship do you want to be part of?

_____

_____

_____

_____

_____

_____

_____

_____

Parenting. Are there any qualities you want your children to see in you? How would you like them to feel around you? How would you like them to remember you?

_____

_____

_____

_____

_____

_____

_____

_____

_____

Wider family relationships. What kind of family member would you like to be? What would you like your family relationships to feel like?

_____

_____

_____

_____

_____

_____

_____

_____

Step 3. Ask yourself, does this match where you are in life now?

After completing this task, many people realise that their current life is not aligned with their values. Are you living a value-driven life? Or has this exercise highlighted an area you want to start working on right away? Does it make you realise you've been working your ass off in an office job, when you really want to be home ensuring your friends, relatives or children get your love, attention and presence? Does it make you realise that you want to move your body (running, dancing or other forms of exercise) to honour it rather than punishing it to reach a goal set out by an Instagram influencer?

If any shame or panic arises due to a mismatch, as always, notice the pain and offer yourself a kind word.

What is the first step you can take today that is in line with this? Write it here as a commitment to yourself.

_____

_____

_____

_____

_____

_____

_____

_____

_____

Start thinking about how you can bring your values into your life each day. Maybe grab a pen and circle the values you wish to focus on first.

Let your values guide you

When we know our values, we have a deep sense of who we are. We have a compass that can guide us each day. Even if the world suddenly changes – if you retire, become ill, have to move forward from a tragedy – and you can no longer work towards your usual goal, you can use your values to decide how to move forward. You can find ways to bring these qualities into your day and to shape your new life. You can ensure that on your deathbed you will look back and know you lived a life you can feel proud of. A hope, I imagine, we all share.

17. Find and Connect to Your Community

*The unconscious fear that seems to always be
lurking in the background is that if we aren't
understood it will be as if we never existed.*
—MICHAEL SCHREINER

This chapter will help you think about ways to:

- Create a community.
- Campaign for causes that are important to you.
- Volunteer your time.

Did you know that our hearts and breath sync when watching an emotional movie or singing with other people? And when around people we love, looking into their eyes or simply sitting next to them causes the same thing to happen. This not only feels grounding in the moment, it helps in stressful times, with one study showing that loving touch helped decrease physical pain.

Humans are not meant to exist in isolation; they are meant to be in communities and feel like they belong.

Throughout this book I have discussed the importance of relationships, the devastating consequences of loneliness and disconnection, and the problems that exist in society (such as prejudice) that we will only be able to overcome if we work together.

If we are truly going to heal ourselves and heal each other, we need to think about how we connect to other people. Ideally, we need to link in with people who can make us feel heard, seen, empowered and like we are contributing. And, ideally, we need to focus on the quality of our relationships rather than the quantity.

Feeling understood by one person is more important than being surrounded by lots of people who leave you feeling isolated.

Don't worry if you are reading this and thinking, *But I don't have a community or a person*. Rethink that thought and add . . . *yet*.

In fact, whenever your brain panics, saying you don't or can't do or manage or have something, repeat the sentence with . . . *yet*!

Getting Involved in Communities

The number of friends we have usually peaks in our twenties. This number gradually decreases as we head through our thirties and onwards, but the friendships that remain tend to be very deep.

Often it isn't until a significant life event occurs that we consider the number or quality of our friendships. Meaning many people don't think about needing to expand their friendship pool till they suddenly look up from their busy lives and realise there are few people to talk to.

But making friends as an adult can feel really hard, so where to start?

Shared experiences and shared values are the most common starting point for most friendships. Therefore, when looking to make new friends, you may choose to look for a group specifically related to:

- An emotional or life experience you are going through, such as a mental health group, a survivors' group or a local interest group.
- Part of your identity, for example, your sexuality, a new parents' group, a local charity, or a campaign group tackling an issue you care about.
- Something you enjoy that aligns with your values.

Face-to-face vs. side-by-side connection

Sometimes the connections we look for involve wanting people to talk to and share with (face-to-face connection). Sometimes we want people to share activities with (side-by-side).

During the COVID-19 lockdown, people often said to me that there was a lot of pressure to talk to people over video link. They said they didn't love this experience for many reasons, including the fact that there was so little to discuss aside from the pandemic. People ran out of things to say, and they missed doing activities side-by-side with people, like watching sports or wandering around town for the day.

Side-by-side activities are an excellent low-pressure way to connect with others. Men, in particular, often feel they lack the skills for face-to-face relationships and find watching sport together more manageable than sitting and chatting.

If any of this speaks to you, think about the activities you already enjoy or want to learn: cooking, sport, craft, photography, languages. Whatever floats your boat.

Do you like to sing? When we sing, we boost our breathing skills, our diaphragmatic breath, and it is even starting to be recommended as a treatment for postnatal depression and to improve the quality of life for people living with cancer and with chronic respiratory disease. You don't have to be good at it! The quality of your voice isn't the point. Sound like a bag of cats? Don't worry, the psychological outcome will be just as good!

If you're not into singing, you could join a walking group, a sports team, a language class or a sewing and crafting group – this can be particularly good for people who are feeling a bit nervy about face-to-face socialising. You can connect mindfully with a physical activity, sitting side by side, not needing to chat. You don't need to talk about yourself.

Side-by-side connection with a common goal is as valuable for giving you a sense of purpose and connection as face-to-face conversation. And, you never know, you may find that when your attention is on the task at hand, you relax, chatting naturally with the others there, who you already share at least one of your interests.

If you meet someone you like, be bold and ask them if they want to meet for coffee sometime. Exchange details. Remember how common loneliness is, meaning it's quite likely that the other person may be looking for a new pal too!

Quick tips

- **Inviting people to your home can ramp up the pressure, so for the first few friend-dates maybe go somewhere you can relax** and don't feel you have to host or perform.
- **Ask questions!** Being listened to is a rare gift. Offer that to someone and you might get to know them quicker than you imagined.
- **Be kind to yourself.** Deep friendships take time to build. And it can be nerve-racking to put yourself out there. So, be a friend to yourself when you go through the process too!

In case you're unsure where to find communities or a group, Meetup.com is a great place to start looking. They have over 225,000 groups in over 180 countries worldwide, with categories including pets, writing, dance, photography, political movements, beliefs, book clubs, hobbies and crafts, LGBTQ+ and many more. If you can't find a Meetup group that works for you, you could even start one.

Online communities

As 2020 showed us that shared physical spaces aren't a guarantee, it is also worth looking online. Online groups offer you a wider reach than your local community, and also sometimes have an offline meet-up option too – the best of both worlds!

Also, online communities have created safe-places, representation and role models for people whose experiences are marginalised and misrepresented in the real world.

For example, for young, queer, gender non-conforming and transgender folx (the collective and inclusive term for folks), online communities offer a chance not only to connect with others with similar experiences, but also a space to explore identity, new self-definitions, a place to hear about other people's coming-out stories, find support that fosters resilience and self-esteem, and find out about community events.

Online communities are particularly special as they offer a place where people can show themselves in the way they wish to be seen. Remember I talked about lack of representation in the media? Social media is tackling this with people showing themselves as they wish to be seen. Empowering! And game-changing. It challenges the narrow representations shown in the media, and tells everyone the truth, which is, whoever you are, you deserve to be seen and you deserve to take up space.

So, if you can't find a community offline, make a point of finding a place online that matches your values, your interests and your lived experiences.

Campaigning

> *Social media is a force for change, which can challenge entrenched hierarchies, redistribute power, democratize information, support mass mobilization and contribute to the building of global movements.*
>
> —CABE & HARRIS, 2020

If we could create a world in which prejudice and traumatic experiences did not exist there would be less of a need for therapy to exist.

Is there a social justice issue that affects you? Racism? Sexism? Ableism? Homophobia? Fatphobia? Transphobia? Ageism? Another form of prejudice or experience that you want to fight against? Or a social justice issue that affects many others, and that you want to co-conspire with them against? If so, and you don't already know of a place to find someone already working to fight these areas, Google it!

It may seem obvious but, if you can find them, look for groups and organisations run by people with the lived experience of whatever it is you are fighting against. Hear from, and be guided by, people who have lived it.

Traditionally, change used to occur when people with high status, power and resources fought for matters that were important to them. Social media has changed this, as previously unconnected people from across the globe can now come together to discuss the hostility they face in the outside world, join voices and become politically active about inequality and inequity. Inspired by people who are on the front lines, fighting for what they believe in, and for more than just survival, every single day.

Many important movements that fight for freedom and justice started online and are working to change the world and bring social justice, including Black Lives Matter (which started as a hashtag in a Facebook post by the American Civil Rights activist Alicia Garza) and the #MeToo movement (which targets sexual violence and was started online by Tarana Burke in 2016). Both have become powerful movements that fight for freedom and justice.

UK activist Gina Martin used social media as the place to start her successful campaign that made upskirting illegal. Scarlett Curtis, Grace Campbell, Honey Ross and Alice Skinner co-founded The Pink Protest, an online community that has successfully changed two UK laws and raised awareness around period poverty and female genital mutilation.

If you want to make change, you do not need to be famous or connected to people in places of power; you just need an internet connection and critical mass.

Once you have found a group, think of the resources you have to offer. Can you offer practical help campaigning, spreading the word, collecting signatures or money? Are there other ways you can volunteer (we will talk about this at the end of the chapter)? Do you have a large audience or social media platform that you could use to spread the word? Or maybe you can donate to support a campaign you believe in

But what if there isn't a campaign running? What then?

Setting up your own campaign

If you wish to set up a community to campaign with, I recommend reading *Emergent Strategy: Shaping Change, Changing Worlds* by Adrienne Maree Brown and *Be the Change: A Toolkit for the Activist in You* by Gina Martin. They offer insightful and often beautiful ways to think about organising to create change.

Consider these steps:

- Find like-minded people you know or who exist online.
- Email or message your local leaders about the issues that are important to you. Organise a face-to-face meeting with local representatives. Contact your local radio stations and talk shows.
- Vote and rally to support leaders you believe in.
- Volunteer to support communities, activists and campaigns that already exist either locally or nationally, or even internationally. If you don't have time to offer, donate other kinds of resources, e.g. money or used clothes or belongings.
- Host a book club or movie night on the topics of your choice to raise awareness. Start a boycott, or a buycott!
- Create stories of lived experiences you want to highlight and share online and/or as part of the campaign you send to local leaders. Maybe set up a social media account on the topic and start a petition.
- Have difficult conversations with people you know.
- Get lots of rest, as creating political and social change is a marathon not a sprint.

Volunteering

Community volunteering soared during lockdown, with one in five people in the UK volunteering (among other activities) to buy and deliver groceries to people unable to leave the house, calling people to combat loneliness, or working on phone lines. Communities were strengthened by individual members offering their time to support others.

But volunteering doesn't solely help those it aims to support; volunteering gives volunteers a sense of purpose, is a great way to meet new people, get new skills, feel good about yourself and, the best part is . . . anyone can do it.

To decide what you might like to do, think about the skills you already have to offer, and where you might be able to share those.

If you know how to write computer code and can offer some time each week or month, then you could volunteer for 'Girls Who Code' and teach those precious skills to close the gender gap present in the tech industry.

If you speak more than one language, there are always organisations that need help with translation, such as the Red Cross, and you can even do this from the comfort of your own home.

If you have green fingers, you could volunteer at a community garden that provides fruit and vegetables for people who live in the area.

If you have experience of working through distress, overcoming your own mental health battles, you might consider passing your hard-learned knowledge onto another person in need. Many people have said this was an important part of their recovery journey. If this speaks to you, there are many mental health charities that would love you as a befriender, a mentor or an advocate. You can be a beacon of light for others who currently find themselves in the dark.

There are so many places and ways that you can volunteer your time. For example, you can work with organisations that:

- Teach future generations by reading to disadvantaged children (e.g. the National Literacy Trust).
- Fight hunger by cooking food for people experiencing homelessness and/or then deliver that food to people who are in need.
- Fight isolation by writing letters to the elderly in nursing homes (e.g. the charity Love For Our Elders).
- Help people know they are not alone even in times of crisis by volunteering for a crisis line (e.g. Crisis Text Line, Childline and Samaritans)
- Fight inequality and expose human rights violations by researching for Amnesty International, or do research teaching and training for the United Nations.

You can also volunteer from the comfort of your own home (e.g. the Red Cross needs support with blood drives, people to manage cases, code and check digital tools). Volunteermatch. org lists global opportunities, but if you want something much closer to home, across the UK you can find your local volunteering centre through NCVO, which is the UK's largest network for charities and volunteering.

Wherever you are in the world, you can look up volunteering opportunities in your local area or online. Or you could simply offer to make tea or pick up groceries for your neighbour. Whatever you choose, there are many people who will be delighted to snap you up.

An old supervisor of mine used to say, 'If you want to improve your self-esteem, do esteemable things.'

18. Get Therapy

This chapter explains:

- The common myths surrounding therapy.
- The different types of therapy and what they are for.
- What to ask yourself when looking for a therapist.
- What to ask a therapist when you first meet them.

This section will be helpful for anyone who feels afraid of therapy and wants to know what it really is. For anyone who is considering therapy but has no idea where to start.

Finally, Therapy

The difference between therapy and the advice in this book is significant. Therapy involves feeling like your mind is being held in the mind of another person. It makes you know that someone else is thinking about you and considering how best to support you, and that you have someone who is rooting for you. I truly am my clients' biggest cheerleader.

Additionally, therapy is tailored to your needs and is confidential. So, if you have further questions or avenues to explore after completing this book, you might want to find someone to work through it with.

Throughout the book I have highlighted times where therapy may be important to consider. For example, if you are experiencing panic attacks that are ongoing, have intrusive thoughts that are scaring you and affecting your life, have an abusive inner critic or are struggling with prejudice and pain in the world. However, therapy is not solely for people in acute distress. It is for anyone wanting to understand themselves, their self-esteem, their patterns and their relationships on a deeper level.

I realise therapy is not accessible to all, hence me writing this book in the first place, so this chapter not only explains how to navigate therapy, get a therapist and leave a therapist, it also includes books based on each type of therapy so that you can continue your reading outside of the therapy room.

Common myths around therapy

It means you're crazy or that you have serious 'issues'
Just no.

Therapists are no different from your friends or family
Therapists are not your friends and they are not your family. They have specialist training and 'know how'. They will hold you in unconditional positive regard and act as a container, confidante and possible guide, but they are professionals with ethical and legal guidelines they must follow. They offer an

objective perspective and have no agenda other than your best interests.

Therapy is just talking

Therapy can be many things. Therapy can be mainly talking but it also – depending on the kind of therapy you choose – involves skills-training, homework and activities to be completed within and outside the session. And sometimes it is mainly physical, such as somatic therapy, which we will talk about later in this chapter.

Everything in therapy is about childhood

I hope I have shown you that sometimes we struggle due to our past. Sometimes we struggle due to our present. Sometimes we can only move forward by addressing our past. Sometimes we simply need someone to teach us practical strategies that will help us right now. Because of this, different kinds of therapy look at different areas of your life.

If you are experiencing panic attacks or intrusive thoughts, for example, the goal of therapy is to stabilise you, to make you feel safe and grounded, teaching you to manage and overcome both of these experiences before considering anything else.

If you are stuck repeating patterns in your relationships (e.g. if you are always drawn to others who make you feel the way people in your early life made you feel), this would require returning to the time when these patterns first started, to understand what the patterns serve and work from there.

Everyone needs therapy

While it's true that we would all benefit from understanding ourselves, not everyone needs therapy. Lots of people are just fine without it. And some people who are struggling just need the right support, a little psycho-education (psychological information to help them make sense of their experiences) and a few trusty coping skills to help them along.

Therapy will fix you

Sorry, no. That's not what we do.

1. Because you do not need 'fixing'.
2. Because we do not have all the answers.

For example, in my therapy sessions I remind my clients that 'You are the expert of you'. I tell them I am up to speed on a ton of psychology and neuroscience, and that I will walk alongside them, or sit in the dark with them, creating a shared understanding and path forward until we, together, find a way towards the light.

It can be true that when you start therapy things can feel a little worse for a while, as you begin to notice the stuff you've been avoiding or unaware of, but, over time, you move through this and onwards. However, this quote sums it up very well:

> *As every therapist will tell you, healing involves discomfort —*
> *but so does refusing to heal. And over time, refusing to heal*
> *is always more painful.*

> —RESMAA MENAKEM,
> author of *My Grandmother's Hands*

So what is therapy?

Therapy is a place to understand yourself, without judgement, and find a path forward with the tools you need to do so.

Therapy offers insight into the parts of ourselves we can rarely reach alone. I have seen this time and time again. I find this still when I go to therapy. My therapist often points out patterns in my relationships that I totally missed during my own introspection and my mind is blown!

For some of us, therapy is our first secure attachment relationship. The first place we can rely on someone to be there for us and listen to us consistently.

Most importantly perhaps: when you are losing hope, a therapist will hold that hope for you until you are ready to hold it too. They will help you create a new story and a value-driven life, and work with you to find the skills that will get you there.

Over time, we start to internalise the soothing voice and words of our therapist, which means that when our inner critic pops up, we have an automatic inner cheerleader whispering soothing words into our ear in our time of need.

Therapy can be engaged in face to face, by video call, over the phone, over text. It can be one-to-one, for couples and/or families, or in groups with people you grow to know. It can involve direct conversation, walk and talk and/or physical movement. It can be an hour a week or many hours a week. It can be offered by your local health service for free, or private and not free. There are so many types of therapy it's enough to make my head spin. Here is some advice on what to do when considering finding a therapist.

What to ask when looking for a therapist

There are some practical questions you need to ask yourself when thinking about therapy. These include:

- What are you looking to gain support with? Are you looking to learn skills to manage and overcome feeling emotionally overwhelmed, such as anxiety? Are you looking to understand your relational patterns and hopefully shift them? Are you looking for trauma support?
- What are your goals? For the short term? And for the long?
- Are there specific aspects of your identity or experience that you feel will be best understood by someone of the same or similar identity to you? If so, which ones? For example, would you like them to be the same sexuality or race as you? Would you like them to have experienced similar lived experiences to you?
- Where will you feel most comfortable seeing a therapist? Online through video? Face to face? Alone? In a group?
- If you have had therapy before, what worked well and what didn't? What do you want more of in the future and what do you want to avoid?

These questions will help narrow down your options when it comes to the therapy model and the therapist you choose. Once you have answered these questions, consider the types of therapy below to choose which would be a good fit.

Types of therapy

The type of therapy you need depends on what you are working on. When I had panic attacks, I didn't know there were different kinds of therapy. The first therapist I met immediately launched into 'Now, tell me about your childhood.' I had told them I was having panic attacks and suddenly we were talking about my mum and dad. I was confused, and my panic attacks were immediately worse, not better. I needed skills, not to dredge up my childhood. I never saw that therapist again. I then found a CBT therapist, listened to breathing exercises and mindfulness tapes 24 hours a day (I'm not exaggerating: I had them in my ears all day and all night) and the panic started to lift.

Now the panic years are over, I have a therapist who often asks me about my childhood and my relationships from that time. It is perfect for what I need right now in my life.

Here are the most common types of therapy (think about how each one could meet your goals).

Cognitive Behavioural Therapy (CBT)
This is a skills–driven approach that teaches us:

- To understand the reasons we feel anxious, depressed or another emotion.
- To identify and challenge beliefs, unhelpful thinking styles and behaviours (such as avoidance) that are keeping us stuck.
- How to use breathing exercises and other coping skills effectively.

CBT is particularly helpful for anxiety and OCD, and is also recommended for people experiencing depression, rumination and PTSD. If you need practical skills-training, this may be for you. Many ideas in this book come from CBT, including how to check if you are overestimating threat, and common thinking errors.

Book recommendations: *CBT for Dummies Workbook* by Rhena Branch and Rob Willson. *Mind Over Mood* by Dennis Greenberger and Christine A. Padesky.

Acceptance and Commitment Therapy (ACT)

This is similar to CBT in that it also looks at thoughts and behaviours and teaches practical coping skills. However, instead of challenging your thoughts and beliefs and behaviours (which can sometimes lead to us fighting against our thoughts, making them feel even more sticky), it teaches:

- Mindfulness techniques that help you accept and let go of thoughts, feelings, urges and behaviours that keep you stuck.
- How to identify your values and live a value-driven life so you can choose how to move forward and live a life that suits you.

This is very good for anxiety, OCD, depression, substance use, chronic pain and for other health conditions. Many ideas in this book come from ACT, including singing your thoughts to a song (Chapter 7), the sky and weather mindfulness metaphor (Chapter 13) and the section on values (Chapter 16).

Book recommendation: *The Happiness Trap* by Russ Harris. It's fantastic.

Dialectic Behaviour Therapy (DBT)

DBT is particularly good if you need to be grounded and regulated hard and fast, and is recommended for borderline personality disorder, eating disorders, ADHD, substance use and managing self-harm. Increasingly, research is showing how useful it is for managing anxiety and emotional regulation for people with ADHD or autism. DBT:

- Teaches emotional regulation skills – focusing on mindfulness, interpersonal effectiveness, distress tolerance and emotion regulation.
- Usually combines individual work and group sessions, meaning you have community and active support, so you know you're not alone.

The ideas I've shared in this book that you'll find in DBT include 'both/and' thinking (which they call 'dialectics') and the grounding technique that tells you to submerge your face in iced water (Chapter 11).

Book recommendation: *Dialectical Behavior Therapy Workbook: Practical DBT Exercises for Learning Mindfulness, Interpersonal Effectiveness, Emotion Regulation & Distress Tolerance* by Matthew McKay, PhD, Jeffrey C. Wood, PsyD and Jeffrey Brantley, MD.

Mindfulness-Based Stress Reduction (MBSR)

This highly structured 8-week programme (2.5-hour weekly meetings + one 6-hour weekend retreat):

- Teaches you to use mindfulness to recognise your emotional and physical pain, and allow it to be present without fighting it, changing your habitual stress responses.
- Is usually provided within a group.
- Entails group discussions that reflect on the meditative process, such as the experiences that arise during body scans and walking meditation.
- Is not tailored to the client in the ways that other individual therapies are.

MBSR is recommended for managing depression, anxiety, chronic pain and multiple health conditions known to cause distress such as hypertension, skin and immune disorders (e.g. psoriasis), HIV, cancer and diabetes.

The ideas I have shared in this book that you will find in MBSR include the mindfulness-practices, including the body scan, found in Chapter 13.

Book recommendation: *Full Catastrophe Living: Using the Wisdom of Your Body and Mind to Face Stress, Pain, and Illness* by Jon Kabat-Zinn.

Internal Family Systems (IFS)

IFS practitioners believe that our personality is split into multiple parts. Each of these 'parts' developed to protect us in some way. For example, our inner critic may be a perfectionist, or a taskmaster, and these represent different 'parts' of ourselves that we have developed in response to the world. If we have experienced extreme distress in our lives, such as psychological trauma and abuse, we may have parts of ourselves that we have exiled so as to stay safe, such as the part of ourselves that was extremely frightened, or the memory of the person who abused us. This therapy helps you to:

- Identify and integrate each part of your 'self', so you can feel safe, whole and self-reliant again.

This can be used to support people with depression, anxiety, panic attacks and physical health conditions. However, I particularly recommend this for people who have an extreme inner critic.

The idea that I shared in this book that comes from IFS is '7 styles of inner critic' (Chapter 9).

Book recommendation: *Activating Your Inner Champion Instead of Your Inner Critic* by Jay Earley PhD and Bonnie Weiss, LCSW.

Psychoanalysis/psychodynamic therapy

This is the therapy you often see in films, where someone lies on a couch speaking to their therapist. It is not skills-based. It instead:

- Looks into the unconscious and is more closely aligned with Freudian ideas.
- Focuses on patterns that may emerge from the past – looking at relationships starting at birth and the unconscious struggles and urges that you may have repressed or are fighting with that are affecting you now.
- Expects you to re-enact these patterns in your therapeutic relationship so that you can see them happening in real time and learn how to move forward.

This is used for everything (unless you are having panic attacks or intrusive thoughts and you need skills training), particularly if the emotional pain you are experiencing has been long-standing. I particularly recommend it for relational issues – for example, if you notice you are repeating the same patterns in your relationships over and over. This kind of therapy is usually long-term.

My book recommendation isn't a traditional psychodynamic book, as they are often difficult to digest. Instead this book explains a short-term therapy model that combines psychodynamic ideas and cognitive theory (Transactional Analysis) and it is utterly brilliant.

Book recommendation: *Counselling for Toads: A Psychological Adventure* by Robert de Board (I recommend listening to the audiobook).

Systemic therapy

Systemic therapy does not believe people are flawed or need a diagnosis, as it sees problems arising in relationships and not within people. It focuses on the present moment (what is keeping you stuck right now) and teaches you to:

- Identify the multiple environments you live in that might be causing you distress (is the distress arising in your family, between you and one other person, or is it arising because of prejudice, structural inequality, or because someone who has power over you is telling stories about you that have now gained so much traction you now believe this narrow story?).
- Identify ways to move forward, knowing that you already have the strength within you to do this.

- If you engage in narrative therapy (an offshoot of systemic therapy) you will learn to look for the exceptions to the stories you (or other people) are telling about you, so that you can create new stories that empower you.

Systemic therapy can be for individuals, couples, whole families, and teams of people who work together. It's recommended for alcohol dependence, anxiety, depression, body image issues, PTSD, relationship problems and many other experiences.

Book recommendation: *Retelling the Stories of our Lives: Everyday Narrative Therapy to Draw Inspiration and Transform Experience* by David Denborough.

Eye Movement Desensitization and Reprocessing (EMDR)

Not only does this therapy teach you coping skills to manage distress, it offers a way to process traumatic memories that cause serious distress and flashbacks. This is quite different from other therapies, as it involves:

- Learning coping skills to manage emotional distress.
- Bringing a distressing moment to mind, then letting your mind run free while your therapist does something called bilateral stimulation (this could involve you having to watch your therapist move their fingers from side to side in front of your eyes, or listening to something that beeps in one ear and then the other). Bilateral stimulation of this kind is thought to work as it helps the brain process memories in the same way it processes information during REM sleep, when our eyes go back and forth.

This therapy is recommended for people who have experienced trauma and other distressing life experiences, including PTSD, panic disorders, anxiety, phobia and depression. It can be particularly helpful if you wish to process memories that have a lot of shame linked to them, as you do not need to share all of your experiences with your therapist.

Book recommendation: *Getting Past Your Past: Take Control of Your Life with Self-Help Techniques from EMDR Therapy* by Francine Shapiro, PhD.

Somatic therapy

This is about connecting the body and mind in ways that teach you to feel safe again in your body. Rather than focusing on talking, somatic therapies focus on grounding your nervous system and safely releasing the physical experience of stress, anxiety and trauma. Through, for example, physical movement, massage and breathwork.

Book recommendations: *Healing Trauma: A Pioneering Program for Restoring the Wisdom of Your Body* by Peter A. Levine PhD. *The Body Keeps the Score: Mind, Brain and Body in the Transformation of Trauma* by Bessel Van Der Kolk.

Some therapists blend therapeutic models to suit their clients, as I have done in this book.

When you have decided what you hope for in therapy, you can now either ask your local healthcare professional if they will refer you to someone (if you are in the UK, please go to your GP and they will refer you to your local NHS service) or, if you are going to pay for therapy, you can ask your friends for a recommendation, or you can do a Google search for therapists in your area. The *Psychology Today* website has a global therapist directory, and you can search for a practice closest to your address.

Ensure you look for a qualified and accredited therapist.

In the UK, the term 'psychologist' can be used by anyone who chooses to use this label. However, 'clinical psychologists' and 'counselling psychologists' must have a doctorate in either clinical or counselling psychology and be registered with the Health and Care Professionals Council. Psychotherapists and counsellors may have a mix of qualifications that allow them to be titled as such, and are usually accredited by the British Association for Counselling and Psychotherapy (BACP). Different countries have different rules around the qualifications required to be an accredited therapist, so search 'How to find an accredited therapist' if you are not from the UK. Wherever you live, ask potential therapists what their qualifications are and which professional body they are registered to.

If you find a private therapist you like the sound of, ask for a free consultation to see if they are a good fit for you.

Your first session

A strong therapeutic relationship is shown time and time again to be the biggest predictor of positive change in therapy. With this in mind, when meeting a therapist for the first time, pay attention to how you feel when you are with them. In your initial meeting I recommend doing the following:

- Arrive with a list of questions, such as: how does this work? How do you make sense of experiences like mine? What will I have to do inside and outside of sessions? How long do you think we will need to work together? What happens if we disagree at any time? What experience do you have of working with situations similar to mine?

- Tell the therapist your goals and experiences but know that you do not have to share anything you do not feel comfortable sharing right away; you can take your time. People often have vulnerability hangovers after oversharing, so do not rush; share what feels safe.

- If you have had therapy previously, tell your therapist what you liked and disliked about the work you have done in the past. Tell them what you would like to do more or less of.

- Throughout and afterwards ask yourself whether you feel safe and comfortable in the therapist's office/online space and presence?

If you feel good throughout, and all these questions are answered, it's a match!

Should you break up with your therapist?

Sometimes you will have to break up with your therapist and that's okay! Sometimes therapy will naturally draw to a close when you have met your goals. Other times you will have to end it early, as you don't feel like you're a good fit. This can feel scary to do, but it is important that we do it when we need to. I have ended therapy with therapists I didn't mesh with and people have ended therapy with me too. All of this is okay.

Reasons you may want to end therapy include feeling like:

- You have met your goals.
- The therapy is not meeting your goals and, when you raise that you would like to work on something specific, nothing seems to change.
- You feel unsafe in the relationship or like you are minimised, judged or shamed.
- Your therapist talks more about themselves and their life than they do about yours.

If you want to see if you can make the relationship a little better, you can talk about this with your therapist too. I realise this is easier said than done, so here are some ways to initiate a conversation if you feel like this:

- 'In our next session can we review our goals?'
- 'Can we talk through how you think things are going?'
- 'Can we talk about how it feels when I share personal experiences?'
- 'Sometimes I don't feel safe when I share how I feel. Can we think of ways to address this?'

These questions will, I hope, signal to the therapist that they need to work together with you to make the change you wish to see. If they don't take your points seriously, then you can still leave.

If you want to finish therapy, you can just say you want to end the sessions. You can use this trusty statement: 'I think I'm ready to go it alone; can we talk about endings?'

Speaking of endings . . .

Wow. This is the end!

It has been a few years since I sat in that car and wrote the notes that became this book. You have in your hands more than the basics that I teach and share with clients, and now I want to leave you with the final message I share with my clients too.

Instead of focusing on resilience, and the ingenuity people constantly show in terms of coping with a sometimes unpredictable and scary world, many therapists like to focus on everything that went wrong, could go wrong, and what is 'wrong' with people.

I don't believe anything is wrong with people. Humans are humans. Distress arises when distressing things happen in our lives. And people are ingenious; they always find a way to adapt.

You are ingenious. You have adapted. You have found a myriad ways to get to this point in your life. You are so many incredible things that the world has possibly trained you to pay little attention to.

I hope that this manual gave gives you an opportunity to start to believe this.

I hope that this manual will be something you return to over and over, finding something new each time you dive back in.

I hope you realise, now more than ever, that you make sense, so much sense, and that no matter how dark it gets from time to time, you are not broken – there is always a way to cope and move forward. You are human.

So much love,

Dr Soph xx

Appendix

Overcoming Avoidance
One Step at a Time

If you have been avoiding supermarkets, the train or another place (or thought or feeling) associated with anxiety, then what you need is a plan. A plan to move from the smallest scary thing to the biggest.

Draw a ladder (or staircase) in the space provided. It can have as many steps as you like (but no more than 10).

Write down the name or thing you have been avoiding:

_____

Ask yourself: what is the least scary first step I could take to going to that place? For example, if you are avoiding the underground like I did. Is it: look at a picture of the underground online? Once you have decided on this step, write it on the bottom rung of the ladder, (or the bottom step).

What is the next one? Is it: go to the top of the underground steps and sit outside for 5 minutes while doing breathing and grounding exercises? If this is too scary, you could go with a friend, or you could even imagine going there. Write this on the next step.

Imagining an action activates the same area of the brain as doing the actual task.

If it's too scary to go somewhere that you associate with anxiety, begin with imagining going there.

Find a comfortable spot at home, start your breathing exercise (from Chapter 12), and this time imagine you are going to do the thing that scares you.

Start doing the breathing exercise as you visualise yourself walking into the underground and onto the train/into the place that worries you. See yourself there, hearing the noises that you might hear, smelling the smells. See yourself doing the breathing exercise, noticing the wave of emotion as it rises

---

and falls, and telling yourself that you are totally safe. Keep breathing, and keep visualising yourself coping. Imagine it going well and that you leave feeling confident.

This will give your brain your first example of this activity going well, and you can build from there. Do this a number of times. When you feel safe enough to imagine yourself doing it, then do the real thing.

If, during the imagery, you see yourself panicking or doing something else that doesn't feel good, don't stop. Simply rewind and replay that moment, visualising yourself doing it calmly this time. In your mind you can rewind and edit any moments, so make the most of that opportunity.

What is next? Is it: go into the ticket hall of the underground for 5 minutes, breathing and grounding? Whatever you choose, write this on the next step.

What then? Is it: go onto the platform with a friend who can do the breathing and grounding exercises with you, again for 5 minutes (or 1, or 2, if this is too much for the first time)?

What then? Is it: go onto the train, with a friend, stay for 5 minutes breathing and grounding.

What then? Is it: go onto the train without a friend, but they are in the next carriage, and you breathe and ground until the next stop?

What then? Is it: do that again but without your friend? Breathing and grounding on your own?

Can you see how this goes? You decide on the steps, and who you would need to support you, and you write them on the ladder.

Then decide when you will put each step into practice. Whatever you do, ensure you know how to use your grounding skills and breathing exercises to your advantage. And if you have a friend supporting you, ensure they do too. I used to have my breathing exercise on audio, playing in my ears while I did this. You can try that too.

Then start. Do the smallest part until you know you can successfully breathe through it. Then move to the next.

Expect that the anxiety will increase the first time you do each step. If your brain thinks what you're doing is dangerous it will ramp up. I know it sounds scary but it is totally normal. Breathe, ground, stay put soothing yourself, and you will notice that the wave of emotion will gradually fade out.

If you progress too quickly and feel overwhelmed, no problem – go back to the previous step, or even two, and start from there. This is not a race.

After each step, give yourself a huge reward. This is an amazing feat. A small step for people who haven't panicked before; a giant leap for the rest of us. Good luck xx.

And remember, there are qualified people who can take you through this, should you need that. I did.

Notes

PART ONE – How You Got Here

p.10 *The wheels of who we are . . .*

Saudino, Kimberly J., 'Behavioral Genetics and Child Temperament', *Journal of Developmental and Behavioral Pediatrics (JDBP)*, 26(3), 214 (2005).

1. Caregivers, Siblings and our Family Environment

Attachment Styles

p.22 *You were given the message that your emotions would not be attended to . . .*

I say this ironically as, while this helped us fundamentally as kids, this is something that can really mess with us as adults.

Siblings

p.27 *Seriously, did you know that siblings . . .*

Perlman, M., & Ross, H., 'The Benefits of Parent Intervention in Children's Disputes: An Examination of Concurrent Changes in Children's Fighting Styles', *Child Development,* 68(4), doi:10.2307/1132119, 690–700 (1997).

p.29 *Research shows that caregivers do often feel closer to one of their children . . .*

Peng, S., Suitor, J. J., & Gilligan, M., 'The Long Arm of Maternal Differential Treatment: Effects of Recalled and Current Favoritism on Adult Children's Psychological Well-Being', *The Journals of Gerontology: Series B*, 73(6), 1123–1132 (2018).

p.29 *44.6 per cent to be exact . . .*

Suitor, J. J., Gilligan, M., Rurka, M., Peng, S., Meyer, J., & Pillemer, K., 'Accuracy of Adult Children's Perceptions of Mothers' Caregiver Preferences', *The Gerontologist*, 59(3), 528–537 (2019).

p.29 *39 per cent of the time . . .*

TED (2016). Jill Suitor, 'So You Think You're Mom's Favorite?' https://www.youtube.com/watch?v=8x_gFJuMONg. Accessed 1 Sep. 2020.

2. The School Years

Our culture

p.53 *that the number of babies who are born 'intersex' . . .*

Office of the High Commissioner for Human Rights, *Free & Equal Campaign Fact Sheet: Intersex*, 2015, https://unfe.org/system/unfe-65-Intersex_Factsheet_ENGLISH.pdf. Accessed 20 July 2020.

p.57 *young women rated their sexual satisfaction . . .*

McClelland, Sara I., *Intimate Justice: Sexual Satisfaction in Young Adults*, City University of New York, 2009.

p.58 *'traditionally masculine qualities'*

Priess, Heather A. et al., 'Adolescent Gender-role Identity and Mental Health: Gender Intensification Revisited', *Child Development*, 80(5), 1531–44 (2009),. doi:10.1111/j.1467–8624.2009.01349.x

p.58 *more likely to punish and shun 'gender violations' in boys than in girls . . .*

Kane, Emily W., '"No Way My Boys Are Going to Be like That!" Parents' Responses to Children's Gender Nonconformity', *Gender and Society* 20, 20(2), 149–76 (2006)

Bullying

p.60 *Young people with long-term illnesses . . .*

Long, Robert, Nerys Roberts, and Philip Loft, 'Bullying in UK Schools' (2020).

p.60 *LGBTQ+ pupils report being bullied*

Stonewall., 'School report' (2017), https://www.stonewall.org.uk/system/files/the_school_report_2017.pdf. Accessed 23 Aug. 2020.

3. Advertising, Media, Social Media

Advertising

p.73 *Chloé Michel and colleagues demonstrated . . .*

This study looked at data of approximately 1 million people in 27 European countries across 31 years, and adjusted for effects linked to other factors that we know affect human wellbeing, such as unemployment and the business cycle (read: the effects this study found were not due to other factors that we know usually cause life satisfaction to drop). Making this finding one we can rely on.

p.73 *dip in life satisfaction across the nation*

Michel, Chloe, Michelle Sovinsky, Eugenio Proto, and Andrew J. Oswald, 'Advertising as a Major Source of Human Dissatisfaction: Cross-National Evidence on One Million Europeans', *The Economics of Happiness*, 217–239, Springer, Cham, 2019.

Selling perfection

p.76 *twice as much weight-based body discrimination as men*

Puhl, Rebecca M., Tatiana Andreyeva, and Kelly D. Brownell, 'Perceptions of Weight Discrimination: Prevalence and Comparison to Race and Gender Discrimination in America', *International Journal of Obesity*, 32(6), 992–1000 (2008).

Social comparison theory

p.76 *father of social comparison theory*

Festinger, Leon, 'A Theory of Social Comparison Processes', *Human Relations* 7, 2, 117–40 (1954).

You are good enough

p.83 *a spike in anti-fat attitudes*

Ravary, Amanda, Mark W. Baldwin, and Jennifer A. Bartz, 'Shaping the Body Politic: Mass Media Fat-Shaming Affects Implicit Anti-Fat Attitudes', *Personality and Social Psychology Bulletin* 45, 11, 1580–9 (2019).

Film and TV

p.85 *girls and Black boys' self-esteem is decreased . . .*

Yuen, Nancy Wang, *Reel Inequality: Hollywood Actors and Racism*, Rutgers University Press, 2017.

Mental health on screen

p.89 *They focus on the rare forensic cases . . .*

Chen, Marian and Stephen Lawrie, 'Newspaper Depictions of Mental and Physical Health', *BJPsych Bulletin*, 41(6), 308–13 (2017).

p.89 *The reality for people with schizophrenia diagnoses*

Wehring, Heidi J. and William T. Carpenter, 'Violence and Schizophrenia, *Schizophrenia Bulletin*, 37(5), 877–8 (2011).

p.91 *in Northern Ireland the number rises . . .*

Samaritans, UK, 'Suicide Statistics Report – Latest Statistics for the UK and Republic of Ireland', 2018.

Social media

p.93 *Instagram has the worst effect on our mental health*

Cramer, Shirley, '#Statusofmind: Social Media and Young People's Mental Health and Wellbeing', in *APHA's 2018 Annual Meeting & Expo (Nov. 10–14)*, American Public Health Association, 2018.

p.93 *Instagram had been directly linked with . . .*

Brown, Zoe and Marika Tiggemann, 'Attractive Celebrity and Peer Images on Instagram: Effect on Women's Mood and Body Image', *Body Image*, 19, 37–43 (2016).

Lup, Katerina, Leora Trub, and Lisa Rosenthal, 'Instagram# instasad?: Exploring Associations Among Instagram Use, Depressive Symptoms, Negative Social Comparison, and Strangers Followed', *Cyberpsychology, Behavior, and Social Networking*, 18(5), 247–52 (2015).

Sherlock, Mary, and Danielle L. Wagstaff, 'Exploring the Relationship Between Frequency of Instagram Use, Exposure to Idealized Images, and Psychological Well-being in Women', *Psychology of Popular Media Culture*, 8(4), 482–90 (2019).

p.94 *'Snapchat dysphoria'*

Milothridis, Panagiotis, 'The Elective Nature of Cosmetic Medicine', in *Cosmetic Patient Selection and Psychosocial Background*, 1–9, Springer, Cham, 2020.

p.94 *#nofilter images are indeed filtered*

Santarossa, Sara, Paige Coyne, and Sarah J. Woodruff, 'Exploring #nofilter Images When a Filter Has Been Used: Filtering the Truth on Instagram Through a Mixed Methods Approach Using Netlytic and Photo Analysis', *International Journal of Virtual Communities and Social Networking (IJVCSN)*, 9(1), 54–63 (2017).

Social media is addictive

p.96 *'It's a social-validation feedback loop . . .'*

'Sean Parker unloads on Facebook: "God only knows what it's doing to our children's brains"', Axios (9 Nov. 2017), https://www.axios.com/sean-parker-unloads-on-facebook-god-only-knows-what-its-doing-to-our-childrens-brains-1513306792-f855e7b4-4e99-4d60-8d51-2775559c2671.html. Accessed 4 Sep. 2020.

4. Pride & Prejudice

Explicit prejudice

p.105 *crimes increased compared to the previous year*

'Hate crime, England and Wales, 2018 to 2019', GOV.UK', https://www.gov.uk/government/statistics/hate-crime-england-and-wales-2018-to-2019. Accessed 26 Aug. 2020.

p.106 *anti-Muslim hate crimes in the UK increased by 692%*

'The Impact of the Christchurch Terror Attack', Tell MAMA Interim Report 2019, https://www.tellmamauk.org/wp-content/uploads/2020/03/The-Impact-of-the-ChristChurch-Attack-Tell-MAMA-Interim-Report-2019-PP.pdf. Accessed 1 Sep. 2020.

p.107 *70 per cent more applications respectively*

Di Stasio, V. and A. Heath, 'Are Employers in Britain Discriminating Against Ethnic Minorities' *Summary of Findings from the GEMM Project* (2018).

p.107 *women, disabled people and People of Colour are more likely to be paid less ...*

Brown, Duncan, Catherine Rickard, and Andrea Broughton, 'Tackling Gender, Disability and Ethnicity Pay Gaps: a Progress Review', *Equality and Human Rights Commission (EHRC)*, 2017. Accessed 22 June 2017.

The layering of prejudice

p.109 *Intersectionality helps us understand how each person may experience the world*

You may notice these layers of identity spell (sort of) 'graces' – well, 'ggrraaaccceeesss' to be precise. This is because John Burnham (a consultant family and systemic psychotherapist) put forward the Social Graces as a framework to help therapists to think about the multiple layers of identity their clients may have.

p.109 *Some people's sexuality may not be immediately visible ...*

You may argue that all sexuality is invisible, and you would be right: you cannot be sure of someone's preferences purely by looking at them. However, some people use physical identifiers (such as their haircuts and clothing) to signal they share a group identity.

Microaggressions

p.117 *What my client was experiencing each day were microaggressions*

Pierce, Chester, 'Offensive Mechanisms', *The Black Seventies*, pp.265–82, Porter Sargent Publishers, 1970.

p.121 *when microaggressions happen in the classroom . . .*

Sue, D. W., *Microaggressions in Everyday Life: Race, Gender, and Sexual Orientation*, John Wiley & Sons, 2010.

Turning prejudice against yourself

p.127 *People of Colour using skin-bleaching products*

David, E. J. R., *Internalized Oppression: The Psychology of Marginalized Groups*, Springer Publishing, 2014.

Mirroring power

p.133 *Indian women who campaigned for women's rights*

Anand, A., *Sophia: Princess, Suffragette, Revolutionary*, Bloomsbury Publishing USA, 2015.

5. Life Events

Heartache and break-ups

p.143 *people who were being burned on their forearm*

Kross, Ethan, Marc G. Berman, Walter Mischel, Edward E. Smith, and Tor D. Wager, 'Social Rejection Shares Somatosensory Representations with Physical Pain', *Proceedings of the National Academy of Sciences of the United States of America*, 108(15), 6270–5 (2011).

p.143 *the brain released its own natural painkillers, opioids*

Hsu, David T., Sanford, Benjamin J., Meyers, Kortni K., Love, Tiffany M., Hazlett, Kathleen E., Heng, W., Ni, L. et al., 'Response of the μ-opioid System to Social Rejection and Acceptance', *Molecular Psychiatry*, 18(11), 1211–17 (2013).

p.147 *dampens down the stress response in your brain . . .*

Moser, J. S., Dougherty, A., Mattson, W. I., Katz, B., Moran, T. P., Guevarra, D., Shablack, H., Ayduk, O., Jonides, J., Berman, M. G., & Kross, E., 'Third-person Self-talk Facilitates Emotion Regulation Without Engaging Cognitive Control: Converging Evidence from ERP and fMRI', *Scientific Reports*, 7(1), 4519 (2017)., https://doi.org/10.1038/s41598-017-04047-3.

Loneliness

p.160 *When chronic (part of your everyday life) . . .*

Holt-Lunstad, Julianne, Smith, Timothy B., and Bradley Layton, J., 'Social Relationships and Mortality Risk: a Meta-analytic Review', *PLoS Medicine*, 7, e1000316 (2017).

NOTES

Loneliness vs. solitude

p.163 *80 per cent of their waking hours with other people*

Cacioppo, John T., Fowler, James H., and Christakis, Nicholas A., 'Alone in the Crowd: The Structure and Spread of Loneliness in a Large Social Network', *Journal of Personality and Social Psychology*, 97(6), 977 (2009).

p.163 *increased to 35 per cent of the British population*

Li, Lambert Zixin, and Wang. S., 'Prevalence and Predictors of general Psychiatric Disorders and Loneliness During COVID-19 in the United Kingdom', *Psychiatry Research*, 291, 113267 (2020).

A Note to You

p.170 *These changes can be seen as quickly as two weeks*

Tang, Yi-Yuan, Tang, Y-Y., Tang, Y., Tang, R., and Lewis Peacock, J. A., 'Brief Mental Training Reorganizes Large-Scale Brain Networks', *Frontiers in Systems Neuroscience*, 11(6) (2017).

PART TWO: What's Keeping You Here

What do I mean by predictions?

p.189 *Wherever you are, whatever you're doing . . .*

This is based on the theory of constructed emotion. For more, see: Barrett, Lisa Feldman, *How Emotions Are Made: The Secret Life of the Brain*, Houghton Mifflin Harcourt, 2017.

Emotions are meant to be fleeting

p.214 *'Name it to tame it'*

Siegel, Daniel J., and Tina Payne Bryson, *The Whole-Brain Child: 12 Revolutionary Strategies to Nurture Your Child's Developing Mind*, Bantam, 2012.

7. The Flight-Fight-Freeze-Fawn Response

Scary feelings

p.219 *you click 'Send' with moments to go*

Additional note to the 'last-minuters': if working like this has paid off for you time and time again, teaching you that, even though it feels dreadful leaving it to the last moment, it doesn't seem to harm your chances, this may be one of the reasons you don't feel motivated to change your behaviour, or why you don't hit the sweet spot of anxiety till the last minute, as part of you may be thinking, *I always get it done in time, why change the habit of a lifetime?*

Fight or flight?

p.222 *22-year-old Lauren Kornacki* . . .

'Super strength: daughter rescues dad pinned under car', https://abcnews.go.com/US/superhero-woman-lifts-car-off-dad/story?id=16907591, 1 August 2012. Accessed 10 Sep. 2020.

p.222 *Tom Boyle* . . .

'How it's possible for an ordinary person to lift a car', https://www.bbc.com/future/article/20160501-how-its-possible-for-an-ordinary-person-to-lift- a-car, 2 May 2016. Accessed 10 Sep. 2020.

8. Coping Strategies That Make Things Worse

Control

p.252 *we will bounce back from shocking events* . . .

Buddelmeyer, Hielke, and Nattavudh Powdthavee, 'Can Having Internal Locus of Control Insure Against Negative Shocks? Psychological Evidence from Panel Data', *Journal of Economic Behavior & Organization*, 122, 88–109 (2016).

10. Modern Love

Dating apps

p.316 *Increased use of dating apps have been linked to decreased body satisfaction*

Holtzhausen, N., Fitzgerald, K., Thakur, I. et al., 'Swipe-based Dating Applications Use and its Association with Mental Health Outcomes: a Cross-sectional Study', *BMC Psychology*, 8, 22 (2020). https://doi.org/10.1186/s40359-020-0373-1.

Push-pull, but this time with compromise

p.327 *They often cycle in and out of relationships* . . .

Levine, Amir, and Rachel Heller, *Attached: The New Science of Adult Attachment and How It Can Help you Find – and Keep – Love*, Penguin, 2012.

How to become more securely attached as an adult

p.331 *Amir Levine and Rachel Heller wrote a seminal book on attachment* . . .

Levine, Amir, and Rachel Heller, *Attached: The New Science of Adult Attachment and How It Can Help you Find – and Keep – Love*, Penguin, 2012.

NOTES

PART THREE: How You Can Move Forward

Maximising your chances

p.353 *'To make a habit-like practice stick ...'*

Fogg, Brian J., *Tiny Habits: The Small Changes That Change Everything*, Houghton Mifflin Harcourt, 2019.

11. Grounding Exercises

Submerge your face in iced water

p.362 *drop our heart rate by 10–25 per cent ...*

Speck, D. F., and D. S. Bruce, 'Effects of Varying Thermal and Apneic Conditions on the Human Diving Reflex', *Undersea Biomedical Research*, 5(1), 9–14 (1978).

A Safe-Place Meditation

p.367 *They learn they have a place to escape to ...*

Zehetmair, Catharina, Claudia Kaufmann, Inga Tegeler, David Kindermann, Florian Junne, Stephan Zipfel, Sabine C. Herpertz, Wolfgang Herzog, and Christoph Nikendei, 'Psychotherapeutic Group Intervention for Traumatized Male Refugees Using Imaginative Stabilization Techniques – A Pilot Study in a German Reception Center', *Frontiers in Psychiatry*, 9, 533 (2018).

13. Mindfulness

Why does mindfulness work?

p.390 *The prefrontal cortex ...*

Kang, Do-Hyung, Hang Joon Jo, Wi Hoon Jung, Sun Hyung Kim, Ye-Ha Jung, Chi-Hoon Choi, Ul Soon Lee, Seung Chan An, Joon Hwan Jang, and Jun Soo Kwon, 'The Effect of Meditation on Brain Structure: Cortical Thickness Mapping and Diffusion Tensor Imaging', *Social Cognitive and Affective Neuroscience*, 8(1), 27–33 (2013).

p.391 *The pons ...*

Shao, Robin, Kati Keuper, Xiujuan Geng, and Tatia MC Lee, 'Pons to Posterior Cingulate Functional Projections Predict Affective Processing Changes in the Elderly Following Eight Weeks of Meditation Training', *EBioMedicine*, 10, 236–48 (2016).

p.391 *The temporoparietal junction ...*

Hölzel, Britta K., James Carmody, Mark Vangel, Christina Congleton,

Sita M. Yerramsetti, Tim Gard, and Sara W. Lazar, 'Mindfulness Practice Leads to Increases in Regional Brain Gray Matter Density', *Psychiatry Research: Neuroimaging*, 191(1), 36–43 (2011).

p.391 *Smaller amygdala . . .*

Hölzel, Britta K., James Carmody, Mark Vangel, Christina Congleton, Sita M. Yerramsetti, Tim Gard, and Sara W. Lazar, 'Mindfulness Practice Leads to Increases in Regional Brain Gray Matter Density', *Psychiatry Research: Neuroimaging*, 191(1), 36–43 (2011).

14. Journalling

p.393 *fewer trips to the doctor . . .*

Pennebaker, James W., and Joshua M. Smyth, *Opening Up By Writing it Down: How Expressive Writing Improves Health and Eases Emotional Pain*, Guilford Publications, 2016.

p.393 *improve 'moderate asthma' . . .*

Smith, Helen E., Christina J. Jones, Matthew Hankins, Andy Field, Alice Theadom, Richard Bowskill, Rob Horne, and Anthony J. Frew, 'The Effects of Expressive Writing on Lung Function, Quality of Life, Medication Use, and Symptoms in Adults with Asthma: a Randomized Controlled Trial', *Psychosomatic Medicine*, 77(4), 429–37 (2015).

p.393 *people with rheumatoid arthritis . . .*

Smyth, Joshua M., Arthur A. Stone, Adam Hurewitz, and Alan Kaell, 'Effects of Writing About Stressful Experiences on Symptom Reduction in Patients with Asthma or Rheumatoid Arthritis: A Randomized Trial', *Journal of the American Medical Association* (*JAMA*), 281(14), 1304–9 (1999).

Rage journalling

p.398 *'seal over' the event . . .*

Tait, Lynda, and Max Birchwood, 'Adapting to the Challenge of Psychosis: Personal Resilience and the Use of Sealing-over (Avoidant) Coping Strategies', *The British Journal of Psychiatry*, 185(5), 410–15 (2004).

15. Self-Compassion

p.401 *formal practice of self-compassion is linked to . . .*

Neff, Kristin D., 'The Role of Self-Compassion in Development: A Healthier Way to Relate to Oneself', *Human Development*, 52(4), 211–14 (2009).

p.401 *Increased emotional intelligence . . .*

Neff, Kristin D., Kristin L. Kirkpatrick, and Stephanie S. Rude, 'Self-compassion and Adaptive Psychological Functioning', *Journal of Research in Personality*, 41(1), 139–54 (2007).

p.401 *we can cope with whatever life throws at us*

Neff, Kristin D., Kullaya Pisitsungkagarn, and Ya-Ping Hsieh, 'Self-compassion and Self-construal in the United States, Thailand, and Taiwan', *Journal of Cross-Cultural Psychology*, 39(3), 267–85 (2008).

p.401 *Increased motivation to make the most of what life has to offer*

Neff, Kristin D., Kristin L. Kirkpatrick, and Stephanie S. Rude, 'Self-compassion and Adaptive Psychological Functioning', *Journal of Research in Personality*, 41(1), 139–54 (2007).

Loving/kindness meditation

p.405 *The positive effects of this exercise on minimising the inner critic . . .*

Hutcherson, Cendri A., Emma M. Seppala, and James J. Gross, 'Loving-Kindness Meditation Increases Social Connectedness', *Emotion* (publication of the American Psychological Association), 8(5), 720 (2008).

p.409 *The loving/kindness meditation, when practised formally, changes the prefrontal cortex . . .*

Berry, Michael P., Jacqueline Lutz, Zev Schuman-Olivier, Christopher Germer, Susan Pollak, Robert R. Edwards, Paula Gardiner, Gaelle Desbordes, and Vitaly Napadow, 'Brief Self- Compassion Training Alters Neural Responses to Evoked Pain for Chronic Low Back Pain: A Pilot Study', *Pain Medicine*, 21(10), 2172–85 (2020).

17. Find and Connect to Your Community

p.423 *hearts and breath sync when watching an emotional movie . . .*

Golland, Yulia, Yossi Arzouan, and Nava Levit-Binnun, 'The Mere Co-Presence: Synchronization of Autonomic Signals and Emotional Responses Across Co-Present Individuals Not Engaged in Direct Interaction', *PLoS One*, 10(5), e0125804 (2015).

p.423 *singing with other people*

Müller, Viktor, and Ulman Lindenberger, 'Cardiac and Respiratory Patterns Synchronize Between Persons during Choir Singing', *PLoS One*, 6(9), e24893 (2011).

p. 423 *This not only feels grounding in the moment . . .*

Goldstein, Pavel, Irit Weissman-Fogel, and Simone G. Shamay-Tsoory, 'The Role of Touch in Regulating Inter-partner Physiological Coupling During Empathy for Pain', *Scientific Reports*, 7(1), 1–12 (2017).

Face-to-face vs. side-by-side connection

p.426 *postnatal depression . . .*

Fancourt, D., and R. Perkins, 'Effect of Singing Interventions on Symptoms of Postnatal Depression: Three-arm Randomised Controlled Trial', *The British Journal of Psychiatry*, 212(2), 119–21 (2018).

p.426 *people living with cancer . . .*

Young, Laurel, 'The Potential Health Benefits of Community Based Singing Groups for Adults with Cancer', *Canadian Journal of Music Therapy*, 15(1), 11–27 (2009).

p.426 *respiratory disease*

Fancourt, D., and R. Perkins, 'Effect of singing interventions on symptoms of postnatal depression: three-arm randomised controlled trial', *The British Journal of Psychiatry* 212, no. 2 (2018): 119–21.

18. Get Therapy

Mindfulness-Based Stress Reduction

p.444 *MBSR is recommended for managing depression . . .*

Niazi, Asfandyar Khan, and Shaharyar Khan Niazi, 'Mindfulness-based Stress Reduction: a Non-pharmacological Approach for Chronic Illnesses', *North American Journal of Medical Sciences*, 3(1), 20 (2011).

Appendix: Overcoming Avoidance One Step at a Time

p.454 *Fun fact: imagining an action activates the same area of the brain as doing the actual task*

Yue, Guang, and Kelly J. Cole, 'Strength Increases From the Motor Program: Comparison of Training with Maximal Voluntary and Imagined Muscle Contractions', *Journal of Neurophysiology*, 67 (5), 1114–23 (1992).